Joseph Huntington

Calvinism improved

The gospel illustrated as a system of real grace, issuing in the salvation of all men

Joseph Huntington

Calvinism improved

The gospel illustrated as a system of real grace, issuing in the salvation of all men

ISBN/EAN: 9783337284336

Printed in Europe, USA, Canada, Australia, Japan

Cover: Foto ©Lupo / pixelio.de

More available books at **www.hansebooks.com**

CALVINISM IMPROVED;

OR,

THE GOSPEL ILLUSTRATED

AS A SYSTEM

OF REAL GRACE,

ISSUING IN THE

SALVATION

OF

ALL MEN:

A Posthumous Work of the late Reverend
JOSEPH HUNTINGTON, D. D.
Minister of the First Church in Coventry, (Connecticut.)

"WHO WILL HAVE ALL MEN TO BE SAVED, AND TO COME UNTO THE KNOWLEDGE OF THE TRUTH. FOR THERE IS ONE GOD, AND ONE MEDIATOR BETWEEN GOD AND MAN, THE MAN CHRIST JESUS, WHO GAVE HIMSELF A RANSOM FOR ALL, TO BE TESTIFIED IN DUE TIME." APOSTLE *PAUL.*

PRINTED AT NEW-LONDON, *(CONNECTICUT.)*
BY SAMUEL GREEN.
M,DCC,XCVI.

Entered as the act directs.

INTRODUCTION.

THE AUTHOR, TO ALL HIS FELLOW-SINNERS,
PARTAKERS IN COMMON WITH HIM
IN GUILT AND WOE.

OUR great and common Parent hath been pleafed to give us a place among his rational, and immortal creatures, and made us capable of great and everlafting happinefs or mifery. Which of thefe fhall be our lot to all eternity, depends on his good, holy, and fovereign will alone. Not many of us are ordinarily much attentive to either, except in regard to the prefent life and world; yet were we wife, our main concern and attention would be converfant with our intereft in a future ftate, and we fhould make the prefent life wholly fubfervient to that intereft.

But however inattentive moft are to thefe things, there are in the world, and always have been, many individuals fcattered here and there, whose minds have been deeply impressed with a sense of eternal things. They of this description and no other, will pay much attention to what I here offer.

The author has often been too precipitate and hasty in many things; but in no wise so in embracing the doctrine here advanced. He is now passing the meridian of life; and this opinion of the way of salvation is the result of his most careful enquiry from the days of his early youth.

His first idea of the way of salvation, was this, viz. That by the grace of God, and by a diligent use of means, he must obtain some *valuable distinction* between himself and other sinners. That when God saw *this*, his heart would be moved thereby, to give him regenerating and converting grace, and then would be holden thereby in a way of *mere grace*, by gospel constitution, to confer eternal salvation.

Upon this plan he labored much in early life, but the result was not as he expected; it ended in total despair. For, the more he labored for a good hope in this way, the more he was convinced of his awful destitution of all such distinctions and qualifications. He was then led to take refuge, and found great relief in that grace, which he saw to be absolutely sovereign, flowing out of the very nature of God, through Christ; not moved by any distinctions or previous qualifications in sinners; but from the nature of God, wholly self-moved, according to the free electing love of God. A view of which might bring a joyful sense of salvation to the most vicious, stupid, hardened sinner, as well as to himself. Yet still he had no idea of any salvation beyond the more common, and *much limited* idea of God's election and salvation.

Being much disposed to a studious life, and always delighting greatly in books, he spent much of his time in reading and enquiry, in the early periods of life. Amidst all the vanities and follies of youth, yet acquainting his heart with wisdom, even while he too much laid hold on folly. Being also much favored, by a kind Providence, with regard to the best means of instruction, and a pious example from his parents in his early days, and afterwards with a more public education; the disposition of his heart inclined him, in great preference to all other employments, to the study of divinity, and to become a preacher of the gospel.

He was now in those principles which we call *Calvinistic;* and met with some acceptance in his public performances, and soon took the pastoral charge of a kind and respectable people, from whom he has ever since received as many kindnesses as most of his brethren in the ministry have. Living in a series of harmony and love, excepting only with respect to a very few individuals, at one time and another, who yet have given him no great trouble.

INTRODUCTION.

He, for several years, understood the way of salvation taught in the word of God, (which he always regarded as the only decisive rule of faith and life,) agreeably, in all essential matters, to the explanations of Mr. *Calvin*, Dr. *Owen*, Mr. *Willard*, President *Edwards*, and the great body of puritan divines since the reformation from popery. Not as yet thinking of any extent of the divine decrees, or God's eternal purposes of love to a lost world, beyond the common orthodoxy of his country; or what, for want of a more significant word, he would call *the limitarian plan*. By degrees, he began to be pressed more and more in his own mind, with regard to the full consistency of it.

He preached, as did other divines, the atonement of Christ, a full and complete sacrifice for the redemption of every sinner in the world; and the divine law wholly satisfied in the obedience of Christ unto death; that every sinner on earth, was alike invited, and most solemnly commanded to believe on Christ to the saving of his soul; that it was the greatest of all sin and rebellion against God, not to believe unto salvation, and alike so, in every sinner that heard the gospel; and, that saving faith did not *create*, or in the least *change* the object or foundation of it, but was wholly grounded on an object and foundation forever immutable.

These doctrines he urged, from the nature and attributes of God; the covenant of redemption; and the dying love of Christ, as displayed in the book of divine revelation. And, on the same principles, always enforced holiness and virtue, as a native and genuine consequence of a cordial belief of them; and also as being most reasonable and happifying in the very nature of things. Meanwhile often denouncing the dreadful wrath of God, revealed from heaven against all ungodliness, and unrighteousness of men. His preaching was of this tenor, with all the uses of it, and inferences that might be drawn from it; on the idea of a *limited* decree, and a *limited* scheme of redemption and salvation.

The author holds all these doctrines *of grace* and *of duty*, more firmly now, if possible, than ever before; except only with regard to the *limitation* of the covenant of redemption, as not according to the eternal purpose of God.

What has lain on his mind with increasing pressure is this. When he had exhibited to his audience the infinite fulness and all-sufficiency of Christ to save sinners, both by price and by power; and the great duty of every sinner to believe it to the salvation of his soul, then to tell them; " *Many sinners, many alas! are left out of the* " *covenant of redemption; many for whom Christ* " *never died*. A part only are comprehended, a " very few in comparison, as we have reason " to believe, or at least to fear. How many we " cannot say, nor who they are. God will cer-" tainly make such as are elected, to believe, " by his own almighty power and grace; and " he will most certainly leave all the rest to "eternal damnation as their sins justly deserve: for they were never comprehended in the decree of God or the covenant of redemption and salvation." I have been more and more pressed and perplexed in my own mind, with regard to the consistency of this manner of preaching with itself, or with the word of God. I have often taken up the objections that have been brought against it, and have attempted to remove them in the common way, and done it to as general satisfaction, perhaps, as other preachers.

The arguments used to silence these objections are so trite and familiar with every one, that I need only hint at them now. I have told my audience that we all justly deserve to be eternally miserable; that God was not obliged to save any; that he is a just, absolute sovereign: the reprobate, or non-elect have no cause to impeach God of any injustice; they shall receive only the due reward of their deeds; that they may believe if they will; that it is the wickedness of their hearts, their wills, and dispositions that hinders them; the heart at enmity with God; and that this is so far from being their reasonable excuse, that it is their just, and most awful condemnation; that they have no business with God's secret, eternal decree, or the extent of the covenant of redemption, and the number given to Christ therein, and for whom alone he died; that they must attend only to what God has revealed; that he will have all men to be saved; that he taketh no pleasure in the death of him that dieth,

INTRODUCTION.

but that he would turn and live; that he plainly commandeth all men every where to repent, and believe to the faving of their fouls; that the fecret decree of God can have no influence on their wills, and ought to have none on their conduct. So I have gone through with all the common arguments as other minifters of the gofpel have fo often done. Thefe the reader has all by heart, if he has paid any tolerable attention to the common preaching of calviniftic divines.

My audience have generally almoft to a man fet down fatisfied. Yet, at evening, much perplexity hath invaded my own mind; thoughts have thus returned upon me. I have this day told my audience, making no difference, and without the exception of a fingle perfon, that if we do not believe that God hath given to us eternal life in his Son, we make him a liar; and quoted the evangelift John in fupport of it. I have told them, that they have, every one alike, all the warrant, that the God of truth can give them, to believe to eternal life; and that it is the greateft of all fin not thus to believe. I have told them that their acting this faith on the Son of God, can lay no foundation at all, but is wholly built on an eternal foundation already laid, the immutable truth of God in his Son. I have told them they muft fo believe; they have right to, they ought to do it; and then every one of them fhall be saved. When upon the *limitarian* plan, I know not that one tenth part of them, or even one of them was ever included in the covenant of redemption, or given to Christ, or that he ever died for one soul of them.

Ought I not to have known for whom among them Christ did indeed die, before I gave out this doctrine; and then to have addressed the same to them only? or ought I not, at least, to have spoken hypothetically and said; *if you are of the number of the elect*, you have full warrant and ground to believe to salvation. Otherwise there is no foundation laid in Christ for your faith; but, on the contrary, you will make God a liar in so believing, as you will believe what he knows is not true, viz. that every soul that hears the gospel has a foundation for his saving faith, laid in Christ?

I have told my audience that the number given to Christ, and for whom he died, is a secret that belongs to God only, and not at all to them. And, that it is their great duty to make their calling and election sure. I have quieted their minds, but not my own. For I cannot avoid many thoughts which have never occurred to their minds, on the *limitarian* plan. I cannot help seeing, that although, *on this plan*, the number and the names are a secret with God alone; yet the principles are what I have been preaching. I have asserted them as revealed in the word of God, I have proclaimed them aloud, as the will of God; and now how, alas! shall I reconcile them in harmonious truth?

INTRODUCTION.　　xi

I can very willingly let alone the *number* and the *names; that* fits eafy on my mind. But what fhall I do with the principles I have advanced, as things revealed and belonging to every finner in the world? How can I, on thefe principles, thefe revealed doctrines, invite and command every finner to believe to falvation, and, in the name of Chrift too, tell every one, without exception, that Chrift has laid a foundation for this univerfal faith and falvation; when I believe he did, in his death, lay a foundation only for a part; that only a part are given to him, and that " other foundation can no man lay than that which is laid, which is Jefus Chrift?" Many fimilar thoughts have unavoidably prefied into my mind, after I have been preaching the gofpel in the limitarian line.

The learned reader will readily recollect the way that feveral learned and pious divines have taken to free themfelves from this perplexity. They affert, that all finners are commanded to believe that which has *no truth* in it, antecedent to their believing it; and that in the devout and obedient exercife of their minds in believing, *that* is turned into a glorious, faving truth, which had no truth in it when their minds firft began to work upon it. This they fay is a moft *inconceivable, aftonifhing myftery*. I think fo too, and can get no relief to my own mind in that way. If I could believe without previous truth, and make truth by believing, I fhould believe myfelf into the enjoyment of many agreeable things, temporal as well as fpiritual: Yet even men of no less worth than, Messrs. *Boston, Marshall, Hervey*, and others I might name, have taken that refuge; and merely, no doubt, because they could not possibly reconcile the *limitarian* doctrines of salvation in any other way.

These embarrassments in my mind, have induced me to look, most attentively, into all opinions that have ever been found among all sects that embrace divine revelation; and especially the *neonomian* and the *arminian* tenets. But, on the most thorough investigation, I find these inconsistent with divine revelation, and the necessary attributes of God; also with the relation of man to his Maker; and with his entire, absolute, and everlasting dependence on God. Still, the evidences, and even demonstrations of the truth, and divinity of the sacred oracles are so clear, that I can never renounce my firm faith in them. I also find, in reading all books of divinity that ever I saw, that the main, leading sentiments in them, will most inevitably infer the same extensive doctrine of grace and salvation that is here advanced: were all just and necessary consequences drawn from those foundation principles which all unite in. But, few just consequences have been drawn, and many things said by *limitarians*, of all denominations, in full and plain opposition to the foundation principles which they hold.

After all researches, I have recurred to the word of God alone. There I find a most glorious, and astonishing system, and exhibitions of divine wisdom, power and love; most harmoniously consistent with itself, and with all the divine attri-

INTRODUCTION. xiii

butes, with pure reason, and with God's conduct in the universe; and in a most blessed way, accommodated and adapted to guilty, miserable man, in all the depth of his *entire impotency* and guilt: A complete Savior undertaking to deliver him alike from both; and that in such a merciful and glorious extent, that I can in the name of Christ, command every human creature, under heaven, to believe in such a Savior, and promise him, on the same authority, he shall be saved by him.

I can now preach the gospel to *every creature*; i. e. I can tell every human creature under heaven, *Good news to* HIM. I can tell every creature of a Savior as complete to *give him* the *qualification*, as to make the *atonement*; to give repentance as well as forgiveness of sins, alike engaging and ensuring both, by covenant with his Father. A blessed Savior, that hath made his salvation sure, before lost sinners ever thought any thing about it; and that did all the work alone without their doing any thing. That, by the power of his own spirit, he setteth sinners to work out their own salvation with fear and trembling: not at all to make it more sure, than he has made it in the covenant of redemption, and the atonement; but only, to communicate the knowledge, and comfort of it to them, and to apply the benefit, by working in them a moral capacity to enjoy it.

Hence I can bid them, in the name of Christ, to work out their own salvation with

INTRODUCTION.

fear and trembling: for it is God that worketh in them both to will and to do, of his own good pleasure. I can tell them that the grace of God, alone, brings salvation to their sight and trust; and that this, in a way of *native consequence*, teaches them to deny ungodliness and every worldly lust, and to live soberly, righteously, and godly in this present world. Because this is God's way, and the only fit way in which God brings them to the final, heavenly inheritance, and makes them meet to be partakers of it. Also, because it is most reasonable, and an exceeding great pleasure and delight to them while on the way: And as in all respects it is most agreeable to the natures God has given them; to their moral agency; and to the honor of his own name, to bring them to the enjoyment of all the sure benefits of redeeming love and grace in such a way.

On this ground, I can assure them that God hath given to us *fallen men* eternal life, and this life is in his Son; and he that believeth not this record, *whosoever he be*, hath made God a liar. So I can charge any unbeliever with the greatest blame, for not believing *immediately* to the saving of his soul, i. e. to a sense and enjoyment of gospel salvation. And I can pronounce every unbelieving sinner damned, i. e. most justly and awfully condemned while in unbelief. But on the limitarian plan, I can charge no sinner with any thing amiss, for not believing to his own salvation; unless I first know, that he is one

INTRODUCTION. xv

that is comprehended in their partial and much limited covenant of redemption; or one of the few, or the party, be it more or lefs, for whofe eternal falvation Chrift died.

The more I have thought on thefe things, the more I am convinced of the utter inconfiftency of the general preaching of proteftant divines, on any other ground than this. *Chrift died alike for all. And all mankind are alike included in the moft glorious and merciful covenant of redemption.*

I fuppofe, at the fame time, that it is not *expedient* that gofpel preachers fhould *dwell* much on this point, viz. proving that God will indeed bring all the fallen race, in his own time, out of their blindnefs, guilt, and mifery, to the knowledge and enjoyment of falvation; or that Chrift will in his own way and time, draw all men unto him, in the plaineft fenfe of the words. But rather to dwell much, and mainly, on the nature and character of God, and that of fallen man, and the way of falvation for fuch a miferable race; with all the duties, and obligations, hopes, and expectations refulting from thefe thoughts.

The great things we want to know, are what God is; and what we are; and how we may pleafe God; and in what way we may be faved. Merely to know how many, or how few, fhall be brought to glory is no part of our faving knowledge. But to know the way to heaven, by saving experience, is the great thing we all need. This is just the same in my view of salvation; as on that of the proteſtant world in general, ever ſince the reformation from popery. Nor ſhould I think it expedient to publiſh the following ſheets, at leaſt at this time, were it not that I find I cannot vindicate divine revelation on any other plan. I likewiſe find many inquiſitive minds, deeply concerned about things of eternal conſequence, preſſed with the ſame embarraſſment.

I am well aware, that ſuch an open *advancing* ſtep to pour light into the minds of men; though it is no other, in the nature of it, than what has been many times done, may, as in former times, in all probability, be an occaſion of great alarms in the minds of many pious, good people. Among the reſt, (which is to me moſt diſagreeable in proſpect) ſeveral of my deareſt and moſt valuable friends and connections will probably be more wounded by this publication, or at leaſt more aggrieved, than any other perſons on my account.

But there is a wonderful force in important truth, preſſed home on the human mind with full conviction. When HE who ruleth the ſpirits of all men, is determined to make it appear to the world, he always makes the truth preſs ſo hard on the human mind as to find vent. Witneſs the caſe of *Elihu*, *Jeremiah*, *Paul*, and many others. Job, 32. Jer. 20. Acts, 18. The moſt of thoſe, whom God has made inſtruments

INTRODUCTION. xvii

to give additional light and guidance to his church and to the world, have felt much reluctance on the part of human nature and worldly confiderations, from the days of *Mofes* to the prefent day. But almighty God always finds an effectual way to draw out of their fouls, whatever he is pleafed to pour in with fpecial defign for the benefit of mankind. It is doubtlefs by connection and acquaintance with the people of God, that the gentiles, in every part of the world, got this idea of their prophets, fybils, and augurs, in all ages. The celebrated Roman poet, as the learned will recollect, paints this thought moft beautifully in the cafe of his prophetefs, in the fixth book of his Æneid. And I apprehend, we may well maintain the doctrine of fuch a forcible energy on the mind, in thefe cafes, without giving any countenance to enthufiafm, in the more common acceptation of the word.

What now appears, is a fmall part of a SYSTEM of DIVINITY, which the author has been meditating more than *twenty years.* A critical view of the religion of the covenant people of God, in every age, and in every part of the world, where divine revelation has been embraced; and alfo of the mythology of all the nations of the earth that have not been favored with the facred oracles, fell naturally in the way of his contemplations, as he was proceeding on a very extenfive fcale. What he undertook was with no other view, than for his own improvement; as he has ever found the use of the pen of very special service to his own mind.

Innumerable criticisms on the original languages in which the sacred oracles were first written, are left out in this publication. Because our English bible is so well done, in the last translation, that there is not one verse, or sentence in it, that will misguide any common, English reader, in any material thought. And because, on the contrary, the author did, and does still suppose, that such a number of criticisms, as he found his own thoughts naturally led into, would, if inserted, much bewilder the minds of most of his readers. And lastly, this would much swell the volume, and embarrass any printer in this country, for want of proper types, and practice.

The following TREATISE is not divided into chapters and sections according to the more common way in later times; but is on the plan of the more ancient compositions. Moreover, the reader will find in many places, that a particular thought, or argument, is taken up and pursued as far as the present connection required; then laid aside for the present, and resumed again, in another connection, and enlarged upon in separate parts of the volume, with distinct views, and in various connections. This is no more repetitions, than if each thought, or argument had been wholly finished in one place by itself. This method, was chosen because the author's desire was to help the reader, as much as possible, to carry along in his mind to the end of the whole, every material idea, without the loss of any.

The author is quite beyond a doubt, in his own mind, with regard to the solid truth of his leading principles and arguments; though he supposes that inaccuracies may be discerned by the more critical part of his readers. With respect to the *due time* of advancing this step forward, and so explicitly pouring in this additional light, he is not so positive.

There are, however, several considerations that have weight in my mind, to make the publication without further delay; such as these. I have spent more than *twenty years* in the most careful reading and attention to every thing relating to this subject; and, I think, with a single eye, and ardent desire to know the truth, and to avoid all false reasoning, and every groundless conclusion. *I have no interest but in the truth.* I am in the same predicament, with regard to the *due time* of publication, that all men since the days of inspiration have been. Any author may misjudge, after his greatest possible exercise of judgment in the matter. Some have done it, as the great and learned *Huss*, who was one century before the *due time*, in attempting to pour in a flood of light upon the world. He offered nothing to the public but what was advanced in the next century by *Luther*, *Calvin*, and others with glorious succefs. I confider that if all ftudents will refrain publication, in advancement of light and knowledge, until they are quite certain the moft proper time is come; every thing of this kind muft be at an end. Alfo that when God's own time is come, for new acquifitions of knowledge, even then, it is his wife and holy pleafure, that truth fhould beat its way through very confiderable oppofition, and that the leaders in it fhould meet with little thanks, and no comfortable reward, from the world in general.

Befides all this, I regard the marvellous hand of divine providence, fince my own day of obfervation, as leading into new acquifitions of every kind more rapidly than in any former period of time. A fpirit of *enquiry*, of *light* and *liberty*, does wonderfully increafe. And it hath been my fteadfaft opinion, with the venerable Edwards and others, who, as I apprehend, have written beft on the prophecies, relating to the latter day glory, that the glorious millennium is now dawning, and hath been ever fince the reformation from popery; and that when fix thoufand years from the creation of the world are compleated, the fun will fairly arife, even the fun of righteoufnefs in all his divine glory. That time now draws near. The fecond or third generation from us may, fome of them, behold that bleffed day.

INTRODUCTION.

I am further fully perfuaded, that the glorious and univerfal revival, and power of true religion in that day, will not be brought on fo much by the awful thunderings of divine wrath, and threatnings of hell and damnation, as by leading the blind fearful minds and guilty fouls of men to fee and know the true character of God, and the Savior. When the world fhall know the living and true God and Jefus Chrift whom he hath fent; then a fenfe and enjoyment of life eternal will abound, and the cords of love will effectually draw dead finners to holinefs and virtue.

The reader may naturally expect that I fhould take notice of feveral writers of late, and fome former writers, on the fubject of the *univerfal redemption* and *final falvation* of the human kind; both in fupport of the fentiment, and in oppofition thereto. I fuppofe I have read them all, from the great *Auguftine* (who advanced the foundation arguments in fupport of this doctrine, with greater ftrength of mind, than any have done fince) down to the prefent day. Several learned men have written on the fubject, in Europe and America; fome on one fide of the queftion and fome on the other. I have purpofely omitted any particular remarks on either: principally becaufe it appears to me, that none of them ever fufficiently attended to the fubject to write with full pertinency upon it. Though, at the fame time, the author regards them as much greater and better men than himself, and would think himself honored to set at their feet, to receive instruction in any matters they have *fully* attended to.

The LEADING THOUGHTS, on which the following TREATISE is built, may be divided into the following particulars. *The attributes of God. His own fixed eternal purposes. His covenant of redemption with the Son of his love. The full and proper contrast between the first, and second fœderal head of mankind. The doctrine of a true and proper imputation of guilt and righteousness. The co-extensive offices of Christ, as prophet, priest, and king. The just desert of sin. The voice of God's holy law, and that of the gospel, sounding throughout the whole of divine revelation. The law wholly satisfied in Christ.* The GOSPEL *announcing these* GLAD TIDINGS. *The nature and office of regeneration, saving faith, and repentance unto life. The indispensible necessity of internal holiness. The awful damnation of all while unregenerate. The only way, in which God will save sinners, and the infinite reasonableness of it. The great power of a real acquaintance with the salvation of God, to move the heart to all holiness and virtue; and to regulate the whole life. The absolute, and everlasting dependance of all the human race on him that made them. And the everlasting glory that will redound to God alone, Father, Son, and Holy Ghost, in this great salvation.*

The above are the principal, leading thoughts,

INTRODUCTION.

illuftrated by a variety of arguments; which are indeed but a very fmall part of all thofe that might have been adduced, with equal force, from the nature of God and from his word.

The author has one requeft to make to all that may fee, or hear of this book. He afks that none would either *approve* or *cenfure* it, until after a careful reading. And that all, who may have read it with attention, and then fpeak freely their own opinion concerning it, as every one in that cafe has good right to do, would alfo communicate this humble requeft from the author, to all fuch as have knowledge of it only by report. This is a juft claim, which every man has on his fellow-men; and which every humane, candid mind will readily grant. The author is the more emboldened to make it, as he never could endure to violate the fame principle himfelf, with regard to any writings he has ever feen or heard of. Having intimated thefe things as introductory, the reader is now led to a direct and immediate confideration of the fubject.

A TREATISE

ON

UNIVERSAL SALVATION.

THE sacred scriptures, or the two testaments, are certainly the very dictates of God to men, on the most interesting matters. God hath spoken as became himself to speak, things most important to the human kind; and things in the most perfect consistency, through the whole of divine revelation. The great design of it is, that the divine Being and character may be manifested, in the clearest possible manner, for the display of his own glory; and mankind guided thereby to the true end of their existence, even the knowledge and enjoyment of God the supreme and consummate good. The duty and happiness of man are inseparably united in the sacred oracles.

It is of the utmost importance to the

comfort of man, to have his mind open, and unbiassed with regard to the truth, heartily engaged to find the very truth, and embrace it with supreme love, for its own sake. This is "a good and honest heart." This is "receiving truth in the love of it." Alas; how hard an attainment for man in his present state!

Now any man that can read the word of God with open candor, will see, that there are two capital points of instruction running through the whole of it, as things to be believed; and that every where virtue, or holiness of heart and life is enjoined upon us, as matter of practice, enforced with the strongest reasons and motives.

The two great doctrines we are taught to believe, are, *First*, What it is just and right for God to do with us, considered in our own personal character, and desert. This I shall call the pure voice of justice to man, without regard to an atonement, or a mediator. *Secondly*, What God will *in fact* do with mankind, as united to a mediator, and one with him by divine constitution, in a federal sense: Or how, in very deed, God hath promised to deal with man, in that union with the second Adam: What his condition shall certainly be, in this life, and the life to come. This I call pure gospel; or tidings from God, which never could have been known but by his own revelation.

It will also appear that these two capital points are, throughout the whole bible, kept in conſtant view, running *ſide by ſide*, in open fight, from the beginning to the cloſe of the ſacred oracles. Theſe points are very different from each other, yea directly oppoſite, except only as harmonizing in Chriſt, which is the moſt wonderful myſtery of the goſpel, and the grand diſtinguiſhing doctrine of divine revelation.

TAKE a few inſtances of this direct oppoſition of ſentiment, if literally underſtood, in an immediate and direct import, without any regard to a mediator, an atonement, or a fœderal conſtitution.—" In the day thou eateſt thereof thou ſhalt ſurely die." "And all the days that Adam lived were nine hundred and thirty years." "Every man ſhall die for his own ſins." "Chriſt died for our ſins according to the ſcriptures." "God will by no means clear the guilty." "I, even I am he that blotteth out your ſins, for mine own ſake." The reader that is well acquainted with the book of divine revelation, will think of thouſands of plain aſſertions, as much to the purpoſe as theſe; and every fair reaſoner will own that words and ideas cannot be ſet in more full oppoſition, if taken in one and the ſame, plain, immediate, literal ſenſe. Yet we find not the leaſt difficulty in reconciling all theſe with each other, and with the truth, when we bring them into one proper analogy: We eaſily ſee one harmonious, perfectly conſiſtent ſcheme, running through the whole.

BUT, it will abundantly appear in the ſequel, that we muſt keep our ear open to the voice of pure juſtice to man, as he deſerves out of Chriſt ; alſo to the voice announcing what ſhall in very deed, through infinite grace, take place with reſpect to man in Chriſt : Or it will be wholly in vain for all the wit, and art in the world, to make any thing better of the holy ſcriptures, than a long, ſolemn, ſeries of the moſt palpable contradictions. I have, with the utmoſt caution, and deepeſt attention, long conſulted the ſacred oracles ; and, perhaps, all of eſſential conſequence, that has been written on them, ſince the chriſtian æra, in various languages ; and I freely confeſs that, without the clue, juſt named, I muſt ſet down in deiſm : But, with it, the whole book of God, *how true ! how beautiful ! how glorious !*

THE whole word of God, centers in Chriſt, and is ſealed in his blood ; the law, and goſpel, otherwiſe oppoſite, are brought into perfect union ; righteouſneſs and peace embrace each other ; and this diſplay ſhines, in perpetual and glorious ſymmetry, through the old and new teſtaments.

BUT now, to reſume the capital argument already alluded to.

WE begin with the firſt threatening ever denounced againſt man, on condition of his rebellion, Gen. ii. " In the day that thou eateſt thereof, thou ſhalt ſurely die." I believe the more common conſtruction of this commination, by proteſtant divines, is right, viz. that total death, temporal and ſpiritual, was to take place on all human nature, on that very day ; and eternal death then begin, and be confirmed and made fure to all human nature, without the leaft intimation of remedy or relief, to endlefs duration. I fully believe this conftruction is juft, and abundantly fupported in the holy fcriptures.

However, as I am acquainted with many learned, and ingenious criticifms on the words, needlefs here to remark upon, I will take a conftruction in which all agree as far as it extends; and which will anfwer what I am now aiming at, as well as that which is more agreeable to my own mind. It is certainly true, as far as it goes; though I fuppofe it does not contain the whole truth. " In the day thou eateft thereof, thou fhalt furely die." Let the fenfe be allowed as in the paraphrafe: viz. " In the day thou eateft of the forbidden fruit, thou fhalt become mortal, even thou Adam, and all human nature now in thee. Thy foul alfo, fhall fuftain great damage and unhappinefs, that is, fpiritual death, in fome awful degree, without the leaft ground of hope that the cafe fhall ever become any better with thee, (with the human kind,) to endlefs duration. Be affured of no felicity for thee; nothing better than forrow and woe; or, at the utmoft, no greater relief than extinction of being." I grant this explanation of the words, at prefent, for two reafons; the one is, it is certainly true as far as it extends; though it by no means comprehends the whole: And the other is, becaufe all that regard the word of God, will acquiefce in it thus far, while moſt will carry it much further. It will plainly appear, that whether this, or the more common idea be taken from the words, it will have one and the ſame aſpect, in ſupport of the following argument: Inaſmuch as there can be nothing plainer than that the threatening never did fully take place, on *mere man* in his own perſon, and never will; and that God never deſigned it as the *voice of certain fact*, on mere man; but as the voice of pure juſtice alone.

I HOPE, that I cannot be miſunderſtood in the uſe of theſe phraſes, " *the voice of juſtice,*" and " *the voice of fact ;*" or, " *language of law,* and *language of goſpel,*" with reſpect to man: Or, " *what ought in juſtice to be done, and what, in God's ſovereign mercy, harmonizing with juſtice, ſhall be done.*" I can think of no terms more accurate, and I find the diſtinction frequent among civilians and divines, viz. " *De jure, and de facto,*" which diſtinction has been found neceſſary in many caſes; and is, as will appear throughout the whole of this eſſay, quite eſſential to a right underſtanding of divine revelation, or even maintaining it with any poſſible conſiſtency.

Now if any will ſay, that the threatening did take place on the day of the rebellion, *in full,* according to the plain ſenſe in which God made Adam to underſtand him, when he uttered the words; or agreeable to pure juſtice in the law alone, or ever will take place, on mere mankind perſonally, or juſt as Adam expected; their minds are, at prefent, not in a condition to be reafoned with. God had a moſt glorious and merciful referve in his own mind, on the preconcerted plan of eternal, redeeming wifdom and love, which he did not communicate to man when he placed him under his holy law; and which he did begin to intimate " in the cool of the day," at the very time when Adam expected the full threatening would have taken place. There was no other poſſible way for God to have fufpended the immediate execution of it, confiftent with his own moſt holy nature and character. He had provided a way, in which all he had faid, might and certainly would be verified on man in a *vicar*, a *fubſtitute*, a *fecond Adam*, or covenant head, in *due time* to be dignified by perfonal union with the eternal LOGOS, or WORD. That, on him, the whole weight of the curfe fhould fall, vindicating the truth of Deity in threatening, though never executed on mere man as Adam expected, and as the plain *voice of juſtice* denounced; which Adam then thought was infeparable from the *voice of fact*; having not the leaſt intimation, when he was placed under the holy law, that there could ever be any feparation of *pure juſtice*, from *very fact*, with regard to man: Nor would any man, or any angel ever have thought of fuch a diftinction; or any poſſible way to make it, confiftent with the immutable truth of God, if God himſelf had not contrived and revealed it. Here we have the two grand pillars of divine revelation. God displayed in an *absolute character*, without any intimation of a mediator; this is moral law and all-glorious. And God displayed to man in a mediator; this is gospel, *pure gospel*, and exceedeth in glory.

In a right understanding of these grand points, we are led into a harmonious, and consistent view of the whole word of God. We find the law and the gospel displayed side by side, through the whole. The law every where sounds with awful terror in accents of pure justice, towards man, without a Savior. The gospel is all mere news, and good news, glad tidings, through a mediator, which man would never have heard or thought of, if God had not made the proclamation. The moral law every where speaks to man in his own personal character; the gospel in that of the Messiah. The law tells what man in justice deserves, in his own personal character; the gospel, what the Son of man, the Son of God deserves, and that he is by divine constitution " a covenant for the people, and God's salvation to the ends of the earth;" and that the head of *every man* is Christ. This intimation began on the day of the rebellion, and at that time was but dark, and for wise reasons, which will appear in the sequel.

The divine law enjoining perfect obedience, on pain of endless misery, runs through the whole of divine revelation from beginning to end; and so does the gospel, exhibiting a falvation fully tantamount. There is as much of the gofpel in the old teftament as in the new ; and as much of the law in the new teftament as in the old. The latter difpenfation hath the whole fubftance of the former, and nothing for the *matter* of it new : The former hath, in like manner, the whole of the latter, and nothing for fubftance has ever been done away, or ever will be, until the myftery of God fhall be finifhed. The new teftament is only a new edition of the old, in much greater clearnefs.

Four things are obvious in the grand defign of divine revelation, viz. To manifeft, and hold clearly in our view the abfolute and rectoral character of God. The character of fallen man. His duty. And God's eternal, fixed and gracious purpofe concerning him, through the whole of his interminable exiftence. The three former of thefe pertain to the law of God ; the laft to the gofpel ; and is all pure gofpel, or good news.

In the law we fee God's all-glorious, and infinitely perfect character as law giver; as alfo the infinitely hateful, and moft abominable *moral character* of fallen man ; and the reafonable duty of man to be wholly conformed to the moral image of God, and keep his whole law, without any deficiency ; and what he deferves, and what the voice of juftice is concerning him, if he is found wanting in the leaft. " Curfed is every one that continueth not in *all things* written in the book of the law to do them," is the invariable sentence of the law every where.

Now this manifestation of God, and of man's duty, and his guilt, runs through the whole bible, old and new testament; just as much in the one as in the other; but much more conspicuous, for the *manner of discovery*, in the latter.

On the other hand, the gospel begins in the third chapter of divine revelation, (as the law does in the second,) and runs through all the old testament, in types, figures, prophecies, &c. The gospel is all *mere news*, and *good news*; and it tells what man never would have thought of, if he had not been told it; nor believed, when told of it, had it not come with sufficient authority. The gospel is *pure tidings**; and more, it is *good tidings*.† Whatever is law, in any part of sacred writ, is founded on the nature and character of God, adapted to man's nature, and his relation to God. Whatever is gospel, in any part of the bible, is founded wholly on Jesus Christ, his character and offices, and adapted to the condition of man, *in all his guilt and misery*, and in all his desperate impotency.

It has pleased infinite wisdom, always to make out his promises to mankind in a covenant way, or under a fœderal head, or representative.

Thus it was in the first man, and thus in

* Ἀγγελία.   † Εὐαγγέλιον.

his contrasted anti-type Jesus Christ, as is most evident from Rom. chap. 5, and many other parts of sacred scripture. Thus it was in Noah, Gen. chap. 9, and with Abraham, Gen. 17. And with David as a type of Christ, Psal. 89. Never, since the fall, can any individual take hold of any promise of spiritual good, but in a fœderal way; and certainly the grand curse including in it virtually all other curses, came in this way: As the reader will see to full demonstation in its proper place.

It has been observed before, that God keeps up the language of justice towards man in his awful guilt. He keeps the voice of strict justice sounding in his ears, through the whole book of divine revelation, and that, no doubt, that man may know and feel what he is, and have an heart to receive the voice of grace, *as grace;* or feeling himself infinitely vile, may bid a becoming welcome to mere, sovereign mercy. The law speaks in righteousness; every where denounces what is *just* and *equal* towards man. It thunders aloud the true desert of man. But it speaks not what shall *in fact* take place on man, and his surety both; or *on man at all*, in faith and union with Christ; or any otherwise than in his surety; any more than the original curse did, in the garden of Eden, which was noticed before. Yet it is manifest, that the wisdom of God saw fit, for a time, to leave man in such ignorance and darkness of mind, that he should mistake that which was spoken only as the *voice of justice,* for a declaration of *very fact,* which should inevitably come upon himself. Man most naturally fell into this misunderstanding, from the inward sense of horrible guilt, in his own soul, and so was exercised with great torment, in a way of servile fear. Great sense of guilt will make an object of fear which hath no other existence ; " the wicked fear where no fear is."

It is not for man to account for all the reasons of the divine conduct, though it is well for us, with humble adoration, to go as far in this way as we can. It is a certain fact, however, that God hath chosen to give light and comfort to miserable, blind sinners of mankind, by slow degrees.

There was some light, some comfort, derived to our first parents from what they heard God say to the serpent, relative to the opposite seed, and the victory announced. The law, and the gospel were both promulgated in paradise. The voice of law then sounded much the loudest ; but it has been the manifest will of heaven, that the sound of the gospel should gradually gain upon that of the law, from that day to the finishing of the mystery of God.

By the institution and import of sacrifices in paradise, and cloathing the naked, shameful, pair in their skins ; and by the sacrifices continued down to the flood ; and by the preaching of Enoch and Noah ; and by oral instructions, &c. the light and comfort of divine grace had some gradual increase, while the law, as we know, still founded very terrible. See the epiſtle of Jude.

By the type of the ark; the ſalvation of the church therein; the covenant made with all mankind in Noah; and by the rainbow as a token ſealing the whole, the good report was conſiderably louder and clearer than ever before.

In the covenant made with Abraham, the light of the goſpel increaſed. For all, of this nature, was *very goſpel* from the firſt; *in nature* the ſame with that preached after the deſcent of the Holy Ghoſt at pentecoſt, only much more obſcure, in *manner* and *degree*. God's promiſe of a ſon to that patriarch, to be given in ſuch a wonderful way; and of the *church*, a *numerous ſeed*, through him; the promiſe of the land of Canaan, &c. all gave further inſtruction, with regard to that moſt intereſting concern of man, the redemption and ſalvation of the guilty ſoul.

At the giving of the law on mount Sinai, and the inſtitution of all the rites and ſacrifices of the moſaic œconomy, both law and goſpel were made much plainer than before: the moral law, or ten commandments, to enlighten and awaken God's people, teach them their duty, convince them of their awful deficiency, the juſtice of their condemnation, and their utter impotency and abſolute dependance on God: And the ceremonial law, all the rituals, ſacrifices, types and ſhadows, pointing to Chriſt, the great anti-type, "the end of the law for righteouſness, to every one that believeth." This exhibited the gospel, or doctrine of atonement and free grace, with increasing perspicuity; and is well called "a school-master to bring us to Christ."

FROM this time down to the fulness of time, in which Christ came, God sent among his people a great number of prophets, every one of whom cast some light on the law, and gave some further knowledge of the gospel. Among these, David, Isaiah, and Daniel, were very eminent. The light of divine revelation, both law and gospel, was much augmented, by John the harbinger of Christ. The Messiah in his own person, doctrines, deeds, and sufferings, made the whole will of God, relating to a guilty world, the methods of his grace, and all the purposes of his love, still far more conspicuous; so clearly expressive, that " his name is well called *the word of God.*"

THE light of the same gospel which had been, by degrees, exhibited from the days of paradise, was much increased in the apostolic times, by the more abundant effusion of the holy spirit; by the preaching of the apostles, far and wide; by their writings, filling up the sacred canon. So that the least teacher under this *new dispensation,* was better instructed than the greatest under the *old;* and understood the doctrines of the kingdom of heaven, better than John the promised Elias. Matt. xi.

AND, when the gospel door was set open to *all nations* of the earth, as well as to the

Jews, the doctrine was so strange, so far beyond all the notions of grace and salvation, ever entertained among the covenant people of God; and so exceedingly mortifying to the pride of their hearts, that it was abhorred and rejected. Just as it now would be, should one assert in the most obvious and plainest sense, that " God will have all men to be saved, and to come unto the knowledge of the truth :" Or, as if a modern believer should assert without any construction of his own, and with all the simplicity of an old patriarch, that Christ died, " not for our sins only, but also for the sins of the WHOLE WORLD." Indeed, when Jesus first gave this intimation, they who had just been gazing at him with pleasing wonder, were so chagrined at the idea that a whole world of *heathen dogs* should be set on a footing, as respectable as themselves, that they wished him nothing better than instant death. Luke iv. They could not bear the thought of losing their fancied monopoly, on which they so much valued themselves.

THE motive, why the Jews were more malicious persecutors of Christ, and the primitive christians, than other men, was quite natural to all mankind. It was not because they were worse than other men, or more malicious by nature; but they had been so long honored of God, and distinguished by peculiar *privileges*, that they felt *them* in their hearts as a monopoly : Even as a man descended from an ancient, noble family, has no idea that it is fit, in the course of providence, that the children of beggars immemorial, should ever become as rich and noble as himself and his posterity. This is human nature in every age. Any doctrine, that will place poor, shameful creatures, who have in time past been most neglected of God, in the holy, sovereign dispensation of his providence, on a level with us, with regard to grace and favor yet to come ; and would break down all barriers which inclose us in the palaces of distinction and honor, will set on our hearts, just as *like* doctrines did on the hearts of the favored children of Abraham, in days of yore.

It has pleased infinite wisdom, however, to cause the light of salvation to increase, down to the present day; though not in every age, or every period of time alike. There have been remarkable æras, in which something like a flood of light has poured into the world, and, at certain times, darkness and ignorance have rather gained ground. But, on an average, light hath been growing, in all sciences ; and the light of the gospel, the light of salvation in particular.

I HAVE already observed remarkable periods and dispensations, down to the close of the sacred canon. After that, there was a gradual increase of knowledge for about three hundred years. Then, for a time, the darkness in general, seemed to gain upon the light ; and sometimes gross darkness seemed as if it would overspread the world. Yet God kept up, in his church, some luminaries at all times. There never paffed one century, without fome great, godly, learned man, who, perhaps advanced fomewhat further than his fathers; witnefs the Waldenfes, and Albigenfes, in the darkeft period; alfo, *Hufs, Luther, Calvin,* &c. And, fince the days of thefe eminent luminaries, there has been an unremitting advancement of knowledge. I believe I may fay, not one year has elapfed without fome increafe of gofpel light, as well as of every other fcience. " Many fhall run to and fro, and knowledge fhall be increafed."

The laft, and prefent centuries have been productive of many great and learned inquirers after truth, who have been happily fuccefsful. At the head of them we may place, in Europe, the incomparable *Owen*, and, in America, the immortal *Edwards*; men of the fame turn of mind, and much the fame channel of thinking. Thefe men grafped the whole circle of fcience in a remarkable manner. And, by the way, every careful reader will fee, that they held all the foundation principles of falvation, on which this *treatife* is fupported, juft as I do; though they drew not the fame confequences, however fully and fairly implied: And like all others, that have advanced forward and beat the way, they met with vaft oppofition. For the moral world is like the natural; he that breaks up new ground, meets with great refiftance from the hard bound, ftubborn foil; after a few years cultivation, the plough runs eafy.

F

I MAY now further consider the law, and the gospel. They were first promulgated, as I have said, very near together, in the garden of Eden, and they run through all the sacred oracles, *side by side.* God keeps them both, every where, in full view; yet they are as distinct in their natures as any two things in the universe.

WHATEVER is law, wheresoever found in sacred scripture, is a rule of absolute perfection, as high as the natures of moral agents can rise, in heart and conduct; on supposition they are wholly without any moral disorder, any want of perfect holiness, in the temper of their minds. This law every where denounces the infinite and everlasting wrath of God, and endless misery to man, in case of the least failure. The law knows nothing of mercy, or of mitigation. This is law, and it is "holy, just, and good."

THE gospel, on whatever page of sacred writ it is found, either in the old testament or new; whether in types, sacrifices, prophecies, epistles, or any other way; knows nothing at all of misery, or torment, or the punishment of any creature under heaven. I should have said, *any mere creature.* It speaks much of the distress, sorrow, pain, and punishment, of Jesus Christ. God-man; by the appointment of the Father, and his own free consent, set apart to suffer and die for the sins of the *whole world:* the anti-type of all the types in the ancient church; "the lamb slain from the foundation of the world!" "The Lamb of God that taketh away the fin of the world." On this one head, the gofpel tells us of juft as much " indignation and wrath, tribulation and anguifh," as the whole law of God does from the beginning to the end of the bible. But, as to any mere man, the gofpel fays not one uncomfortable word ; quite the reverfe. Every word is a word of comfort, it is every where "*glad tidings* of great joy, which fhall be to *all people.*" So Jefus as the prince of peace, and as the great preacher of it, and as mediator between God and finners, fays, " do not think that I will accufe you to the Father; there is one that accufeth you, even Mofes in whom ye truft."

The voice of the whole law, and the voice of the gofpel, are exceedingly diftinct, and diametrically oppofite. The *law demands perfection ; curfes for want of it ; and cries vengeance.* The GOSPEL *points out perfection; highly approves of it, and the imputation of it ;* and PROCLAIMS SALVATION. The law fays do well, and thou fhalt live. The gofpel fays thou *fhalt* live, becaufe Chrift lives, and fhalt do well. The moral law is no news at all ; it is what our reafon dictates and approves. The gofpel is all news. We never fhould have thought of it, had it not come in a way of tidings from heaven. It is all *good news ;* and there is not one word of *bad news* in it.* It is all good news to fin-

* 'Αγ[ελι'α, *may be bad as well as good; but* Ευαγγέλιον, *cannot be bad.*

ners, to creatures that might never have expected a word of that kind. It is wholly glad tidings to hell deserving rebels, who could expect from God no tidings but very bad; even as bad as their nature and ways, and as horrible as all their guilt.

Hence it appears, that, when we are told of a *gospel law*, the meaning (to make any sense of it) must be the law spoken of in Jer. xxxi. 31, &c. and afterwards quoted by the apostle, Heb. viii. Even a living principle of obedience, wrought and excited by understanding and believing the gospel; which will ever be the case, as will appear in the sequel. But, in a strict and proper sense of the phrase, (which is however not found in the bible) a *gospel law* signifies the condemning *power of good news*: Which, at best, carries an odd sound with it.

The gospel tells us of the most important facts; things of infinite weight and everlasting importance; and things, in all respects, as independent of us, as any things we ever heard of transacted in *Asia*. The news that comes from heaven, is as independent of us, as if we should this day hear some news from the planet Saturn, well attested. All news makes its way into our minds, and commands our belief; not according to our choice, but, by the weight of its own evidence. Thus it is with this emphatically, *good news*. God brings it to our souls with evidence enough when he pleases, and it has its effect, according to its nature and importance, as all other information has: The heart being firſt prepared by almighty power.

It appears fit and worthy of God, to keep his law every where in our ſight, in his revealed will; that we may ſee the true character of Jehovah; and our own character; and our whole duty; with the juſt conſequences of departing from it, even endleſs miſery, as great as our natures are capable of. Rebellion againſt ſuch a God, violation of ſuch obligations, juſtly merits *this*, or *nothing*.

If our obligations to obedience, are not infinite; God is not a Being of infinite perfection and worthineſs. To aſſert which, is equal to atheiſm; for if there is not ſuch a God, there is none. Our ſin can be an infinite evil only in one ſenſe; as oppoſed to a Being of infinite perfection: For finite natures are not capable of diſpoſitions, or deeds infinite in themſelves. Our puniſhment can be infinite only in one ſenſe, viz. endleſs duration: For finite natures are not capable of infinite pain, in any given time.

Thus, endleſs duration of torment, appears obviouſly juſt; no more than we deſerve; and not in the leaſt cruel for God to inflict. Should we, *in fact*, fall under it, every mouth would be ſtopped, and every ſoul would be convinced of ſuch guilt before God, as to render this puniſhment equal, in reaſon and juſtice. And this muſt have been our doom, if another had not, by divine appointment, come in our place.

Now, as I hinted before, it is necessary that we know and feel this conviction, deep in our own souls, that we may receive *grace* as *grace;* and have proper impressions affecting all the powers of our souls, in the reception of mere, sovereign, *infinite mercy.*

To argue, as some do, that it is not *just* for God to punish us eternally, for transient sins in this world, is the perfection of absurdity; and arises from a total ignorance of God and ourselves, in the true character and relation of each.

WE proceed now to consult the word of God a little more attentively: Not what we imagine God ought to have said; but what he hath verily said. The sacred oracles came from God, and he hath said in them a great many things, which we should not have put in, had we made a bible. Many things in it appear, not only above my reason, but as opposite to it, as my command does to my little children when I tell them not to eat a certain fruit, which to them appears exceedingly pleasant, and greatly excites their appetites, and they have no sense of any harm in it, though I know it is poison. Or, when I bid them go to school, and not play, when, *to all their sense and understanding,* play is far more eligible.

THEY, who read sacred scripture, only with a view to make it speak what they judge it ought to speak, and that, after they have owned that it came from God, seem to me rather wanting in common sense, or honefty. I am quite fatisfied with what God has faid, in its plaineft meaning; and as well fatisfied with it, if it is quite above my reafon, as if it is otherwife. Yea, if wholly oppofite to my beft reafonings, I only thence infer my own ignorance and weaknefs, and fully believe and obey my God : even as I will have my little children believe what I tell them, and do what I bid them, though extremely contrary to their puerile ignorance and perverfenefs. There never was uttered a fentiment more juft than this, " *The foolifhnefs of God is wifer than men.*"

Now, does the bible plainly fay that finners of mankind fhall be damned to *interminable punifhment* ? It certainly does; as plainly as language can exprefs, or any man, or even God himfelf can fpeak. It is quite ftrange to me, that fome who believe that all mankind fhall in the end be faved, will trifle as they do with a few words, and moft of all with the original word, and its derivatives, tranflated forever, &c.* All the learned know that this word, in the greek, fignifies an *age*, a *long period*, or *interminable duration*, according as the connected fenfe requires. This word, with all its repetitions, fometimes fignifies no more than a long, limited time; ages of ages ; and fometimes, endlefs duration, when applied to the exiftence of Jehovah.† But there is

* AI"ΩN.

† *Rev.* iv. 9.--- εἰς τ᾽ ὒς αἰῶνας τῶν αἰώνων.

not the least need of any criticism on this word, or any other single word, or phrase, in the bible.

There are express propositions and assertions enough, in the word of God, to exclude any possible termination of the misery of the damned, as well as to assure us, in the plainest manner, that mankind shall be damned. Matt. v. Luke xii. Mark ix. In which chapters we are plainly taught, that sinners' shall abide in hell until they can pay the debt they owe to divine justice; which we know is forever impossible; and that the fire shall *never* be quenched. Plain assertions of this tenor, are almost innumerable. They, therefore, who would deny that the endless damnation of sinners, is fully asserted in the word of God, are unfair in their reasonings and criticisms. Beside, all common sense indicates that if sinners deserve any punishment, they deserve an endless one. Their misery will be as everlasting as the happiness of the saints, and is expressed in the same words, Matt. xxv. Here it is plainly declared, that when final judgment is closed, they shall then " go away into everlasting punishment."

Again; does the bible plainly tell us that *all the human race shall certainly be saved, and be happy forever, through the merits, power, and faithfulness of the Son of God? It does; as fully and plainly, as it is possible for any language to express: and that in several places.* John i. 29. " Behold the Lamb of God, which taketh away the sin of the world." John iii. 17. "For God sent not his Son into the world to condemn the world; BUT THAT THE WORLD THROUGH HIM MIGHT BE SAVED." John iv. 42. "- - - the Christ, the Savior of the world." John vi. 33. "For the bread of God is he which cometh down from heaven, and giveth life unto the world." John xii. 47. "And if any man hear my words and believe not, I judge him not: For I came not to judge the world, but to save the world." 1. John ii. 2. "And he is the propitiation for our sins: And not for ours only, but also for the SINS OF THE WHOLE WORLD." 1. John iv. 14. "And we have seen and do testify, that the Father sent the Son to be the Savior of the world." All these are taken from only one of the sacred writers. It is certain, neither he, nor any other man could have spoken plainer, on supposition his only intention was, to assert the final salvation of every human creature. And never any person in the world, would have thought of putting a different construction on any of these passages, had it not been for a previous opinion, fully settled, that sinners of the human race shall personally, not vicariously be damned to all eternity. They build on as plain scripture assertions as are in the power of language, *in case a vicar or substitute be excluded.* But personal misery being a truth not in the least to be examined or scrupled by them; they have put a construction on whatever is expressly opposite,

G

as foreign to plain, common underſtanding, as the power of ſophiſtry can invent. Not knowing any other way to make the whole of the bible true : It being referred by infinite wiſdom to later times ; at leaſt to be uttered with leſs reſerve than in former times.

BESIDES plain aſſertions, as direct and brief as words are capable of, the doctrine of the perſonal ſalvation of all men is clearly taught more at large, and quite as fully, in many parts of divine revelation ; if we will only attend to them with a fair unbiaſſed mind.

WE ſhould be likely to conclude, that if the people of *Sodom*, are finally ſaved, all ſinners will be ; but their final ſalvation is fully aſſerted, though not as the ancient people of God underſtood the covenant of redemption and grace. Ezek. xvi. 53. "When I ſhall bring again their captivity, the captivity of Sodom and her daughters, and the captivity of Samaria and her daughters, then will I bring again the captivity of thy captives in the midſt of them." Ver. 60, to the end of the chapter. " Nevertheleſs, I will remember my covenant with thee in the days of thy youth, and I will eſtabliſh unto thee an everlaſting covenant. Then thou ſhalt remember thy ways, and be aſhamed, when thou ſhalt receive thy ſiſters, thine elder and thy younger : And I will give them unto thee for daughters; but not by thy covenant. And I will eſtabliſh my covenant with thee ; and thou SHALT know that I am the LORD: That thou mayeſt remember and be confounded, and never open thy mouth any more becaufe of thy fhame, when I am pacified toward thee for all that thou haft done, faith the Lord God."

AND though, in the true fenfe of divine revelation they fuffer the vengeance of eternal fire, as all finners muft; yet in this chapter it is plain enough, without any comment, that infinite, fovereign power and grace will finally triumph over the utmoft guilt and wretchednefs of Sodom. Not as man had thought; not as the Jews had ever underftood the covenant of redeeming love. "NOT BY THY COVENANT."

IN the prophet Ifaiah, falvation is fairly extended as far as the human race extend. Read chap. xi. and his prophecy at large. So it is in feveral paffages in the other prophets. The point may be fairly inferred from the prophet, where God exprefsly tells us his will and difpofition is the damnation of none, but the falvation of all : Since we know that by his own Son every obftacle, every claim of juftice, every poffibility of ftaining his own character, by faving whom he will, is wholly removed out of the way. Ezek. xxxiii. 11. "Say unto them, as I live, faith the Lord GOD, I HAVE NO PLEASURE in the death of the wicked, but that the wicked turn from his way and live: Turn ye, turn ye from your evil ways; for why will ye die O houfe of Ifrael?"

WHAT would I have more, to fecure my falvation, than the infinite power, infinite benevolence, and exprefs will of God : Being assured, by the same God, that he can save me if he will, fully consistent with his own honor, and glory ; or that the way is clear and open, in and through Christ, for his infinite good will and all his attributes natural and moral, to be exerted and displayed to the highest advantage in my salvation ? I take this reasoning from Paul. When he would engage us in the great duty of prayer, for the salvation of all men, heathen persecuting kings, and all men in authority, though many of their hands were daily stained with the blood of the saints ; he tells the church, they had a good foundation to pray for the final salvation of such men, and every vile sinner, on the face of the earth. It is that which is the only foundation of all our faith, and all our prayer ; the express *will of God.* 1. Tim. ii. at the beginning. Paul in the sixth verse tells us, that the time infinite wisdom had appointed for a free preaching, and a general understanding of this glorious doctrine, was future. " *To be testified in due time.*"

He well understood God's wise method of gradation, in giving light and comfort to such miserable sinners. In the case of a poor, distressed criminal, condemned to die, and shuddering at his impending fate ; if there is a pardon for him, through the mercy of the Judge, it is kind to open to him the good news gradually ; lest the sudden shock be too mighty for him. Paul had no direction from his master to speak out clearly all he knew to be true ; therefore he ordinarily used milk, and not strong meat; though he had great store of it.

  In the fifth chapter to the Romans, Paul sets up Adam and Christ, each as a fœderal head of the human kind, as plainly as words can express; and repeatedly declares, that salvation by Christ shall be quite as extensive, as ruin by Adam. No man in the world would ever have thought of any other construction of that chapter, had it not been for an antecedent, settled prejudice, that most of the human race shall certainly be damned *in their own persons*. Any one that will read the chapter, divested of such a prejudice of mind, will acknowledge the above representation is indisputable. But what will not a firm, fixed prejudice do? It will even make us say, that " *all men,*" signifies *a few men*; and that " *much more,*" means *much less*. Or it will lead us to read the 21st verse thus, " That as sin hath reigned unto death, even so might grace NOT reign, through righteousness, unto eternal life, by Jesus Christ our Lord."

  I HAVE no idea that Paul could have spoken plainer than he did, 2. Cor. v. On supposition his design had been to announce the final salvation of all men, through the almighty power, and grace of God, and the infinite merits of Christ. 2. Cor. v. verse 18, to the end. " And all things are of God, who hath reconciled us to himself by Jesus Christ, and hath given to us the ministry of reconciliation; to wit, that God was in Christ, RECONCILING THE

WORLD UNTO HIMSELF, NOT IMPUTING THEIR TRESPASSES UNTO THEM; and hath committed unto us the word of reconciliation. Now then we are ambassadors for Christ, as though God did beseech you by us: We pray you in Christ's stead, be ye reconciled to God. For he hath made him to be sin for us, who knew no sin; that we might be made the righteousness of God in him." No man can make a comment on this; for no words can make the passage plainer. Here is the all-sufficient atonement; here is the infinite love of God, and his grace and mercy infinitely free; his purpose fixed, and his power wholly irresistible; and all so of God, that no creature, nothing found in any creature, can in the least set aside his immutable decree.

I HAVE discoursed with several that believed in the sovereign grace of God, in the widest extent; but never saw one that was able to express the idea with so much precision, perspicuity and majesty, as Paul does, Coloss. i. 19, &c. "For it pleased the Father, that in him should all fulness dwell; and (having made peace through the blood of his cross) by him to reconcile ALL THINGS unto himself; by him, I say, whether they be things in earth, or things in heaven. And you that were sometime alienated, and enemies in your mind by wicked works, yet now hath he reconciled in the body of his flesh through death, to present you holy and unblameable, and unreproveable in his sight: If ye continue in the faith grounded and settled, and be not moved away from the hope of the gospel, which ye have heard, and which was preached to every creature which is under heaven ; whereof I Paul am made a minister." Perseverance is necessary to salvation ; that we know. God will take care of that. Lest there should be a possible idea of limitation, Paul assures us, that this gospel " was preached to every creature which is under heaven," i. e. to all *mankind ;* every other creature receiving as much advantage by *their* salvation, as disadvantage by *their* apostacy. And this is explanatory of Rom. viii. 19,—23. where the whole lower creation appears groaning under the total lapse of human nature, and obtaining full deliverance, in the universal restoration of the human kind.

It is exceedingly clear, that all who hear the gospel, are commanded to believe it ; that all who believe it, have life eternal, and have a witness of their title thereunto, on their believing; that their believing, does not make the foundation of their faith and salvation more true than it was before ; but their faith is built on previous truth. This is the foundation, which neither faith nor infidelity in man, had any hand in laying, or can have any power to remove. For " if we believe not, yet he abideth faithful ; he cannot deny himself." 2. Tim. ii. 13.

If we do not believe that to be true, the belief of which centers in a sure title to salvation, we make God a liar. Any man in the world does this, that does not believe. But if God had not laid a sure foundation, for the sure eternal life of *all*; *some* would make him true in *not believing*; and a liar in *believing* it. John lets us know, that he that believeth not a record, or testimony, which, if believed, would give him a witness, make him sure of eternal life, maketh God a liar. Now, if faith does not create its own object, or lay its own foundation, what can be plainer, than that God hath made salvation as sure to sinners, *in the object and decree*, before they believe, as afterwards? But I cannot speak plainer than one divinely inspired. See 1. John, v. 10,—13. " He that believeth on the Son of God, hath the witness in himself: he that believeth not God, hath made him a liar; because he believeth not the record that God gave of his Son. AND THIS IS THE RECORD, THAT GOD HATH GIVEN TO US ETERNAL LIFE: AND THIS LIFE IS IN HIS SON. He that hath the Son hath life; and he that hath not the Son of God, hath not life. These things have I written unto you that believe on the name of the Son of God; that ye may know that ye have eternal life, and that ye may believe on the name of the Son of God." The apostle here assures us, that we cannot have the sense, comfort and enjoyment of life, until we have the Son of God, in our souls, the object of our faith, and fountain of our life.

But, it is clear that neither our faith

or hope, can have any influence on the previous object of our faith, or foundation of our hope; both thefe are immutable and eternal. Let the ftate of our minds, at prefent, be whatever it may, " neverthelefs the foundation of God ftandeth fure, having this feal, the Lord knoweth them that are his." And when we come to know the truth, then will follow, as a fruit and confequence, all holinefs and virtue. " And let every one that nameth the name of Chrift, depart from iniquity."

The apoftles, in all their preaching, commanded every one of their hearers to believe faving truth, on pain of damnation, knowing, at the fame time, that their belief, or unbelief, would not in the leaft alter that truth. Yet their comfort in the truth, depended on their acquaintance with it, and belief of it; and without belief they muft be damned. But Chrift has engaged for their knowledge and belief of the truth, in his own time, as furely as he hath laid the foundation for it, or become the object of it. For his three great offices apply to every poor finner alike. To whomfoever he is a prieft, to him alfo he will be a prophet and a king. Illumination, regeneration, fanctification and perfeverance to eternal life, *are as abfolutely from God as the atonement was.* " All things are of God." " Of him, and through him, and to him, are all things, to whom be glory forever, Amen." The Redeemer of finners, *fo fallen as we are,* faith it not in vain, " I am Alpha and Omega, the beginning and the ending, the first and the last. " Let him that is athirst come: And whosoever will, let him take the water of life freely." He hath engaged to give the appetite, as well as its object: " Him hath God exalted, with his right hand, to be a Prince and a Savior, for to *give repentance* to *Israel* and *forgiveness* of sins, i. e. to all given to Christ in covenant, all families of the earth in Abraham. Repentance and pardon, faith and justification, holiness and heavenly glory, are all alike the gift of the Son of God, and alike within his divine commission and engagement.

HERE the reader may wish to see the extent of the covenant, or engagement between the Father and the Son ; whether it extends to all mankind, or only to a part. This shall be most carefully, and impartially attended to, in a proper place ; as I would, at present, continue my chain of thought, on the apostolic manner of preaching, as well as the matter of it.

THE whole which the apostles preached, as gospel, was the atonement of Christ, and its whole import ; with all things connected with it, and all the fruits and consequences of it. Indeed they kept the law every where in view, in all their preaching. The design of this was, that the hearts of men might be well disposed to receive and obey the gospel.

THE pure gospel which they preached, was just what I have now mentioned;

"nothing but Jesus Christ and him crucified," i. e. the character and offices of Christ, with his obedience unto death, and the whole import of it. They held up Christ as a compleat Savior, in whom God shews mercy to sinners. They excluded every thing in man, from having any, *the remotest* share in the matter of his justification, or reconciliation to God: Every thing, I say, good as well as bad; grace after the implantation of it, as well as enmity before. They considered justification and acceptance with God, not as any real change in the sinner, but a change *wholly relative*. "To him that worketh not, but believeth on him that justifieth the *ungodly*, his faith is *counted* for righteousness."

FAITH is, in the nature of things, necessary to an experience and enjoyment of the benefit, as well as by express divine appointment. But faith does not create the benefit; or change the divine purpose; or make any alteration in the previous certainty of any thing in the universe: As my hearing any piece of news from afar, well attested, and believing it, makes no alteration as to the fact, which is the object of my belief.

SUPPOSE, my kinsman in Judea died ten years ago, and left me all his large estate, by will, well authenticated. I never heard of his death or good will to me, until two years ago, and then I did not believe it. The evidence I then had did not command my assent. Ten days ago, the intelligence came with such demonstration and weight of evidence, that I could not help believing it, and was much affected with the wonderful love and rich kindness of my good kinsman. For I knew I had always been a most injurious, ungrateful wretch to him; and had always dishonored him as much as was in my power; and would have killed him, many a time, had I been able. I was certain that he knew all this. Which, by the way, was the grand reason why I could not before believe the good news, on former reports; and continued to wander about starving, in rags, beggary and shame. But the evidence, at last, was attended with such light of truth, and the power of demonstration, that it commanded my entire belief.

I now enjoy the comfort of a rich inheritance, and my whole soul is much moved with the kindness of my abused kinsman. I think of him and all his goodness, and of myself, and all my horrid wickedness, very differently from what I did in the days of my vile enmity and malice against my best friend; and it affects all my conduct. Yet the inheritance was as surely mine two, or ten years ago, or even at the moment of my kinsman's death, as it is now, or ever will be.

BEFORE I believed this news, I was *condemned*, or *damned* to beggary and infamy, and should have been so all my days, had I not heard and believed it; but now I am rich, and abound in all things, through my *blessed, good* benefactor, and in full opposition to all my deserts. I have no heart, *now*, to feel towards him, or speak of him as I once did. So "the grace of God that bringeth salvation, hath appeared to *all men;* teaching us that denying ungodliness and worldly lusts, we should live soberly, righteously and godly, in this present world; *looking for that blessed hope,* and the glorious appearing of the great God and our Savior Jesus Christ: Who gave himself for us, that he might redeem us from all iniquity, and purify unto himself a peculiar people, zealous of good works." Titus ii.

The apostles every where preached, *as pure gospel,* God wholly reconciled, *but sinners not.* Rom. v. 2. Cor. v. Coloss. i. Heb. ii. 17. In preaching the *pure gospel,* they always affirmed, that God hath nothing, *nothing at all,* against any sinner, in the world, to effect his *final condemnation;* that all he ever had against them, was fully satisfied by their surety; that he had borne all their sins, in his own body on the tree; that "he was bruised for their iniquities, and wounded for their transgressions; that the chastisement of their peace was upon him, and that by his stripes they are healed;" "that Messiah was cut off; but not for himself." Many a glorious hour they founded the gospel in this very strain; but then, as a proper introduction of it as a message of grace to the hearts of men, they always seasoned it with the fiery and dreadful law. Yet this was no part of the gospel; but quite the counterpart.

Thus, the preaching of all the prophets,

that of Christ and all the apostles, was mixed preaching. The law and gospel were carried along together, though distinct, and even opposite in their natures. Thus all skilful preachers do, in these days, and will to the end of the world. The propriety of it is very great, for the reason I have mentioned. Yea, I say further, that the same thing will be kept in view in heaven to all eternity; the law and the gospel, both in full life and vigor, on the minds of all the redeemed of mankind. This will be necessary to keep up their emotions of gratitude, and their warmest sense of the infinite obligations they are under to their God and their Redeemer. They will often name their Redeemer in their anthems and hallelujahs; but cannot call him by that name, without calling to mind what they once were, and what they were redeemed from. Their song will be in this divine strain, " Thou art worthy; for thou wast slain, and hast redeemed us to God by thy blood." Rev. v. 9.

SAINTS in heaven, to all eternity, will feel themselves *in themselves*, as worthy of damnation, as the devils in hell. They will know that they themselves have made no amends to justice, *because infinite power and grace hath made them holy*. They will see, and feel, that *separate from their head*, the lowest hell is their just due: They will *see* and *feel* this, *deep in their souls* forever more; and *in this sense* " the smoke of their torment will ascend up forever and ever." And this view of the damned, *in the glafs of juftice*, will give them the keeneft relifh of grace, *free grace, mere mercy, fovereign mercy*, and forever animate the body of Chrift, with raptures of love unutterable.

The apoftles, in what they preached *as gofpel, good news, glad tidings*, to all people; never made any the leaft diftinction between the certain falvation of one finner and another. They, every where, *mixed in the law;* and *this* again made no diftinction: For every word of it damned the preacher, and all his hearers. It condemned every thing fhort of abfolute perfection. With one juft and awful voice, it always damned all *human nature;* and even the human nature of the Son of God, in a way of furetifhip, or imputation. "He who knew no fin was made fin for us, that we might be made the righteoufnefs of God in him."

But, the apoftles always made a great and clear diftinction, between one finner and another, as to prefent privileges and enjoyment, and alfo with regard to the degree of future bleffednefs. The penitent, believing finner, they declared juftified, pardoned, entitled to eternal life, and a blefled degree of comfort, *even now*. The impenitent finner, and the unbeliever, they pronounced *unpardoned*, unjuftified, condemned already; and affirmed that the wrath of God did abide on him.

They every where afferted, that early piety, and eminent holinefs in this life, would have a great advantage over a long life of sin, or later piety, or less holiness and usefulness: Not only in regard to peace and tranquility, comfort and delight of soul, in this world; but even with respect to the weight of glory in the world to come. Yet, they always, *as gospel*, affirmed the final salvation of all mankind alike. Paul, and his brethren were indeed very earnest on this head; and ready to labor this point effectually; and to suffer any reproach they might meet with, on the account of this glorious doctrine. 1. Tim. iv. 10. " For therefore we both labor and suffer reproach, because we trust in the living God, who is the *Savior of all men, specially* of those that believe; these things command and teach;" i. e. build on this principle, with such degree of explanation as the divine spirit may direct, at the present period of time: It being the will of God that light shall yet increase. The difference beforementioned, is very *special*, very great indeed, between those who now believe, and repent, and obey the gospel, and delight their souls in all the consolations of it: And those who are now in unbelief under the damnable power of impenitence, and every hateful lust. Christ is the Savior of the *former especially*,, but, *if Paul is not mistaken*, he is the SAVIOR OF ALL MEN, at last.

THE interspersion of the law with the gospel, is exceedingly manifest, through the whole word of God. This consideration is necessary, to vindicate the holy scriptures against the charge of contradiction. There is no other possible way to do this; neither is their need of any other way. It is so common every where, that it is scarcely expedient to single out any passages in particular. I will refer, however, to one or two, as a general specimen. Isai. xliii. 21, &c. "This people have I formed for myself; they shall shew forth my praise. But thou hast not called upon me, O Jacob; but thou hast been weary of me, O Israel. Thou hast not brought me the small cattle of thy burnt-offerings, neither hast thou honored me with thy sacrifices. I have not caused thee to serve with an offering, nor wearied thee with increase. Thou hast brought me no sweet cane with money, neither hast thou filled me with the fat of thy sacrifices; but thou hast made me to serve with thy sins, thou hast wearied me with thine iniquities. I, even I, am he that blotteth out thy transgressions FOR MINE OWN SAKE, and will not remember thy sins. Put me in remembrance: let us plead together: declare thou that thou mayest be justified." See also, Isai. lvii. 13. to the end. Isai. lxiii. throughout.

INDEED, all the prophets abundantly use this method of keeping law and gospel in view; and would be guilty of the grossest contradictions in the world, upon any other supposition. The apostles do the like. The same well connected scheme runs on to the final judgment, with an aspect to endless eternity. For, when judgment is closed, and the mystery of God, in this world finished, this same thought extends into eternity, and, as I said before, shall forever be kept in full view. "These shall go away into everlasting punishment; but the righteous into life eternal." Matt. xxv. i. e. The voice of law and justice is *everlasting punishment* to sinful men, considered in their *personal character;* but in the *righteous character* of their atoning Sponsor, the gospel proclaims life eternal. Two different characters are the very things here in view. And this is not at all uncommon in laws and rules, divine and human. The character is often named, and the person omitted, though some person always stands connected with the character, and is understood in that connection.

MANKIND, in the passage just quoted, are considered in *two characters*: In their own *personally;* and then the voice of the righteous law is, "these shall go away into everlasting punishment:" And, in *Christ, the righteous,* by union of faith, (and all shall certainly have this before the judgment day, as will appear in its proper place,) and, in this character, the gospel speaks, and the law also, as satisfied in the atonement: "But the righteous into life eternal." The *person* is designated by the *character*, which is frequent in the common language of mankind, as when we say, *the ruler, the judge, the subject, the king, the creditor, the debtor,* &c. some person is always understood, to whom the character applies.

I KNOW that a character cannot suffer

pain, or enjoy happiness, separate from the person; and an objector may here say, "this destroys the force of the argument." But I think it does not at all: For the person designated by the character, can enjoy, or suffer. All mankind will sustain both of these *characters*, at the day of judgment; *that* of the wicked *in themselves personally;* and *that of the righteous*, in the Son of God, by union and imputation.

The objector may say, "this doctrine as much proves that all shall go to hell, as that all shall go to heaven; or, that all shall go away into everlasting punishment, and also into life eternal, which is impossible; for the person can go but one way." It is true, the person can go but one way, and the person only can suffer, or enjoy; but the wicked *character* is capable of remaining an everlasting object of wrath, shame, contempt, and damnation, or condemnation, and will so, in the view of God, and all holy intelligencies. The righteous character will remain an eternal object of approbation, worthy of life eternal.

But which way shall the persons of mankind go? They are designated both ways, and opposite ways, by their opposite characters, and they can go but one, and they are all, you say, to go together; by the voice of the law and justice to hell; by the voice of redeeming love in Christ, to heaven. Which way shall they all go? Which shall get the victory? The sentence of personal justice; or the declaration of grace through the atonement ? Which voice, or sentence shall triumph ? Which shall reign ? It is a weighty, all important question ; the man of inspiration shall decide it. " But where sin abounded grace did much more abound : that as sin hath reigned unto death, even so might GRACE REIGN THROUGH RIGHTEOUSNESS TO ETERNAL LIFE, BY JESUS CHRIST OUR LORD." Rom. v. 20, 21.

WHOEVER will, with a mind entirely unbiassed, read the whole chapter with due attention, will see this grand point fairly stated, fully discussed, and as fairly decided, as the power of language can express. There the first and second Adam, each a fœderal head to *all men*, are set in full contrast : Justice and grace, the law and gospel, death and life, condemnation and justification, obedience and disobedience. The *approved term* has all along a " *much more*" affixed to it ; and every where triumphs over its *opposite*. Christ and the gospel, grace and life, justification and obedience, every where abound, reign, and triumph, over all the rebellion and guilt of the first Adam, and that of all his race, even, in the deepest colors, most awful malignity, and *widest extent* of it.

AND the general tenor of divine revelation, bears this uniform aspect ; exhibiting and ascertaining the universal victory of the seed of the woman, over that of the serpent. " As I live saith the Lord, every knee shall bow to me, and every tongue shall confess to God." " Look unto me and be ye saved, *all the ends of the earth;* for I am God and there is none elfe. I have fworn by myfelf, the word is gone out of my mouth in righteoufnefs, and fhall not return; that unto me every knee fhall bow, every tongue fhall fwear. Surely fhall one fay, in the Lord have I righteoufnefs and ftrength; even to him fhall men come, and all that are incenfed againft him fhall be afhamed." Ifai. xlv. 22, &c. " Being found in fafhion as a man, he humbled himfelf, and became obedient unto death, even the death of the crofs. Wherefore, God alfo hath highly exalted him, and given him a name which is above every name; that, at the name of Jefus, *every knee* fhould bow; of things in heaven, and things in earth, and things under the earth; and that *every tongue* fhould confefs, that Jefus Chrift is Lord, to the glory of God the Father." Phil. ii. 8, &c.

WHENEVER the apoftles preached to a mixed multitude, as they often did, they commanded them by divine authority to believe, every one the felf fame truth. And it was the duty of every one to believe the fame, and a great fin for any one not to believe. The warrant of faith was the fame to all; the *object*, the *foundation* the fame, as prefented to all. They, who believed, refted on fure falvation; yet their faith made nothing true that was not true before, as to the foundation on which their whole dependance refted. Had they not believed, at that time, " neverthelefs the foundation of God would have ftood equally fure, and with the fame feal." " And what if fome did not believe ? fhall their unbelief make the faith *(faithfulnefs)* of God without effect? God forbid : yea let God be true and every man a liar." Rom. iii. 3, &c.

Now reader, turn to the bible and read that chapter to the end. You will fee the falvation of all the human kind alike fecured, in the firm decree, and fovereign love of God, and in the atonement, power, and faithfulnefs of his Son ; and all diftinctions among men removed out of the way, as fully as words can poffibly exprefs. The preaching is mixed, as ufual ; the law, in all its infinite purity and amazing terror, condemning all mankind *alike;* and the gofpel, in all its triumphant glory with the fame afpect of *fure falvation* to every child of Adam. This idea being every where attended to by the infpired writers, viz. that faith alone gives every poor, apoftate finner, fenfe, enjoyment, and final affurance of falvation, in his own foul. The law is eftablifhed, and the gofpel triumphant in the final redemption of human nature.

It is manifeft enough, that all could not take the benefit, in cafe they did believe, unlefs there was a previous, fure foundation, alike for every one. No one lays the foundation by his faith ; but all build upon it. " Other foundation can no man lay, than that which is laid, which is Jefus Chrift." Faith, agreeably to every juft idea we can form of it, never had, never can have, any other province than this ; to give us fenfe and enjoyment of an unalterable fact or object, if comfortable; or diſtreſs, if the reverſe. Oppoſite objects are equally the objects of our belief. Two men are deſtined to certain death, by an enraged band of furious aſſaſſins, in cloſe purſuit. The *one* can ſee and hear well, and knows he muſt die immediately, and is in awful terror; the *other* is totally blind and deaf. Is not the death of the latter as ſurely impending as that of his fellow? The *one* hath *ſenſe*, the *other* not; but the dreadful decree is alike ſure to both.

I proceed now to conſider the decrees of God, or doctrine of election, according to reaſon and divine revelation. It manifeſtly ſtandeth thus.

There was a period in eternal duration, which God inhabits, or filleth up, (as in ſcripture phraſe he is ſaid to inhabit eternity) in which there was no exiſtence but God only, and when deity had in full view all poſſible exiſtence. Out of which infinite comprehenſion, or view of all things, he might create what he pleaſed. He ſaw what was beſt to be brought into actual exiſtence, and what not; or what would form the wiſeſt, beſt, moſt perfect, and moſt benevolent ſyſtem of creation. This his wiſdom and goodneſs moved him to determine to bring into actual exiſtence, in the fitteſt time and manner. On this choice, his knowledge of all actual, future exiſtence was founded, according to our beſt manner of conception. He determined what should be, when he might as well have determined otherwise, if he had seen it best; and, in that case, would have otherwise decreed. Then the system would have been different from what it now is, or ever will be; also, he would have foreknown it as a different system. But, seeing as he did, with infinite wisdom and goodness, what would be best, he eternally determined what should, in due time, take place in the scale of existence.

On this, according to all the rational conceptions of man, was founded his certain foreknowledge of all real, future being, or existence, in the universal system; I say his foreknowledge of *every thing*, without the least exception, from the greatest world and highest creature that ever he did, or will create, to the very least and lowest; from the highest angel to the minutest reptile or insect; and from the greatest world to the least particle or atom of dust; including every thing of a moral nature, every thought, volition or inclination of all moral agents, that should ever come into being; all their different measures, capacities, powers, talents, motives and dispositions; and the universal connection and result of the whole, as well as every single and particular operation. In a word, he eternally foreknew all actual, future existence, moral and natural, without a possibility of mistake.

This knowledge was founded in his own infinitely wise choice, and unalterable determination or decree: Or, if you please, his infinitely wife and good election. And every thing moral and natural, every being and mode of being, every circumstance, every connection and consequence throughout the whole scale or system of being, did originally, absolutely depend on the choice, election, decree, or predestination of the eternal, immutable Jehovah. And all things, in actual being, have now the same entire, absolute dependance, and ever will have to all eternity.

I can conceive of no God at all, but in the above view. If I recede in the least from this idea, I fall into complete atheism. Divine revelation is plain upon this subject. "Of him, and through him, and to him, are all things." "He is of one mind and who can change him? and what his soul desireth that he doth." "Of whom took he counsel?" "He doeth according to his will, in the army of heaven; and among the inhabitants of the earth; and none can stay his hand, or say unto him, what doest thou?" I might recite a thousand sentences full to the same purpose; but it is needless. Read the whole book of Job, and you will see every argument there founded on the doctrine of the divine determinations, and the insuftrable accomplishment of them all; and the infinite fitness it should be so. Indeed there can be nothing more conspicuous every where, through the whole bible. And in the reasonings of man, there can be no step between this idea of God, and atheism.

K

I HAVE said, that God's predestination, foreknowledge, election, choice, decrees, (or whatever name by which you indicate the same thought) are alike concerned with all existence, and all modes of existence, both natural and moral, to all extent of space, and to all endless duration. This is indeed true, and thus far gives us a becoming view of God. But I am now to apply this grand truth to the concerns of our salvation alone, according to the plain word of God. *Therein* the doctrine of God's fixed election, or choice; his determinate counsel and foreknowledge; his sure, unfailing predestination; his purposes in himself before creation began, are expressed as plainly as any thing can be expressed, and exactly agreeable to all our rational ideas of a Supreme Being.

IN divine revelation, we find the election, decree, predestination, or appointment of God, with respect to several objects; but in every case alike fixed and certain. It may suffice to consider the doctrine only in four respects; from whence we may easily make application to every other case. In regard, *First*; To particular men. *Secondly*; To some particular events. *Thirdly*; To particular communities of men. *Fourthly*; To the eternal salvation of men.

IN God's *revealed will*, his election, or predestination hath sometimes special regard to some particular men, in distinction from others; and is always sovereign, and becoming God, who never can foresee any distinctions among creatures, but what, from all eternity, he was determined himself to make.

Thus, he elected Abraham to be a favorite of his, the father of his covenant people, rather than Nahor. Thus, for wife and holy ends, he chose that Pharaoh should be an example of great obstinacy, rather than Moses. Rom. ix. Thus he elected Jacob to many blessings rather than Esau; David, rather than Shimei, or Saul; Cyrus, rather than Nebuchadnezzar; Paul to know and enjoy the consolations of the gospel, in early life, and, for a happy season in this world, rather than Pilate. It is needless to multiply particular instances. In a word; it is founded on God's election, choice, or predestination, that any man in the world, is, *in this life*, in circumstances more eligible than his neighbor, or any other man. All these things are wholly of God, and of his eternal purpose, however they may be effected by the instrumentality, or different conduct of moral agents: For even all their different conduct, and every different inclination in the universe, has an equal and absolute dependance on the eternal, fixed purpose and plan that was unalterable, in the mind of Jehovah, before creation began. This may serve as a specimen of what is intended by election, or the choice of God, as to all distinctions among men in this world. With regard to God's eternal election, or choice relative to all events that take place in time, predestination is of the same general consideration.

Thus, it was predestinated that the deliverance of Israel, and the overthrow of their enemies, should be at the time, and in the manner it was at the red sea, rather than at a different time, and in another manner: That the deliverance of God's people from their captivity in Babylon, should be in all circumstances as it was, when it might have been effected with a thousand different circumstances, had Jehovah seen fit, and so determined. There was the choice and election of God in all this. Isai. xlv. and xlvi. So with regard to the crucifixion of Christ, the time, manner, and whole instrumentality, was eternally fixed, in the divine purpose. Acts ii. 23. "Him, being delivered by the determinate counsel and foreknowledge of God, ye have taken, and by wicked hands have crucified and slain." It is just so with all events, from the greatest to the least, and all distinctions among them.

The same reasoning applies with regard to all communities of mankind in the world, and all their distinctions. The eternal choice or election of God, before there was any creature, established the future certainty of all these things; and thereupon was God's foreknowledge of all these *then* future events founded.

Thus the Jews were elected to enjoy the special privileges of divine revelation, for a long season, in distinction from all their fellow-men beside. Also, a few among them were elected to know and enjoy inward saving consolation, in this world; in distinction from the great majority of that nation. So the Greeks and Romans, in ancient times, were elected to enjoy the many blessings of civilization, learning, and extensive empire, in distinction from the ignorant and barbarous nations of the world. Thus also, many particular persons of those learned and polite nations, were predestinated to special acquirements and blessings of knowledge and usefulness, in distinction from the body of those nations. Innumerable instances of the like kind, in a greater or less degree, have been found among men, and bodies or communities of men, wherein the eternal predestination of God, has, in due time, appeared.

Not only all particular persons that are wise and virtuous, holy and good, in this life; but also all churches or holy communities, that, *as such*, sustain the character now mentioned, enjoy also, all the privileges and comforts connected with such a character, *in this life*, in consequence of the eternal election, or free, sovereign choice of God. And they are, in this proper and very important sense, *the elect;* in contradistinction from those that yet live in blindness, and are tormented by the cruel power of unsanctified nature, and distressed in the awful slavery of sin. They likewise, *as holy, virtuous and useful communities*, are elected to a superior and distinguished reward of grace in the world to come.

In this view, they stand distinguished from those that yet live in ignorance of God

and falvation, and without ufefulnefs in the
world; thofe that are yet haters of God, and
oppofed to the higheft good of his creatures.
From all fuch, I fay, thofe who now know
God, love and ferve him, and ferve their
generation by his will, are greatly diftin-
guifhed, by the election of God. This is
abundantly taken notice of in the word of
God; for a fpecimen, read Ephef. i.

WHENEVER election, or predeftination, in
facred fcripture, *doth diftinguifh one perfon,* or
one community, or *defcription of perfons, from
another,* it never hath the leaft regard to any
thing *beyond the grave;* excepting a difference
in degree of felicity.

IN the laft place, the doctrine of predeftination hath, in the facred oracles, great
and frequent refpect to our everlafting falvation after death.

IT is a miftaken apprehenfion, in fome,
that *election, decree, predeftination,* &c. necef-
farily implies diftinction between fome and
others of mankind. The words do not *ne-
ceffarily,* or even *naturally,* imply any fuch
thing. It may, or may not be included in
the idea, or fignified by any of thofe terms,
with equal propriety. This diftinction is
fignified, as I have fhewn, as to advantages
and difadvantages in this world, and degrees
of happinefs in the world to come. But, the
words, decree, predeftination, election, and
the like, might be ufed with equal propriety,
were there never any diftinction at all to be
made between one man and another, either
in this world or that to come. All words

of this import, only fignify a firm and fixed purpofe; an immutable determination of God; an eftablifhment irreverfible; an unalterable plan of conduct, laying out what fhall take place and what not.

If God had *chofen, decreed,* or *predeftinated* that never any evil fhould exift, either moral or natural; the whole plan would have ftood upon God's election, predeftination, or decree, as much as it does now. It is therefore wholly a miftake, to fuppofe the words carry in them naturally any idea of diftinction. If all the other planets in the folar fyftem, are full of rational inhabitants, as is very probable, and if they are all holy and happy, which may be the cafe; yet their condition is founded on the eternal choice, decree, and predeftination of the Creator as much as ours. The eternal plan, whatever it be, whether more fimple or mixed, is alike built on God's election, decree or predeftination. On any fuppofition, it is juft what God determined it fhould be, in every relation and circumftance.

To know what the decrees of God are, or what his election, choice, or predeftination is, in regard to mankind after this life, we muft confult what he hath told us, and abide only by what he hath revealed to us in his word. I have before faid, that there is not one thought of diftinction between one man and another, intimated to us in the whole bible, with regard to their *certain falvation,* in the life to come; though, as to the *differ-*

ent degree of happiness, the distinction is manifest.

The divine will, puprose, election, decree, predestination, or by whatever term you would signify the eternal, immutable plan of Jehovah, does, every where in his word, *fully secure the certain happiness of* ALL *the human race,* after death. This assertion is bold, the reader may say; I therefore now appeal to God's own word for the truth of it.

The words, *decree, predestination, purpose, and election* (which, the learned will bear me witness, are terms promiscuously used in translating the same original *hebrew and greek*) with their derivatives, are brought to our view one hundred and twenty four times, in the old and new testament. They mostly refer to things of a temporal kind; and in this sense, a distinction between one man, or one body of men and another is generally clear enough. Some are elected to privileges and enjoyments, in this world, either civil or religious, and others omitted. This is frequent, as to temporal matters, or enjoyments during this life, or any period of time pointed out. Of this description is the case of Esau and Jacob; in which nothing at all is included but what is of a temporal nature with regard to them and their posterity: Also, that of Abraham and his seed; in which nothing after death is made peculiar to them, only, as Abraham and his seed were typical of Christ and the church universal. In this view, all mankind share alike in the election of that patriarch, and that people, as will soon appear. So in the election of Cyrus, for great purposes in this world; and almost every where in the sacred oracles, these terms denote only what was to begin and end in a certain period of time. And, it is always so, when any distinction is made between one man, or one description of men and another, excepting the decrees of future happiness.

WE now further attend to the divine purpose, or election, only as it respects the eternal salvation of mankind, after this life. Here, every reader, that hath that rare attainment of reading and thinking wholly without previous bias of mind, will see there is no distinction at all, as to the *certain salvation* of the human kind. In this view, God has *one elect head* and no more; and *one elect body* and no more. The *elect head* is BEN-ADAM, the *Son of man*, in equal connection with all human nature. The *elect body* is all human nature.

THE forgetful reader may here cry out, where then is the distinction which election implies? But have I not sufficiently shewn, that the term implies no such thing necessarily, or even naturally. There may be a distinction, or there may not, consistent with the natural meaning of this word, or any other word of like meaning, as predestination, purpose, decree, determinate counsel, &c. All these phrases import a certain, fixed, unalterable plan of Deity; whether that

L

plan contains many diſtinctions, or none at all. The reader will pardon this ſudden repetition, as the idea is of eſſential importance.

I now ſay again, that election, or predeſtination, as it reſpects mankind, after death, centres in one head, CHRIST *the Son of God, the Son of man, the only mediator* between God and man; and *all human kind, as his kindred body.* This head is in a like *natural* and *fœderal* connection with the whole body of human nature. Hence we find the Meſſiah never calling himſelf the *Son of Abraham,* or the *Son of David,* (though others might ſometimes call him ſo) but *Ben-Adam the Son* of *man.* We find ſome of the prophets frequently ſo called of God, as types of Chriſt. The mediator, in his perſon and in his types, is pointed out by this epithet, about one hundred and fifty times, in the prophets and in the new teſtament; and almoſt every time he ſpeaks of himſelf, he uſes this term. I do not recollect that he ever called himſelf the Son of Abraham, or of Noah, or the Son of David, or of any man that ever was, except the firſt Adam.

THE reader will remember, as I have intimated, (and the learned all know it well) that the Son of man is in the hebrew, literally *the Son of Adam,* and the meaning the ſame in the original greek. This is the phraſe our Savior generally uſeth, when ſpeaking of himſelf; and manifeſtly for no other reaſon, than to keep in our view his relation to, and connection with *human na-*

ture, *in the univerfal extent of it*, without any diftinction, or any more connection with one man, or one defcription of men, than with another.

It is true, he is pointed out fometimes by the prophets, as the feed of Abraham; the branch of Jeffe; the fon of David, &c. But thefe defcriptions of him are only to direct the church or people of God, and all that waited for the Meffiah, how to know when the true Meffiah did indeed come. And the tribe of Judah, and town of Bethlehem are mentioned for the fame end, with many other defcriptions, that we may know the true Meffiah, and be guarded againft all impoftors. But Chrift, in his human nature, never had any more intimate connection with Abraham, Judah, or David, in contradiftinction from human nature in general, than he had with Judea, or Bethlehem, in contradiftinction from any other country, or town in the world. We know he had none with thofe places, that made him a peculiar Savior to them, in diftinction from other parts of the world; though he was born in that country, and in that town.

Indeed, human nature is identically one now, juft as much as it was, when all were in Adam. Eve was of him, and all human nature is fo. The fhooting out of many branches, does not, in the leaft, alter the nature of the tree. We have had no intermarriages with any other fpecies to divide or alienate the blood. All human flefh is called "*thy own flefh.*" All human blood is one blood.

". God hath made of *one blood* all nations to dwell upon the face of the earth." Hence, with me, there is no doubt, that the *second man, the Lord from heaven* hath chosen this epithet, when speaking of himself so many times, both typically and personally, to impress on our minds a sense of his common, equal union and connection with all human nature, as our *Goel*, or kinsman Redeemer.

Now, I say this Son of man is God's only object, as an elect head in regard to our eternal salvation; and all human nature is his *one entire elect object*, in union with Christ, as a body with a head. The Savior expressly says "he came to seek and to save, not some of those that were lost; but" *that which was lost, that humanity; that nature; that complex body;* which he so often by the spirit of inspiration calls *the world; the whole world; all men; all nations; all people.* " Glad tidings of great joy shall be unto *all people.*" But I may speak more of the elect body, after I have further attended to the elect head. The second man, or the Son of man is often called *God's elect*, or *chosen*, by way of emphasis; and the fountain of life to all men; and a substitute, or surety in the place of a whole fallen world; or covenant head of all human nature.

No believer, I think, ever will doubt but that the Son of man, the Savior of the world is spoken of, under the type of David. Psal. lxxxix. 1,—37. There we find him God's elect, or chosen, connected with all the world, by way of command and subjugation.

This all allow, *in Chrift*, denotes fpiritual conqueft and victory. There we find God has entered into covenant with him, as one he has chofen out of the people. The Father fpeaks to him as Son of man; and fpeaks to him fome things peculiar to the divine nature, and many things to him as mediator and redeemer. Particularly, that the heavens fhall praife his wonders; that none in heaven or among the fons of the mighty can be compared with him; that the heavens are his, the earth alfo and the fulnefs of it; that the people are bleffed, who become acquainted with him, or know the joyful found of his grace and love. God gives him full dominion to the utmoft extent of the earth; to every fea and every river; and makes every mountain to rejoice in his ftrength, i. e. the power of his falvation; attributes to him a redeeming power, equal and extenfive as his creative power. Here is God's elect head of mankind, God's chofen, and here is defcribed the extent of his dominion in the world. In the fecond pfalm, he is fet up with like elective appointment, and extenfive dominion; with power to break and dafh effectually, until all bow to him, from the loftieft king, to the moft obfcure peafant in the uttermoft parts of the earth.

In the lxxii. pfalm it is declared that his faving power fhall be extended over the whole earth. All nations, the greater with the lefs, it is faid, fhall partake of his peace and righteoufnefs, and bring forth the fruit of the fame. " The mountains fhall bring peace to the people and the little hills by righteousness." "They shall fear him, as long as the sun and moon endure, throughout all generations." "He shall have dominion from sea to sea, and from the river to the ends of the earth;" including the most barbarous and obscure inhabitants of the world. "They that dwell in the wilderness shall bow before him; all shall be subdued to him," "his enemies shall lick the dust." All rulers and potentates; all distant princes shall bring him tributes of praise and obedience. "His name shall endure forever, be continued as long as the sun, and men shall be blessed in him; *all nations* shall call him blessed." It is declared that from a very small beginning, like the confined discoveries of redeeming love, then among the Jews, its blessings should be, in due time, extended as the grass of the earth, and the fruit be copious and astonishing. In metaphor thus expressed, "there shall be an handful of corn in the earth, upon the top of the mountains; the fruit thereof shall shake like Lebanon, and they of the city (i. e. the city or people of God, extended all over the world) shall flourish as the grass of the earth." Read the whole Psalm and view the elect head and elect body.

I know, that in all declarations of God's eternal decree, the idea of distinction and limitation among the elect body, is kept up: Some shall sooner become acquainted with these things, and some later: Some in a higher, and some in a lower degree: Some more happily affected than others, and bring forth more fruits of holiness, and enjoy more consolation in consequence thereof. But all these distinctions and limitations are confined to the present world; none reach beyond.

The Son of man saith, "all that the Father hath given me shall come unto me, &c." The question is, how many? The answer is "He shall give thee the heathen for thine inheritance, and the uttermost parts of the earth for thy possession." i. e. To be in due time subdued and conquered, by the king anointed on the holy hill of Zion; and made to serve the Lord with fear, and rejoice with trembling, and to kiss the Son. Here also, the idea of the holy and dreadful wrath of God is displayed, and the voice of justice announcing terrible destruction.

I wish the reader cautiously to keep in mind what I have observed before, that the whole of divine revelation is every where mixed from beginning to end, law and gospel side by side; the voice of justice and that of grace; and that the latter, by the sure decree of heaven, and by the merit and power of the Son of God, is to get the final victory. " Grace shall reign through righteousness unto eternal life, by Jesus Christ our Lord."

This elect head is fully equal to his great work of saving all men, taking away the sins of the world. As he died, not only for our sins, who are now distinguished from others by an early sense of his grace, and early manifestations of his fulness; but al-

so for the sins of the whole world. He can
and will extend, in due time, his all efficacious
offices, and exertions of prophet and
king, co-extensive with his work as a priest.
He will seek and save that *lost thing*. The
utmost perverseness of human nature will be
overcome, until " the earth shall be full of
the knowledge of the Lord as the waters
cover the sea." This elect head of human
nature "shall stand for an ensign of the
people, to it shall the Gentiles seek, and his
rest shall be glorious;" read Isai. xi.

Again, the elect of God in whom his soul
delighteth, shall manifest to all nations the
judgment of the law, or justice of God,
wholly satisfied in him. All, that his obedience
unto death hath merited, his power
and faithfulness will apply to the human
kind, in the most distant times and regions.
In spite of all opposition he will not fail nor
be discouraged, until the most distant islands
in the world have bowed to the all commanding
power of his grace, the almighty energy
of his spirit; so that they shall sing to the
Lord a new song, and his praise from the
end of the earth. The wilderness and the
cities thereof shall lift up their voice; the
inhabitants of the rock shall sing, and they
shall shout from the top of the mountains.
Read Isai. xlii. from the beginning to the
16th verse.

This glorious head and the elect body are
one, in the predestination of God. " I will
bring forth a seed out of Jacob, (i. e. Christ)
and out of Judah an inheritor of my moun-

tains, and mine elect (that is, the body of Chrift) fhall inherit it, and my fervants fhall dwell there." Ifai. lxv. 9. "For thus faith the Lord I will extend peace to her like a river, and the glory of the gentiles like a flowing ftream," it is again faid in the prophet "as the days of a tree are the days of my people, and mine elect fhall long enjoy the work of their hands." "The Lord fhall be king over all the earth; in that day fhall there be one Lord and his name one:" i. e. All people fhall be united in his character. We might compile a volume of citations from the prophets, all of the fame tenor, as *pure gofpel*; and, at the fame time fee many limitations and diftinctions among mankind, of a *prefent* different character, and the voice of juftice every where intermixed, and crying aloud for vengeance; but the voice of grace and the blood of Chrift fpeaking better things. "Lo the lion of the tribe of Judah, the root and offspring of David hath prevailed."

I could wifh that every reader might attend to Paul's difcourfe on the doctrine of election, efpecially in the ninth, tenth and eleventh chapters of his epiftle to the Romans. There we find an eternal, fixed plan of Deity, infuring the final falvation of all the *literal*, or *natural* feed of Abraham, all the Jews. Yet, in the courfe of this life, in the courfe of time, and God's difpenfa- tions *on earth*, with that nation, the apoftle takes notice of as great and fovereign dif-

M

tinctions, as between Jacob and Esau, in temporal matters; and makes the latter an emblem to illustrate the former.

He bewails, from his own former bitter experience, hardness of heart, and enmity against Christ; the miserable case of that nation as a body. They wished themselves at the greatest distance from Christ and all his offered grace, as he once did, or could do, in his blindness and enmity. He could sympathize with them, and greatly pity them, from his own experience. He saw but a very few of them reconciled to their Messiah, or in the knowledge and enjoyment of the benefit; only a remnant possessing the knowledge, sense, and comfort of salvation.

Many more gentiles had come to the knowledge and comfort of eternal salvation than of the Jews; though they were very zealous, and followed after righteousness in their own blind way. They rejected an all-sufficient atonement, and eternal life, on the same footing that any publican might have it, or any poor, scandalous, filthy *dog* of the gentile world. For they gave other nations no better epithet. They did not at all understand how, *in Christ* (the only character that God hath the least respect unto, in the final salvation of all men, or *any* man) every valley was filled, and every mountain and hill made low, and all crooked things straight, and all rough things plain, and the Lord alone exalted: How all boasting was cut off, and God would stain the pride of all glory. These things they did not underſtand ; therefore they ſought ſalvation by ways of diſtinction, or as it is expreſſed by the works of the law." They ſuppoſed that they muſt, ſome how, be marked different from other men ; before, any thing God had ever done, would be a *ſure foundation* and a *ſole foundation* of their hope.

THE apoſtle tells them that this was a moſt miſerable ſtate of mind to be in, and a moſt comfortleſs condition; that they were awfully blind, as to all preſent knowledge, love, and ſervice of God, or conſolation ; and that the preſent temper of their hearts involved in it wickedneſs, *injuſtice*, demanding eternal damnation, in their own perſons. He labors with the utmoſt concern, to bring them to know better, to enjoy the comfort of hope, and to love and ſerve God in conſequence of it. Yet he fully aſſerts that God had *ſecured*, and, in his own time, would certainly *effect* the final ſalvation of every Jew that ever had exiſtence. He declares that although their blindneſs was ſo awful at preſent; yet it ſhould not finally prevent their ſalvation.

AFTER all he ſays againſt their moſt abominable obſtinacy, and the doleful effects of it, *in this world ;* he aſſerts that the final ſalvation of his whole kindred nation, ſtood on a foundation very different from any thing *in them*, or in *any creature*. " And ſo all Iſrael ſhall be ſaved : As it is written, there ſhall come out of Zion a deliverer, and ſhall turn away ungodlineſs from Jacob:

For this is my covenant unto them, when I shall take away their sins. As concerning the gospel, they are enemies for your sakes;" i. e. they are left in awful blindness, *for the present*, and will be for a season, that the gospel may have a greater spread among you Gentiles, " but, as touching the election, they are beloved for the fathers' sakes." i. e. Their salvation is secured in the elect body of Christ, together *with*, and as fully *as that* of their fathers, the patriarchs and prophets, who walked ever so humbly and uprightly before God, and enjoyed great consolation: " For the gifts and calling of God are without repentance." Rom. xi. 25.

God never rested one atom of his eternal plan and fixed purpose, on any creature, or any thing that should ever, at any particular time, be found in creatures. They all rather subserve the accomplishment of it, Indeed, they can by no means frustrate " the determinate counsel and foreknowledge of God," in any one instance.

God cuts off all mankind, *wholly, in every view*, but in his *own Son*, Jews and Gentiles alike, and there is not the least difference. He concludes, or shuts all mankind up together, in total wickedness and unbelief; and even in that very predicament, ascertains their salvation, and that of all alike. " For God hath concluded them all in unbelief, that he might have mercy upon all." Rom. xi. 32. This is most astonishing; but, I wish men would not cavil about it, and quarrel with it as they do. Let them rather feel in their hearts, towards the great God and his sovereign will, wisdom, and grace, as Paul did; and say, with him; " O the depth of the riches, both of the wisdom and knowledge of God! how unsearchable are his judgments (i. e. decrees) and his ways past finding out! For of him, and through him, and to him, are all things: To whom be glory forever, Amen. I wish the reader carefully to attend to the Epistles to the Romans and Galatians, in particular, although all the writings of Paul, and the whole sacred scripture centre in the same great point; *Chrift, and the falvation of his myftic body.*

In a word; the doctrine of God's election, or eternal, fixed choice, decrees, predestination, by what name soever you are pleased to call it, as it respects his grace to the human kind in this world, and their salvation in the world to come, stands exactly thus, in all the reason we are capable of, and in all the sacred oracles. All is fixed and immutable, in the mind of Jehovah, from eternity to eternity; involving innumerable distinctions among men, communities, and nations of men; and, as many in regard to privileges, light, comfort, influence and effect, *in the prefent world;* and great, and innumerable distinctions and differences in the life and *world to come,* in regard to *different degrees* of happiness, dignity, and glory. Yet the divine purpose alike secures all men *in Chrift alone;* in his union with, and covenant for human nature, *as a covenant for the people,* and Gods falvation to the ends of the earth ; and by the exertion of his office of prieft, prophet, and king, in equal extent with each other. In this way, I fay, alike fecures every part of human nature, from any pain or forrow in the world to come : And alike fecures real happinefs and glory to every one, in that proportion of grace, which infinite wifdom and goodnefs hath appointed.

We now look into the atonement, the fource of all hope to guilty man. Some have, in late years, imbibed a fentiment concerning the atonement, exceedingly different from that of the prophets and apoftles, that of the primitive fathers in the chriftian church, or that of our chriftian fathers in later times, fuch as *Luther, Calvin, Owen, Flavel, Watts, Hooker, Edwards,* and indeed every man in Europe and America, that has paft under the denomination of a calvinift, fince the reformation.

Their idea is, that the atonement is nothing of a vicarious nature. They admit nothing like a fubftitute ; nothing like a legal transfer of guilt and righteoufnefs, by divine conftitution and appointment ; nothing like a bondfman paying for an original debtor ; nothing like a redeemer, under the Jewifh law, ftepping into the place of his kinfman, and redeeming by price his forfeited inheritance ; nothing like a good character prefented and accepted, *in law,* in the room and ftead of a bad one,

&c. &c. But thefe have been uniformly, the fentiments of thofe I before mentioned, fince the chriftian æra; and the uniform fenfe of the Jewifh church, with refpect to the great atonement pointed out by all the facrifices, fubftitutes, propitiations, and atonements of that œconomy; and have ever been the invariable fentiments of all nations of the earth, fo far as they have made ufe of propitiations and atonements.

Those ideas, and indeed, the idea of any proper atonement, or legal transfer of guilt and righteoufnefs, is now wholly difcarded by fome. They have, to the great aftonifhment of many, boldly afferted that all the oblations and facrifices of the ancient church, had no direct meaning in them; but that they are a vague and indefinite kind of premonition, that a Meffiah fhould, in due time, fuffer, not however, as an *oblation*, *vicar*, or *fubftitute*, for any man. Hence according to them, he did not bear any man's fins in his own body on the tree, in any direct and proper fenfe; was not wounded for our tranfgreffions, or bruifed for our iniquities; the chaftifement of our peace, was not upon him, nor are we healed by his ftripes: Only as in a mere metaphorical, indirect, and improper fenfe.

Having denied the transfer, and every thing of the nature of a direct and proper imputation, they explain the whole import of Chrift's obedience unto death, in the following manner. " That God being in his free fovereign goodnefs, determined to fave sinners, of his own mere mercy, was yet equally determined to vindicate his law, and give the highest possible testimony of his everlasting approbation of it, to all intelligent creatures. Therefore, with the free consent of his own Son, brought him under this same law, in human nature, and then exacted the whole demand of it. Hereby shewing, that God so highly esteemed the law, as to honor it, at the greatest possible expence; and that he was willing to do nothing, but as he would be done by. But in the like predicament, he was willing his Son should suffer just as his law demands of man: And having given this greatest demonstration of the infinite excellency of his law, he now pardons and saves whom he pleases, of his own sovereign grace and mere mercy." This they call the atonement; though in full opposition to all propriety of language, as will fully appear.

They have no idea of setting this atonement to the account of man; or laying the iniquities of men on Christ, by any legal transfer, or any vicarious covenant of redemption, or any thing like imputations on either side. They only say, that the door is now wide open for God to save sinners, and fully maintain all the honors of justice, and that God now acts, according to the free propensity of his own nature, in this great affair.

This doctrine, if true, would, at first sight shew us that the eternal happiness of all sinners is made sure. For what will not infinite love (GOD IS LOVE) joined with infinite power do, when there remains not the leaft claim of juftice, or any other divine attribute in the way? We may fafely abide by what God hath fo often, and fo clearly told us; that nothing but the claim of juftice can ftand in the way of our happinefs. All his moral attributes are on the fide of our happinefs, this only excepted. All his natural attributes are ready to carry into effect all that his infinite grace, mercy, and love point out; faving only that the honor of his law, the copy of his infinite holinefs and juftice, ftands in the way.

THAT the moral nature of God is infinite love, is moft certain: That this love pleads infinitely for fparing every finner from eternal death, he hath often faid, and confirmed by folemn oath, Ezek. xviii. and through the whole tenor of his word. Now what can any defire more, to infure their own falvation, than the declaration and oath of God, that his whole difpofition is infinitely oppofed to the final deftruction of any man: being alfo affured, that every attribute of his nature, may appear infinitely glorious and honorable, in the falvation of all; and that infinite, uncontroulable wifdom and power, are ever ready to accomplifh all the divine will?

I THEREFORE fay again, that, if the aforementioned, new notion of the atonement were juft, the final falvation of all mankind would be as fure, as infinite love and power can make it; and there would need no more to be said on the subject. But I would not avail myself, at all, of this principle: For it is entirely opposite to all reason, and the whole word of God.

THE TRUE DOCTRINE OF THE ATONEMENT is in very deed this. A *direct*, *true*, and *proper setting all our guilt to the account of Christ, as our fœderal head and sponsor*: And a *like placing his obedience unto death, to our account*. In the covenant of redemption and divine constitution, God regards both parties, just as though the Son of man had personally done all, man hath done; and man had done and suffered all that the *second* man hath himself done and suffered. Rom. viii. 3, 4. "For what the law could not do, in that it was weak through the flesh, God sending his own Son in the likeness of sinful flesh, and for sin condemned sin in the flesh: That the righteousness of the law might be fulfilled in us, who walk not after the flesh, but after the spirit." In the atonement, JEHOVAH looked on his Son, in the glass of fœderal stipulation, in the very character of sinful man, and, *for him a true and proper substitute*, and treated him in justice as such; and took complete satisfaction of him, for all sinful man deserved. This being done, he looks on sinful man in the *true* and *proper character* of his substitute or vicar, even the Son of man, and will be sure to treat him accordingly. The assertion is most astonishing, and far from what man or angels would ever have thought of, had it not been revealed by God himself. This, agreeably to the divine oracles, is a conſtant mark of the truth.

HERE ſome may cry out and ſay, guilt and righteouſneſs is of a perſonal nature, and cannot be transferred. But I now promiſe, that in its proper place, I will fully demonſtrate, that although both theſe are perſonal, they may be transferred, fully according to reaſon and common ſenſe, as well as agreeably to the divine conſtitution. But firſt, I muſt adduce my evidences to ſhew that the ſcripture doctrine of atonement is exactly as I have ſtated.

HERE are four engliſh terms, frequent in the bible, which promiſcuouſly convey the ſame idea, viz. *atonement, ranſom, propitiation*, and *redemption*. The learned will bear me witneſs, that the ſame original hebrew and greek words, with all their compounds and derivatives, are promiſcuouſly tranſlated by theſe engliſh words, with the derivatives and compounds of the ſame. The ſubſtantives are uſed *ſeventy two* times in the old and new teſtament, in the original, and alſo in the tranſlation. They, every where, either directly import, or fairly allude unto a true and proper transfer, or ſetting the doings or ſufferings of one, to the true and proper account of another; or dealing with one, not in his perſonal character, but in the perſonal character of another, *by him aſſumed*.

I MIGHT fill many foolſcaps, ſhould I bring up to view diſtinctly, every paſſage in ſcripture that is to the purpose, and make only a brief comment on each. I shall only adduce a few, and leave the reader to add many more, at his leisure, if he please. The plain import of all the sacrifices and oblations, which God appointed by Moses, first meet our view. Their whole meaning centers in the antitype, which all, that pay any regard to revelation, allow to be Christ. There is no figure no metaphor in a *type*, any more than in the most plain and simple proposition. All types only speak in the most direct manner to the *eye*, what the most simple proposition does to the eye, if read, or to the ear if pronounced. Our mouths speak words; types speak things more directly, and admit no metaphor.

The term is first used, to give us the true and proper idea of a propitiation, ransom, &c. in Exodus xxi. 30. "If there be laid on him a sum of money, then he shall give for the RANSOM of his life whatsoever is laid upon him." Here the money mentioned, comes directly and properly into the place of the man's life; one or the other must be laid down. Again Exodus xxx. 12, 16. "And thou shalt take the atonement-money of the children of Israel, and shalt appoint it for the service of the tabernacle of the congregation; that it may be a memorial unto the children of Israel before the LORD, to make an atonement for your souls." An atonement is called *atonement-money*, the whole idea of which is negotiable, or transferable. In the case of the redemption of an inheritance that has been alienated, the word is often used to signify a proper price. Levit. xxv. 23, 24, 25. Paul, with the plainest allusion to this chapter, comments upon it, applying it to the redemption by Christ. Ephef. i. 14. " Which is the earnest of our inheritance, until the redemption of the purchased possession, unto the praise of his glory." How directly is the victim put in the place of Isaac? See Gen. xxii. No language can possibly speak plainer than the type of the two goats, Levit. xvi. The high priest killed one goat *for the people;* shewing that they all deserved to die; and that the antitype should indeed die *for them.* Then, by a plain signal, with full confession of all their sins, laid them on the head of the scape goat, to be carried away into everlasting oblivion, as to any punishment that should come on them in another world, for their sins; though the very symbol, so often repeated, would keep them in perpetual remembrance, for a proper effect on their own minds.

DAVID applies the direct and proper import of all these types, to redemption by Christ, and makes use of the same words, Psalm xlix. 7, 8. " None of them can by any means redeem his brother, nor give to God a ransom for him: For the redemption of their soul is precious, and it ceaseth forever." Solomon understands the same term to mean *one thing directly for another,* Prov. xiii. 8. " The ransom of a man's life are his riches." Read Paul's comment on the import of all these terms, centering in Christ, Rom. iii. 21. to the end. The apostle here and every where, notices the abundance of grace connected with our justification; and also shews us that there is much more of grace and mercy connected with our justification, by a *true* and *proper imputation*, than could be in any other way, which I shall fully confirm in its proper place.

In the fifth chapter of the epistle to the Romans, Paul considers the atonement in this view: That Jesus paid the whole price for us, or exhibited his own character to God in the room and stead of ours, when we were in our worst state, without repentance, without faith, in all our enmity, and in every view most unworthy: That he did justify us, not as *penitent;* but as *impenitent;* not as *believers,* but as *unbelievers;* for penitence and faith are exercises of a new heart, and godliness; not as *godly,* in the least degree; but as wholly *ungodly:* And then brings the knowledge and comfort of this previous transaction to our souls, by giving us a *heart prepared* to have light and full evidence operate properly upon; also, communicating to us full evidence of what he hath done, so that we receive a *previous atonement,* and " know the things that are freely given us of God."

John tells us, if *any man,* any of the human kind sin, we have an advocate with the Father, Jesus Christ the righteous: that they who *at present* are convinced of this, have *present special comfort* in it; but that the propitiation and the advocate would surely extend to all, in *due time*. For he declares that this advocate for any man, "is the propitiation for our sins, and not for ours only, but also for the sins of the WHOLE WORLD." He also declares, that a man must have a good and obedient heart given him, in order to take this comfort. "And hereby we do know that we know him, if we keep his commandments." 1. John, ii. 1, 2, 3.

JESUS tells us, Matt. xx. 28. and Mark x. 45. what the end of his death was ; " to give his life a ransom for *many*." He does not, in these places, tell us *how many*. The word *many*, may comprehend a *part*, or *all* of the human race. In John i. 29. the extent of the ransom is declared. " John seeth Jesus coming unto him, and saith, Behold the Lamb of God, which taketh away the SIN OF THE WORLD." Paul understands this ransom for many, to signify just as many as there shall ever exist of the human kind, and so calls it " *a ransom for all.*" 1. Tim. ii. 6.

THE same apostle speaketh of the exceeding comfort resulting from predestination and adoption, as first communicated to present believers, and equally sure in God's time, to extend to all the children of men. Ephes. i. 4,—14. " According as he hath chosen us in him, before the foundation of the world, that we should be holy, and without blame before him in love: Having predestinated us unto the adoption of children, by Jesus Christ to himself, according to the good pleasure of his will, to the praise of the glory of his grace, wherein he hath made us accepted in the Beloved: In whom we have redemption through his blood, the forgiveness of sins, according to the riches of his grace; wherein he hath abounded toward us in all wisdom and prudence, having made known unto us the mystery of his will, according to his good pleasure, which he hath purposed in himself: That in the dispensation of the fulness of times, he might gather together in one ALL THINGS in Christ, both which are in heaven, and which are on earth, even in him: In whom also we have obtained an inheritance, being predestinated according to the purpose of him who worketh all things after the counsel of his own will: That we should be to the praise of his glory, who first trusted in Christ. In whom ye also trusted after that ye heard the word of truth, THE GOSPEL OF YOUR SALVATION: in whom also, after that ye believed, ye were sealed with that holy Spirit of promise."

THE whole book of divine revelation gives us the same idea of the propitiation, atonement, ransom, redemption; by whatever term is imported our *meritorious* justification, ascertaining our final salvation. *Meritorious*, I say; for never was there a clearer distinction in the word of God, than the three different significations of the term *justification*: 1st. By the atonement *meritoriously*: 2. By faith *instrumentally*, for comfort and enjoyment: 3. By works, *declaratively*, or as evidence of our juftification. If the reader reads as he ought on fuch a fubject, he will certainly have his bible before him : I will therefore only further refer to a few paffages, which he may confult and comment upon for himfelf. John i. 29.—iii. 16, 17.—iv. 42.—vi. 33, 51.—viii. 12.—xii. 47.—xvii. 21, 23. Rom. iv. 13. —xi. 12, 15. 2. Cor. v. 18, to the end, compare Pfal. lxiv. 9, with John xii. 32. Ephef. iii. Titus iv.

In thefe laft two chapters referred to, the infinite, fovereign, all conquering grace and power of God appear moft aftonifhing. Here the apoftle confiders the whole preaching of the gofpel, and faith wrought in the foul, as having no other concern with their glorious objects ; but only by comfort in them, and perfonal improvement: Not at all altering God's purpofe and grace, or Chrift's merits, or his fure determination to apply them to finners ; but only giving them an apprehenfion and fenfibility of all thefe things, and fo laying a foundation for meet fruits.

PAUL fpeaks of the whole as completed by God, in Chrift, and nothing more remaining to be done, but the communication of it to finners by regeneration, repentance, faith, and every grace ; which are all, wholly the gift of God. " Unto me who am lefs than the leaft of all faints, is this grace given, that I fhould preach among the Gentiles the unfearchable riches of Chrift; and to make *all men see*, what is the fellowship of the mystery, which from the beginning of the world, hath been hid in God, who created all things by Jesus Christ." "That Christ may dwell in your hearts, *by faith ;* that ye being rooted and grounded *in love*, may be able to comprehend with all saints what is the breadth and length, and depth, and height ; and to *know the love of* Christ, which passeth knowledge, (i. e. far beyond all that mankind have hitherto conceived, otherwise there would be a flat contradiction) that ye may be filled with all the fulness of God." Ephes. iii. " For the grace of God that bringeth salvation, hath appeared to *all men*, (i. e, presents one and the same aspect to all the human kind, and the influence when known is alike on the hearts, and in the lives of all) viz. teaching us that, denying ungodliness and worldly lusts, we should live soberly, righteously, and godly, in this present world ; looking for that blessed hope, and the glorious appearing of the great God, and our Saviour Jesus Christ : Who gave himself for us, (with as fixed a purpose of effectual application, as ever he had of meritorious impetration) that he might redeem us from all iniquity, and purify to himself a peculiar people (standing in such a relation to him, as neither angels, nor any other creatures do) zealous of good works ;" i. e. as grace appears, and salvation is brought to the soul by evidence of faith, a zeal for good works does follow. Also those men who, have manifestations of this grace and salvation, are distinguished from those who are not as yet acquainted with it, "*a peculiar people zealous of good works.*" Titus ii. 11. &c.

It has been often said, that guilt and righteousness being of a personal nature cannot be transferred; and that the word of God confirms this, in that it is said, "the soul that sinneth it shall die."

It has been with wonder and astonishment, that I have heard some very sensible men make this remark. Guilt and righteousness are of a personal nature, we all allow; but the consequence does by no means follow, that they cannot be transferred by order of JEHOVAH. Nor can there lie one argument against such a transfer, but what will lie with equal force against any transfer of property, ever made in this world. What gives my neighbor a right to transfer his goods to me for money, or some other valuable consideration? certainly nothing but this, viz. the goods were his property, and the money mine. God gives us the whole warrant and right of contract, transfer, and disposal, and it is the same in every case. *The disposer must be the proprietor*, so far as the disposal is made; this will make it warrantable in every case in the universe, and nothing else can. "May I not do what I will with mine own?"

Now a creature cannot be an absolute proprietor in any thing: This is peculiar to God. Yet creatures have delegated property, within God's limitations. They have no property in opposition to the claim of the Creator; yet they have in opposition to the claims of their fellow creatures. Thus, this paper is mine, and not my neighbor's: But I cannot say it is mine, and not my Maker's. This applies to all that ever can be called the property of any creature. All our property, all that we are owners of, is ours only, in opposition to the claim of our fellow creatures. God is still as much the owner and proprietor of all things, as if he had never given any property to any creature, under any directions or limitations whatever.

I have a right to dispose of my horse, my labor, my land, &c. and my neighbor has no right to controul me. Yet herein, and in all my conduct, I am bound to obey the will, and attend to the orders of the great, and absolute Proprietor of all things. Under this limitation, so far as any thing is my own, I may transfer or dispose of it as I please; and so may every creature of God, in like manner. Has not God himself the same right without limitation of a superior? most certainly. It is only then to shew that God has as real property in all things, moral and natural, temporal and eternal, as I have in the pen I now hold in my hand; and this will prove he has an equal right of disposal, by transfer or any other way. I can easily demonstrate this and much more.

There are several ways, in which mankind acquire property, in the limited sense aforesaid, or such property as we are capable of; particularly by difcovery and occupancy, by purchafe, labor, free gift, &c. In thefe ways we have a right of difpofal and transfer, under the direction of the great and abfolute Owner of all things.

But we fee in a moment, that no property or right we claim, in any of thofe ways, is in any meafure equal to the right arifing from *creation*, or the right of one who gives *whole, intire being* to what he claims. God has this right in every thing without poffibility of exception; in every exiftence natural and moral; in all creatures, and in all done by creatures; and in every difpofition found in creatures, evil as well as good. All guilt and all righteoufnefs are the abfolute property of the great God. He is the origin and fountain of all holinefs, goodnefs, righteoufnefs; " there is none good but one, that is God." As all creatures are his abfolute property, fo are all their difpofitions and actions. Whether good or evil, it alters not the cafe.

In this view of God, as being the abfolute proprietor, and having the fole right of abfolute difpofal; the devil with all that pertains to him, moral and natural, are as wholly and intirely God's property as Gabriel is. A man may be owner of bad property as well as good, and fo may God.

You have two fons in their minority, the one the beft, and the other the vileft in the world. They are both alike yours, and at your difpofal. One of your hands is wounded and in extreme pain, the other perfectly well; yet they are both alike your own. You have a flock of sheep in your pasture, and there is also a den of serpents on your land, which you bought with all its appurtenances. You are the owner and proprietor of those venemous serpents, as much as of your sheep, and have an equal right to kill them both; the one for the supply of your table; the other for the sake of being out of danger from their poison. You have an equal right to transfer them both. Some eminent physician may appear, who knows well how he can turn that den of venemous serpents to more advantage, and greater good to mankind, than he can all the sheep you possess. They are yours; and you may transfer them to him.

So far as man is owner and proprietor of any thing, whether that thing be good or evil, it alters not the right of disposal in the least. If I could exercise true benevolence to my fellow men, in healing them, and in furnishing them with sure antidotes against mortal poison, by keeping a den of the most deadly serpents, under proper restraint; I would do it. No man would say I did wrong: Or that I was not the proprietor of them, and had no right to transfer them; because they are such evil, hateful creatures. Thus, the MOST HIGH turns his whole cave of devils to good account, and to the greatest perfection of benevolence, in a system replete with love. And so he does all the moral evil in the universe. He makes use of creatures and things of the moral kind, which are infinitely hateful to him, *in their nature*, to anſwer great and good ends, *in the whole ſyſtem*.

But God never made ſin. Who did? The devil and wicked men. Be it ſo. Yet this devil and all his aſſociates, and all wicked men, are God's property, *abſolutely* and *wholly* ſo; and of conſequence all their doings are equally his property. Sin is a property infinitely hateful in its nature; but it is not therefore the leſs at God's diſpoſal, as his *own property*, by transfer, or any other way he pleaſes. God is an abſolute ſovereign in diſpoſing of it juſt as he pleaſes. "May I not do what I will with mine own?"

On the other hand. As to all righteouſneſs; God is the original fountain of the whole, that ever did, or can exiſt in himſelf, and in all creatures. It is all abſolutely his own property, as much after communication as before. And all the creatures to whom it is communicated, are in like manner his own. All the holineſs found in their temper, character and conduct is ſo in every view; and Chriſt, as mediator and ſavior of the world, is as abſolutely his, as any creature he ever made. "*Chriſt is God's.*"

Now, in the name of reaſon and common ſenſe, what hinders a transfer, if God pleaſes? does he meddle with any thing but his own abſolute property; to which no other Being in the univerſe has any oppoſite claim, any more that I have now a right to claim Godhead, as my own? Shew me, that Jehovah is dealing in ſomething that is not his abfolute property; and I will then, and not till then, deny that he hath a right to transfer guilt and righteoufnefs, at his pleafure.

But if God is fuch a fovereign as this comes to, where is the fafety of creatures? where is the fafety of man? Be patient, kind reader, I will open to you a glorious foundation of fafety, in its proper place. Take only this hint for the prefent. All the fafety, hope, and happinefs of man, and of the whole, intelligent fyftem, lies in the *nature, moral character, eternal decrees,* and *fovereign will* of JEHOVAH alone. But this is a digreffion, to be refumed in its proper place.

It is expedient here, that I fhew what it is that ever induced any man, that hath acknowledged divine revelation, to draw a confequence fo palpably erroneous, from a pofition that is very true. " *Guilt and righteoufnefs,* fay they, *are of a perfonal nature:* Certainly, there*fore, God himfelf has no right to transfer them*" !!! That is to fay, God has no more property in the moral fyftem than I have! JEHOVAH has no more right to give law to his creatures, than any one man has to another. The MOST HIGH has no right to covenant for his creatures, his own abfolute property; though I have a good right to covenant for my children in many things, and effectually bind them to abide by what I have done.

It is true, a man has no right to covenant for his own children, in matters of a *moral nature,* matters of *guilt* and *righteoufnefs.*

What is the reason that he may not do this, as well as in *pecuniary* matters? It is only because God has given him his limits. Man is an absolute proprietor of nothing. He has a *limited* property, within certain bounds, and that under divine regulation; and thus far he may plead the general warrant of disposal, "*may I not do what I will with my own?*" Beyond this he may not presume. The same may be said of the highest angel; but not of God. He is wholly without limitation, with regard to his own absolute property, in all things *moral*, as well as all things *natural*. And in regard to *righteousness* and *guilt*, they are in all reason, and by every dictate of revelation, as absolutely and justly at his disposal, as a sparrow, or a single hair of your head.

If any should here say, This makes God a guilty being, and his nature like the nature of sin. The cavil would be worthy of no other answer than this; If you own a very wicked servant, whose temper and conduct is hateful to you every day; you are certainly as wicked as he.

We now conclude, that God may according to reason and common sense, transfer and impute guilt and righteousness. His word declares abundantly that he hath this right, and that he hath exercised it, to the most benevolent and glorious purpose. This is the grand distinguishing doctrine of divine revelation, which Paul considered as comprehending the whole. *This*, with its glorious corrections and consequences, claimed his whole attention. "For I determined not to know any thing among you, save Jesus Christ and him crucified." "God forbid that I should glory, save in the cross of our Lord Jesus Christ, by whom the world is crucified unto me and I unto the world." "God hath laid upon him the iniquity of us all." "He was wounded for our iniquities, he was bruised for our transgressions, the chastisement of our peace was upon him, and by his stripes we are healed." "Christ our passover is sacrificed for us." "He who knew no sin was made sin for us, that we might be made the righteousness of God in him." "Thou shalt make his soul an offering for sin."

REASON doth most fully warrant or support a salvation by a proper *vicar*, by *substitution*, transfer, imputation of guilt and righteousness. Not a single reason can be offered against it, but what will lie, even with greater apparent force, against your right of transferring one shilling for a supper; or redeeming your own brother out of prison, by the *vicarious transfer* of one pound. Reason, I say, tells us in the clearest, possible manner, that God may so redeem man, if he pleases. But we are wholly indebted to divine revelation, to know that he hath so done. If he hath not there told us so; it is utterly beyond all the power of language ever to communicate that idea. Give up this doctrine, and we may still reckon the Bible among good books, and even call it the best on the whole. Yet there will be nothing left, to distinguish it from the works of Plato, Cicero, Seneca, &c. otherwise than as any one good writer may somewhat excel another. If all mankind would abuse *all words* as they do *some terms*, who deny that the salvation of sinners is founded on a *proper substitution;* all use and benefit of language would be forever at an end.

The reason why any run so wild in this matter, is, because they have not a true knowledge of Jehovah. They reason about " the possessor of heaven and earth," who is under no limitation, " and who worketh all things according to the counsel of his own will ;" just as they would about the conduct of creatures, who have no absolute property, and are capable of none.

Here, many have found fault with that most clear doctrine of divine revelation, that God constituted Adam a fœderal head for all his race; in language like this. " *I was not present ;*" " *I knew nothing about it ;*" " *I did not agree to it ;*" therefore it is unjust that I should be holden by it." Unthinking man! Do you not so far as you have property, make bargains and covenants to bind your heirs and successors, and those unborn too? Will you not hold fast a privilege acquired in a covenant way, by your great grandfather, or any predecessor at the distance of many generations, and descending to you by right of heirship? What if your neighbor should come and claim your farm, and say, this was my grandfather's; and he sold it; and I was not present. I never gave my consent; and I will not be holden by what he did. I will have the farm. Would you not tell him that his predecessor did nothing but what he had a right to do; and bid defiance to his claim?

But God hath a better right to the disposal of all things, *moral* and *natural*, than ever any man had to that of his land. Besides, he covenanted only for his *own children*, his *own offspring*. In this view, all mankind stand in a much nearer relation to the common Parent of all, than ever any child did to an earthly parent. And we can no more dissolve this relation by all our sins, than the wickedness of your son, can make him cease to be *your son*. Moreover, the covenant God made with Adam, was infinitely better than we could have made for ourselves, had we been present; as will abundantly appear in the sequel. However, God had full right to make it, and *confirm it*, and that on both sides too, upon the ground of absolute and universal property.

When you covenant with your neighbor it is proper for you to say, *I will if you will*: I propose, and wait for your consent. Otherwise there can be nothing binding. You make one part of the covenant, your neighbor the other: for you are equals. It is not so with you, and that Being, "of whom, and through whom, and to whom, are all things." He every where makes both parts of the covenant, and would descend infinitely beneath his right and dignity if he did not. His language to man is, *I will, and you shall;* and never leaves it at the election of man, to comply with his covenant, or refuse with impunity.

But, some have imagined that this idea of justification, by a *true* and *proper atonement, substitution,* or *ransom,* is inconsistent with free justification by grace, or free salvation by mere mercy, so often spoken of in scripture. This is so far from being a just remark, that I am bold to affirm, that free grace and mere mercy abound to sinners in this way, more than could be possible in any other way. *It is all grace,* displayed and communicated to sinners, *in the most gracious way.* Was it not infinite, sovereign grace and mercy in God that first moved in this grand affair? in the Father, to give the Son of his love to suffer and die for sinners, and in the Son to consent, and undertake? Is not the whole purchase, all of mere, sovereign grace and mercy as it respects sinners, in all their guilt and enmity against God? " While we were without strength, in due time, Christ died for the *ungodly.*" " God commendeth his love, i. e. displays it to the very best advantage, in that while we were *yet sinners,* Christ died for us." Hence the apostle argues the certainty of the application of the salvation thus purchased for sinners, while in their *very worst condition.* Because they were *even then justified,* by the blood of Christ, before they knew any thing of it; before repentance, or faith, or regeneration, or any change in their hearts towards God: Justified, I say, by Christ their surety and Redeemer, in the presence of God, long before they had any knowledge of it by faith; or any comfort in the great work that the second man had finished. What can be plainer than the following words? "Much more then, being now justified by his blood, we shall be saved from wrath through him. For if, *when we were enemies, we were reconciled to God, by the death of his Son;* much more *being reconciled,* we shall be saved by his life." Rom. v. 8, &c. Thus the atonement is so far from any thing inconsistent with free grace and mere mercy, that God thereby displays and communicates it to the utmost advantage, "*commendeth his love.*"

Men often greatly derogate from the free grace which they bestow, by the manner in which they communicate it. Your neighbor received from his father, as good an inheritance as you did from yours; and in both cases, the gift was of mere parental love, or free grace. Whenever he petitioned his father with regard to the expected plantation, he was answered with frowns, and kept much in suspense, for forty years. His father used often to tell him; "Son, I will have you to know, that I will make you sure of nothing; I will keep you doubtful, and will do as I please." After forty years, his father, at his death, left him the estate; but he might rather thank death for the comfort of his fortune, than his father.

Your father gave you just as much, of his free grace likewise; but in a different mode. When you was twenty two years of age, he called you to him, and with a paternal complacency in his countenance, addressed you thus. "My son, you are sensible God has blessed me with a plentiful estate, for which I wish ever to be thankful. One half of my estate is more than I can use to any advantage, otherwise than to communicate comfort to others. You, my child, are in the bloom of youth, and I wish to make you as useful and happy as I can, in early life, and all your days; I have therefore given and confirmed to you my house in the next street, and the five hundred acres of land adjoining. The deed was executed last year; and that you may have the comfort of your estate, and every encouragement and motive to industry and usefulness, I now give you the deed, by which I have made the whole sure to you." Then he gave you the instrument under his hand and seal, well executed: Adding; "paternal affection is a mighty principle in the human soul; I wish divine Providence may give you experience of it ere long, in domestic connection." You went immediately into the possession of your fine estate; and have had great comfort in it these forty years.

Your neighbor is now at last, as wealthy as you are; but he has been in doleful suspense and anxiety this forty years, often surmizing he should die a beggar. He hath not enjoyed the comforts of life as you have;

nor had those encouragements and motives to industry; nor loved his father half so well as you have yours. True, at last, when covered with gray hairs, he has received the same free grace from his father that you have from yours; but in a manner very different. You had a title, by *firm* covenant in early life, founded on *mere grace:* He was kept at *sovereign mercy*, in distressing suspense until he was an old man, and then was made rich by *free grace* likewise. Now, my reader, is there not as much grace in the conduct of your father towards you, as your neighbor has experienced from his father? Was not the manner of communication as gracious, and much more so? Just so, our heavenly Father not only makes us rich by *mere grace;* but in the most *gracious manner*, giving us all possible sense of his infinite good will; and all possible comfort in the enjoyment; and every motive to gratitude and usefulness. And, the exercise of goodness through his own Son, *in fœderal capacity*, doth much enhance and commend this grace.

No person of ingenuity, will cavil at a similitude; because it is not in all respects a resemblance. None are so. If they illustrate the point aimed at, it is enough. The above is intended only to illustrate this truth, viz. Much of mere grace lies in the manner of bestowment.

In the great affair of our justification; though it is legally due *from the Father to the Son*, in consideration of the atonement he has made; yet the grace connected with it, is, in every view, infinite, and displayed in a manner gracious in the highest degree. It is grace, free, sovereign grace, in the eternal counsels of heaven : All grace in the decree : Grace in the gift, and in the undertaking : Infinite grace in all Christ has done and suffered, as it respects sinners: Sovereign grace in their regeneration, conversion, the gift of repentance, faith, holiness, consolation, perseverance, eternal glory : All grace, free grace, sovereign grace, unsearchable riches of grace, *from God to man;* though the Son hath a claim of righteousness on the Father, and pleads for the *unjust* and the *ungodly*, on the ground of the covenant. From the foundation to the top stone thereof, all is " brought forth with shouting; crying grace! Grace! unto it."

If we attend to the threefold office of our SAVIOR, as *Priest*, *King*, and *Prophet*; we shall find the final salvation of every human creature made sure in him.

THAT Christ doth sustain these three distinct offices, as our Redeemer, I suppose, none will deny; since he is expressly designated by each of these appellations, in sacred scripture, in a great many places; and since kings, priests, and prophets, as types of Christ, speak of his doings and sufferings as their own. " They pierced my hands and my feet." " They shall look on *me* whom they have pierced, and shall mourn for *him.*" " A priest forever, after the order of Melchisedec." " Give thy judgments to the King." " A King shall reign in righteousness." " King of Kings." But I suppose it wholly needless to adduce proof of this matter, and would only exhibit the demonstration arising from the character of Christ, as *prophet, priest,* and *king.* It is manifest that *all these offices are equal,* as to their extent and operation. Christ is just as far, and as extensively a King over mankind, as he is a Priest and a Prophet; and as far as he doth exercise these offices at all, among the human kind, he doth exercise, and engage to exercise them all unto perfection.

Now, it is universally allowed that Christ is a Prophet, Priest and King, in some respect, and in some degree, to *all* mankind: that the world enjoys many common favors through his atonement, and government of the world; and that all the light, knowledge, and instruction mankind enjoy, is through him, as his gift. But then, the *limitarians* would make one office of Christ, much less extensive than another. " His atonement, say they, is abundantly sufficient for all. As a Priest, he wears an equal aspect to all, presenting his infinite atonement to every man alike. As a King, he governs and will govern all creatures, by his almighty power, with uncontrouled effect, according to his own will; either to make them dutiful subjects, or to punish them as rebels. He will dispose of all men, and all things with an irresistible arm; saving only, that the moral dispositions of most of the children of men shall be exempt from his kingly government, and remain unconquered. He will subdue *some things*, but not *all things*, to himself. He will make *some knees* to bow, but not *every knee*. He will bring down *some high thoughts*, but not *every high thought*." Thus they extend the *sacerdotal* far beyond the *regal* office of Christ.

As to his *prophetic* office, they restrain and limit that very much indeed. They allow that he gives common light and knowledge to mankind in general; but not that saving light which is, by way of distinction, called the *true light*. They allow that he is the *common light*, but not the " *true light*, that lighteth every man that cometh into the world." They will make a great distinction, or limitation, where the inspired Evangelist makes none at all. They will not allow that " in him was life; and the life was the light of men," without a word of limitation. John i. 4. But make the three offices of Christ aforementioned, quite unequal, as to their extent and efficacy.

Paul represents the offices of Christ as co-extensive. Effectual calling is by virtue of the prophetic and kingly office of Christ: Justification pertains to the sacerdotal, or priestly office, by the atonement: The sanctification, perseverance, and glorification of sinners, result from all the offices of Christ alike. This apostle tells us that where one of these offices is exercised, the other two are, in every instance. Rom. viii. "Whom he did predestinate, them he also called: and whom he called, them he also justified: and whom he justified, them he also glorified. What shall we then say to these things? If God be for us, who can be against us? He that spared not his own Son, but delivered him up for us ALL, how shall he not with him also freely give us all things?" - - - - - - "For I am persuaded that neither death, nor life, nor angels, nor principalities, nor powers, nor things present, nor things to come, nor height, nor depth, nor any other creature, shall be able to separate us from the love of God which is in Christ Jesus our Lord." As to the extent of this love, we are left at no loss, being told that "God so loved *the world*, that he gave his only begotten Son, that whosoever believeth in him should not perish, but have everlasting life." If you would know how many shall believe and be saved, Jesus tells you in the next words: "For God sent not his Son into *the world* to condemn *the world*, but that *the world* through him might be saved. John iii. 16, 17. Would you know how far the light of Christ, and his prophetic office to mankind, shall finally extend, see John i. 7. "The same came for a witness, to bear witness of the light, that *all men* through him might *believe:*" The same is affirmed John xvii. 21. "That *the world* may believe that thou hast sent me."

I HAVE before shewn that the eternal decree of JEHOVAH, the firm predeſtination of heaven, or the infinitely merciful election of God, as it reſpects mankind after death, comprehends all alike.

IT appears that " the head of *every man* is Chriſt," 1. Cor. xi. 3. and that in the covenant of redemption, all mankind were given to the *Second Adam*, as they were once included in the *Firſt ;* that he undertook to redeem them by *price*, by *power*, and by *application* of the atonement he engaged to make; and which, in the fulneſs of time, he did make : That nothing can reſiſt his power as King eternal, immortal, inviſible : That our whole ſalvation is committed to him, in every view, and in every part of it, as *Alpha* and *Omega*, the beginning and the ending, the firſt and the laſt : That " other foundation can no man lay than that which is laid, which is Jeſus Chriſt :" That he is of one mind, and who can turn him? and what his ſoul deſireth, that he doeth : That of him, and through him, and to him, are all things : That he hath placed himſelf on the mountain of his holineſs and ſtrength, and that, in his own time, he will take away the veil of darkneſs, and covering of ignorance, that hath been ſpread over all the nations of the earth ; and will ſhew them that death, *ſpiritual* and *eternal*, is ſwallowed up in victory ; and exhibit the goſpel feaſt of joy and glory to all the world.

THUS, as on a glorious and holy mountain, doth he take his ſtation, and, in divine majeſty and love, proclaim aloud, ſaying,

"In this mountain, shall the Lord of hosts make unto *all people* a feast of fat things, a feast of wines on the lees, of fat things full of marrow, of wines on the lees well refined; and he will destroy, in this mountain, the face of the covering cast over all people, and the veil that is spread over all nations. He will swallow up death in victory; and the Lord God will wipe away tears from off *all faces;* and the rebuke of his people shall he take away, from off *all the earth:* for the Lord hath spoken it. And it shall be said in that day, lo, this is our God, we have waited for him, and he will save us; this is the Lord; we have waited for him; we will be glad and rejoice in his salvation; for in this mountain shall the hand of the Lord rest." Isai. xxv. 6, &c. This well agrees with what has been said of the progressive manifestations of grace and salvation to men. Infinite wisdom hath seen best to keep a veil and a covering over all nations, in a greater or less degree; and to draw it aside a little, by slow gradations, until the glorious removal of it, in full display, on the mountain of the Lord.

The certain salvation of the human kind, may be argued from the doctrine of repentance, as preached by Christ and his apostles.

All will allow that repentance is certainly connected with pardon and salvation. Now, wherein does this certain connection consist? Does it merit pardon? No: Does it at all change the eternal, immoveable purpose of

God ? No : Does repentance save us, as a meritorious good work, or good difposition in the foul ? No : How then is repentance furely connected with pardon and life ? As God's ordinance, and as a fit temper of mind; without which, in the very nature of things, pardon and heaven itself could be no blessing. This is, indeed, the true anfwer.

Now, who gives repentance to finners ? Who makes this gofpel qualification fure to them, before they go to heaven ? Does it depend in the leaft on themfelves ? So far from this, their whole fouls oppofe it with all their might. Can any creature give it to another ? No : Do finners ever before they are penitent, do any thing to render it reafonable that God fhould give to them repentance rather than to others ? No. Repentance is a free, fovereign gift of God in Chrift, who will have mercy on whom he will have mercy, for his own name's fake, and for his own praife. And Jefus is exalted to grant this grace, juft as much as the remiffion of fins, in confequence of it. He gives the former, only as the neceffary channel, or medium by which pardon and falvation can come to the foul. The gift of this grace is juft as much within his commiffion, as *Mediator* and *Savior* of the world, Savior of all men, as is the beftowment of pardon and heaven. " Him hath God exalted, with his right hand, to be a Prince and a Savior, for to give repentance to *Ifrael*, (all are fo, in union with Chrift, by human nature, and by covenant) and forgiveness of sins." Acts v. 31.

The prayer of Christ is efficacious. "Him the Father heareth alway." He has prayed for the pardon of those that you would exclude, if you exclude any of the human kind; even *Judas*, and *Pilate*, and *Herod*, and the malicious chief Priests, and murderous, bloody band of soldiers, and all that mocked and derided him, on the day when he finished the great work. For all these he surely poured out an effectual, fervent prayer; "Father forgive them, for they know not what they do." In this prayer which the Father certainly heard, (as he does alway without a single exception) Jesus comprehended every sinner in the world; for every sin doth crucify the Son of God. By this, and his other effectual intercessions, he ensured the promised grace, to take hold of their hearts in his own time. "They shall look on him whom they have pierced and mourn."

The gift of repentance as well as of faith, and every other grace, is only that the sure pardon and salvation may be known and *enjoyed* by the soul, in God's chosen way, and in the only *proper*, or even *possible* way. Thus, as *peculiar to the gospel*, all men every where are commanded to repent. Acts xvii. 30. "And the times of this ignorance God winked at; but now COMMANDETH ALL MEN EVERY WHERE to repent." Repentance is preached for the remission of sins, which remission was made as certain before as afterward. It was by the atonement of Chrift afcertained, *in itfelf*; but by way of repentance it is made fenfible to finners.

CERTAINLY; repentance, *as an exercife* in the human foul, does not create its own object, or lay its own foundation, any more than faith does, or love, or hope, or joy, or any grace whatever. They all agree in this, that they are all built on a firm foundation which they had no hand in laying. This foundation of God ftandeth as fure, when thefe graces are not in exercife, as when they are, and before their implantation as after their utmoft perfection. The foundation of God hath the feal, *not of alterations in creatures*, but of his own eternal decree, and his knowledge of our falvation founded thereon. Let the mind of man, *at prefent*, be in what ftate it may, " neverthelefs the foundation of God ftandeth fure, having this feal, the Lord knoweth them that are his."

WHEN all men are commanded every where to repent, no doubt, faving, evangelical repentance, is the thing commanded, and this, we know, is the exercife of a new heart, and implies union with Chrift by regeneration, or a new creation in him. The very command implies, that this is made fure, and all the benefits connected with it, as what Chrift has laid a foundation for. The doctrine preached is only a piece of good news, founded in *truth* and *certainty*, as all other gofpel doctrines are. The doctrine is an object of faith, as all other gofpel doc-

R

trines are. It has a reasonable duty connected with it; which is common to all gospel doctrines.

When the doctrine of repentance is preached for the remission of sins, this remission is always considered as sure in Christ. Repentance as a fit temper of mind to receive it and enjoy the benefit, is also engaged by him, who orders the doctrine to be preached. Christ considers all nations of the earth, and every human creature as reconciled to God, by his blood, and God to them. What remains, in the preaching of the gospel, is that they be brought to the knowledge, sense, and enjoyment of it, that it may have proper influence on their hearts.

Before Peter thus understood the matter, he had an objection against preaching the doctrines of faith, repentance, and salvation to the gentiles. He had no idea they had any right, *secured in Christ*, to these favors; therefore he had no news of that kind to tell them. His objection would have been founded in all the reason in the world, had the position been true, that the gentiles were *not cleansed in Christ*, and reconciled to God *by him*, and God to them. Had this been the case, Peter ought not to have preached to them the gospel of repentance and reconciliation. But Christ tells him, that his fundamental principle in this matter was not true, forbidding him to assert it again; " What God hath cleansed that call not thou common;" i. e. *unclean*, or *unsanctified* in Christ; or unaccepted of God, *in him*. See the vision of the sheet and its explanation, Acts x. and xi.

Hence it appears that all mankind, " even *while enemies*, are *reconciled* to God, by the death of his Son, and much more, *being reconciled*, shall be saved by his life :" i. e. because he lives at the Father's right hand, to make effectual application of his atonement, which he does by sending his Spirit into the hearts of men, to renew them; and by conveying to them in his own time, the doctrines of repentance, faith, and every grace and virtue; and making these doctrines take effect. We are after reconciliation saved by his life, *much more*, i. e. most evidently and certainly, as he lives an almighty and faithful Savior, exalted with God's right hand, a Prince and Savior, to make *application* of the benefits of redemption, to give repentance to his redeemed (called his Israel) and forgiveness of sins.

Regeneration, repentance, faith, love, hope, joy, every virtue, and every good work wrought in us, or exercised by us, all agree in this, viz. They are all so many fit and necessary steps, which the almighty Redeemer takes with human souls, to acquaint them with his meritorious impetration, give them comfort in it, and affect them suitably by it in their hearts and lives. There is no strict propriety in preaching any of these doctrines *as gospel*, i. e. as news founded in facts, that ought to be believed; unless all is made true and sure in Christ before we have any acquaintance with the tidings, or any operation from them. The whole preaching of the gospel, in every article of it, is only the announcing of immutable truth, not created or altered by our hearing of it. Which truth it is good for us to know, and hath a good effect and consequence.

In hearing the doctrine of repentance, we learn the nature of it; the good effect of it in our great comfort and usefulness; the meet fruits of it, which are all very good; and also that Christ is exalted by God's right hand, to give it to the world, whose sins he died to take away. Thus the pardon comes, to their conviction and comfort, by the doctrine of repentance for the remission of sins.

They, who would make repentance, faith, regeneration, or any other grace, means necessary to our salvation, say right. But they who make them terms of distinction *in us*, to give us a sure title to salvation, put our safety now on the same footing or ground, on which Adam stood at first, as to the general nature and reason of it. Adam must have had a good heart and a good life, and then he would have been safe; yet *all* would have been *of God's grace*, or free gift, as every body will allow: For his whole being was so. Now, say they, we must have *good, penitent, believing, holy hearts*, in a good degree, *all of God's grace*, and then we have a title to his favor, and not otherwise. We need not be quite so good as Adam must have been; but our safety stands on the same general ground, and in a good degree too. The degree alters not the nature or ground of our safety: The general reason is wholly the same. Both stand on personal qualifications.

But the truth is, Adam stood wholly on his personal qualifications: We stand wholly on those of Christ; and enjoy the comfort and operation of them, by regeneration, faith, repentance, and every virtue. To suppose otherwise, is, at best, falling into the *neonomian* scheme. The retainers of which, say, that the terms of our acceptance with God, are much lowered since the fall of Adam, the conditions much mitigated; but that we stand upon personal qualifications, such as they be, *in the gospel demand*, as much as Adam did, on the higher qualifications of the first covenant.

Any impartial mind, with proper attention, will see, that we fall into the self same doctrine, as to the general and real nature of it, if we insist on any kind or degree of qualifications in creatures, as *terms* of acceptance with God; or, otherwise than as the work of God's almighty power, and free grace in us, in order to give us the knowledge of our previous acceptance with God in Christ alone; and to form and attemper our souls to the enjoyment of life and eternal salvation, made sure by the covenant of redemption, and the faithful engagement of the Son of God, and sealed on his cross. If we depart from this plan of hope, it is indifferent whether we call ourselves *papists* or *proteſtants, arminians* or *calviniſts, neonomians, antinomians, new divinity men,* or *quakers;* inaſmuch as we ſhall all agree in the grand principle, the cardinal point: viz. *That our acceptance with God, and our certain ſalvation, does reſt on valuable qualifications, whereby we are diſtinguiſhed from other men.* Yet all agreeing in this, even that God by his mere mercy and free grace, hath made the ſaving diſtinction. Thus we all, in our hearts, join with him of old in pleaſing devotion; " God I thank thee that I am not as other men." He acknowledged the free grace of God, as much as any *limitarian* ever did.

It is a further ſymptom that the way of life I am pleading for, is agreeable to the goſpel; that believing in it will certainly make us hate all ſin, all ungodlineſs. Or to ſpeak with more accurate propriety, where this faith is, there certainly will be a bitter hatred and averſion to all ungodlineſs. The very diſcovery of God which I am ſpeaking of, that view of the Redeemer, that exhibition of the divine character, neceſſarily involves in it a perception and ſenſe of infinite amiableneſs, beauty and glory. The infinite lovelineſs of God, and ſalvation by grace through Jeſus Chriſt, are the eſſential objects of the faith I maintain. This wholly agrees with the old calviniſtic doctrine of ſaving faith. No acquaintance with God or divine truth, without a feeling impreſſion of the divine lovelineſs on our ſouls, was ever thought to be saving faith, by *Calvin, Owen*, or any eminent promoters of the protestant cause. Their object of faith is exactly the same which I contend for; and the manner of communication and operation is the same, as wrought by the power of God, working by love, and purifying the heart, even as God is pure.

We do not consider assurance of our salvation to be of the essence of saving faith; but merely consequential, even as hath been usual with protestants. The faith we contend for, has nothing immediately and directly to do with ourselves, but with the object of our faith. When this faith is wrought in us, by the power and grace of God, and proper fruits ensue; thence we argue our own safe estate by way of consequence, and so make our calling and election sure. We unite with the orthodox in all ages, in saying, that hatred of all sin is the fruit of faith; or that saving knowledge and supreme love of God are through faith.

The universal extent of Christ's saving power and grace, is further taught us by metaphors and emblems, which the divine Spirit hath made use of in the word. As that of the *dew*, the *wind*, the *rain*, &c. which are known to be of universal extent over the whole earth, at such various times and in such manner as God is pleased to direct. Perhaps no emblem is more significant than that of a *sun*, often made use of in the scriptures, as Psalm lxxxiv. 11. "For the Lord God is a sun and a shield: the Lord will give grace and glory: no good thing will he withhold from them that walk uprightly." Mal. iv. 2. and in other places.

SIMILITUDES do not quadrate in all respects with the things illustrated by them; but wherein they do, we may argue with safety. Take the similitudes now referred to, and we shall find universal extent and operation, to be principal ideas suggested. A comment might be made on each of them, perhaps, with equal propriety. Omitting the rest, take that of *a sun*. It very well presents to our view the Sun of righteousness, the great Redeemer, in the extent, and benign efficacy of his mediatorial character.

THE sun is an object highly exalted above the world: So is Christ highly exalted. The sun is the fountain of light to the world: So is Christ the brightness of his Father's glory and the express image of his person. The natural sun revives, quickens, gives life to all things in the natural world: So doth Christ with regard to the whole spiritual world. The sun hath various times and seasons of special influence, and does dispense his favors variously to various parts of the world, at different times, seasons, and periods: So it is with the Sun of righteousness, in the spiritual world. Under the influence of the sun in the firmament, there is the vernal and the autumnal season, the summer and the winter, the darkness and the light, in various degrees, and the heat and cold in perpetual variation: So it is with the various difplays and difpenfations of the great Redeemer, the Sun of righteoufnefs. Something of this has been taken notice of before in the gradual progreffion of gofpel light; and in the decrees of God, making many and great diftinctions among mankind in this world, both of an outward and of a fpiritual nature, and alfo in the world to come, with refpect to degrees of exaltation and glory; though none as to the certainty of future falvation, to the body of Chrift, who is the " head of every man."

The natural fun is certainly and greatly beneficial to the whole world; though not to every part in the fame manner and degree. The frigid zones feem leaft of all to feel the bleffings of that glorious luminary; though they have their day, and a long one, and many other benefits derived from the fun. The torrid zone is, on the whole, favored far beyond thofe laft mentioned, in many refpects; yet the inhabitants of thofe climates have not near fo many benefits from the fun as the regions included in the temperate zones. Moreover, each of thofe parts of the earth, is more bleffed with the benign influences of the fun at one time than at another; and all of them more in the day time than in the night; more in the ferene and clear day than in the dark and gloomy day. Many other remarks of this kind, will naturally occur to the mind of the reader.

It is to be obferved, in general, that there is no feafon of the year, no period of time, no hour in the ſtormy day, or midnight darkneſs, in which any part of the world is left wholly without any benefit, or even conſiderable benefit from the ſun. Even in dead of winter, the ſun is a great bleſſing to men : So even at the darkeſt or coldeſt midnight, it is neither ſo dark nor ſo cold as it would be if there were no ſun. When any particular climate ſuffers moſt in the abſence of the ſun, yet the inhabitants of that particular climate, have ſuch a connection with the world in general, and with thoſe parts of the world where, at the ſame time, the influence of the ſun is moſt replete with bleſſings, that they receive great benefit, though in a mediate and direct way. Each part of the world has at ſome times, the immediate and direct beams of the ſun ; at other times his indirect and reflected influence, by the moon and ſtars. And, even when theſe appear not, ſtill many and great benefits are derived to them ; without which they would be far more miſerable than they ever yet were, in their moſt torpid or benighted circumſtances. They always have ſome " *precious things brought forth by the ſun.*" Juſt ſo with regard to the " true light which enlighteneth every man that cometh into the world." The Lord is good to all ; and his tender mercies are over all his works. All the human kind are at all times much the better for Chriſt. 'He hath always a deſire to the work of his hands.

The covenant people of God, under every diſpenſation, may be compared to thoſe climates and regions moſt peculiarly under the bleſſings of the natural ſun. Different diſpenſations among them compare with different ſeaſons of the year. Special providences, propitious or adverſe, are like the interchange of calm ſunſhine and angry ſtorms. The firſt openings of divine revelation are ſimilar to the firſt ſtreaks of dawning day: Increaſing light is like the gray of the morning. The jewiſh diſpenſation was, at firſt, like the horizontal beams of the riſing ſun. As light was added, under that diſpenſation, the ſun advanced towards the meridian. Chriſt and the inſpired apoſtles, with the light at that time poured in upon the world, may compare with the ſun in his ſtrength. "His countenance was as the ſun ſhineth in his ſtrength." "I am come a light into the world." And "ye are the light of the world." There is much in ſacred writ to ſupport this analogy.

As it is demonſtrated concerning the ſun in the firmament, that his influence is more intenſe ſome time after the meridian is paſt, than before; ſo the bleſſings of the great Redeemer have been increaſing, ſince he was on earth in the form of man, ſince "he aſcended up on high, led captivity captive, and received gifts for men; *yea for the* REBELLIOUS *alſo*, that the Lord God might dwell among them." Pſalm lxviii. 18.

EVERY part of the pagan world, all nations of the earth unacquainted with divine revelation directly or immediately, have indirectly ſomething valuable of the ſame light and knowledge, in various degrees and measures, by connection with the people of God, more or less, by tradition, communication, &c. Even as every part of the earth, has always, both in winter and summer, in every season of the year, by day and by night, some benefit more or less from the sun; if not by his direct beams, yet by the reflected or refracted. There are no people in the world, but what have some religion. Yet probably there never would have been any in the world, had there been no revelation from God. Yea, perhaps, the existence of a God would never have been thought of, had he made no sort of revelation more than in the works of nature and providence. It has been the opinion of some of the greatest of men, that the first intimation of a Supreme Being, was owing to divine revelation: Although, when the hint was thus given, the nations of the earth, with this leading thought, could demonstrate his existence from the works of nature. However this may be, there is no nation on earth, which is not enlightened by Christ, in some degree or other, by his word, spirit and providence, in such manner as infinite wisdom and goodness hath seen best. In this sense is the apostle to be understood, when he says, " the gospel was preached to every creature under heaven." For this never had been done by express revelation, or direct communication of the knowledge of Christ.

ALL mankind have some religion, which

came to them through Chriſt; though many have never heard of his name. All people know the truth, in ſome degree. All are orthodox in ſome points, and right in ſome meaſure. God manifeſts himſelf, and gives knowledge and inſtruction of all kinds, to the inhabitants of this world, and indeed to all intelligent creatures, only in and through Chriſt. All common ſenſe, all extraordinary endowments of mind, all ſcience and learning, all new inventions of every kind, all acquaintance with moral and ſpiritual things, are by Chriſt. Hence he is called the word of God; becauſe as men convey knowledge and inſtruction by their words, ſo doth God by the Mediator.

When man fell, he was then immediately in total darkneſs, as to any impreſſions on his mind, or mental exerciſes that might profit him. The mediation of Chriſt began that very moment. The guilty pair were immediately put in better circumſtances, by the Son of God, than otherwiſe they would have been. And it is the general opinion of divines, I think, with good reaſon, that they were ſoon regenerated and brought back to the ſaving knowledge of God, in a way of ſpecial illumination, repentance, and faith. There was, however, a bleſſed degree of the power and influence of the Mediator on their minds, immediately after their fall; and there ever has been on the minds and diſpoſitions of all their children. None have ever been nearly ſo bad, as if there had been no Mediator. Common grace, as we term it, having always been an unspeakable favor to all the fallen race. And this is as truly and really by and through Christ, as eternal salvation is.

The influence of the Second Adam, the Lord from heaven, on the hearts of men, has always been sovereign, and very various; as much so as the light and influence of the sun on the earth has been in the various parts of it, and in the various seasons of the year: Yet all are much the better for the Sun of righteousness. It is a universal proposition and every where true, that " the people that walked in darkness have seen a great light ;" i. e. with a vision more or less perfect ; with some degree of illumination; " and they that dwell in the land of the shadow of death, upon them hath the light shined." So in Isaiah li. when God speaks of his fixed determination to save sinners, his established purpose and judgment in that matter, he saith, " I will make my judgment to rest for a light to the people, my righteousness is near, my salvation is gone forth, and mine arms shall judge the people. The isles shall wait upon me, and on mine arms shall they trust." " My salvation shall be forever : and my righteousness shall not be abolished." " My righteousness shall be forever, and my salvation from generation to generation."

The Most High speaks of the light of Christ, as a growing and spreading light, until, in the end, all the world shall behold his glorious beams, and feel his saving power. Ifaiah lx. " Arife fhine; for thy light is come, and the glory of the Lord is rifen upon thee." " And the gentiles fhall come to thy light, and kings to the brightnefs of thy rifing." "'The abundance of the fea fhall be converted unto thee ; the forces of the gentiles fhall come unto thee." "Who are thefe that fly as a cloud, and as the doves to their windows ? Surely the ifles fhall wait for me, and the fhips of Tarfhifh firft, to bring thy fons from far." And it is obfervable, as God is fpeaking of his covenant mercies in Chrift to the ends of the earth, it is fubjoined towards the clofe of the chapter, " Thy Sun fhall no more go down, neither fhall thy moon withdraw itfelf : for the Lord fhall be thine everlafting light, and the days of thy mourning fhall be ended." And to the fame purpofe it is faid,. " The earth fhall be filled with the knowledge of the Lord, as the waters cover the fea."

In all this provifion, and diffufion of faving light and grace to men, God is as free and fovereign as in creating the fun in the firmament, and in difpofing of all his benefits. And as " he maketh his fun to rife on the evil and on the good," fo likewife hath he no regard to any diftinction feen in the human kind, in the beftowment of faving mercy. Many differences is he pleafed to make in this world, and that as becometh his holy fovereignty ; but none, *none at all*, as to the final extent of falvation, or the efficacy of the Sun of righteoufnefs.

THE DOCTRINE OF THE TOTAL DEPRAVITY OF HUMAN NATURE, is so plain a scripture doctrine, that we cannot deny it, without rejecting the whole authority of divine revelation.

THE doctrine is this: That the whole human nature, included in the first man, was, by the fall, left totally destitute of any moral or spiritual good; and that fallen man became as bad in a moral view, as fallen angels, at their first apostacy, according to their inferior natural capacity.

THE angels who had fallen sometime before man, had increased their wickedness, by the exercises of it; and man was in the like sure way to increase his, and by the same cause. Every power, every faculty of the soul, was left without any, the least degree of moral good; all dreadfully polluted; "every imagination of the thought of man's heart was evil only, and that continually." The depravity was total. And there was nothing left in the soul of man, of a moral kind, but enmity against God. I should here take up the demonstration of this at large, were it not so fully done already, by the most able divines, in a way of the plainest scripture reasoning.

I HAVE said, and I here repeat it, the mediation of Christ, in favor of all human nature, began the moment after the fall. In Adam and Eve was all human nature included, or, in Adam alone: For the woman was from him. Christ, by his merciful energy, began immediately to withstand the force of man's depravity, and has done so ever since, in a greater or less degree, in all human nature, in every child of Adam. Otherwise, mankind would all be as bad as the devils, according to their measure of being; but we know they are not. The Mediator was a sovereign in the measure of good influence he granted at first to the fallen pair, and in all additional measures of grace of what kind soever; and is so still, and always will be, as it highly becomes his character always, and in every thing, to keep up a view of his holy sovereignty. At what time he regenerated the souls of our first parents, we cannot say, or what measures of grace he was pleased to give them while they lived.

He now gives unto some, much more of his kind influence from their infancy, than others; and to some increasing favors of this kind, all their days. Some have less and less of it all their days, and so grow worse and worse. But none, in this life, are ever found without some degree of grace or favor from the Mediator; such as preventing goodness, restraining grace, some checks of conscience, some humanity and kindness to their fellow men. Be it granted that all this is from merely selfish motives, and destitute of all moral good, and that there is sin worthy of damnation, in regard to deficiency, in all their honor and honesty, in all their industry and the public good they do, and in all the benefits they communicate.

Grant all this, which indeed is true; yet there is much of the grace of the Mediator in hindering their being and doing worse. Christ, by his providence and spirit, mercifully and powerfully resists the awful force of their depravity, at all times, even though he has not yet renewed them in a saving manner.

To illustrate the above remarks. God says to Abimelech, "I with-held thee from sinning against me." Though he was guilty of great sin in all he did, even in dismissing the wife of the patriarch, not doing even that in faith and from a principle of friendship to God; yet a blessed degree of God's grace was granted him. God in his providence, and, it should seem, by some special influence on his mind and inclinations, kept him from a great sin. There never was any man on earth left to the whole force of his natural depravity: No, not Cain, or Ahab, or Jezebel, or Judas himself. If otherwise, Cain would have killed his parents as well as his brother; Ahab would have murdered many besides Naboth, thousands more than ever he did. Jezebel's whoredoms and witchcrafts were many; but they would have been many more, had not the Mediator's grace resisted. And, were it not for this grace, Judas would have been a much greater thief and murderer than he was. It was this that made him repent, and bear his last testimony in favor of the Redeemer. And even this good almighty government of Christ so ordered, that he hanged himself, before he had further added to his wickedness; though this was done by the inſtrumentality of ſatan, as the immediate agent.

The reader may now want I ſhould ſhew, if I can, that Judas did not go to an eternal hell. I will take notice of this, in its proper place, and ſo of every thing elſe that he may think of, as he goes along, as impatient to have at that moment diſcuſſed.

But, not to digreſs further, I would add concerning the grace which the Mediator afforded even Judas, in his higheſt pitch of wickedneſs. Had it not been for the gracious, reſiſting power of Chriſt, he would have boaſted of his treaſon; ſtrengthened his malice; been foremoſt, with his own hands, in nailing Jeſus to the croſs; been the loudeſt to mock and deride his dying agonies; and then gone on to murder all the diſciples of Chriſt: And where would he have made a ſtand? Surely not until he had hanged himſelf, which he would have done at laſt. The ſame may be ſaid of the moſt horrid monſters of wickedneſs that ever have been in the world; *Herod, Nero, Alexander, Richard* IIId. of Britain, *Beadle, Benedict Arnold,* &c. Not one of theſe, or any other on earth, were ever, in any meaſure, ſo horribly wicked as they would have been, had all reſtraints been taken off. And all the reſtraints that ever were kept upon the wicked, are by the grace and power of the Mediator, and the purchaſe of his blood. The mercy, power, pity, and grace of the Redeemer is great and wonderful, even where souls are not renewed. " The Lord is good unto all ; and his tender mercies are over all his works."

I READILY grant there is a difference *in kind*, a *specific difference* between common, and saving grace ; or that grace which the renewed have, and that which is common to men. But in these particulars they do indeed agree ; both are free : Both are good, and valuable in their nature : Both from God only through Christ : Both wholly unmerited by sinners : Both bestowed on sinners who have equal dependence on God : Both are the fruit of the Mediator's undertaking for a guilty world, bestowed in God's own time and manner. So that the great excellency of one above the other, does not, in the least, militate against the present argument, to prove a real connection of the Messiah in a fœderal way with all mankind; but does fully confirm this doctrine, even as fully as if there was no specific difference between them.

THERE are innumerable good things of a nature specifically different, that are equally the gift and grace of the Mediator, as wisdom and wealth ; health and a good name ; all the five senses : All these are good, and all alike from the Son of God, as Creator and Governor of the world. Man could have enjoyed no good at all, had not a Mediator interposed ; but the curse, in its most literal, plainest meaning, would have been executed. God was able to make Adam and Eve understand what he said to them. They knew what was meant by the word *day*; and God was able to make them underſtand what was meant by the word *die*, or *death*. Otherwiſe he did, in effect, ſay nothing to them. If he did not make them underſtand him, there was no threatening at all, *as to them*, in what he ſaid. They knew the day meant twenty-four hours, or a diurnal, apparent revolution of the ſun. God made them to underſtand, that to *die*, ſignified, with reſpect to the body, a total ceſſation of all vital functions, all ſenſibility; and, with reſpect to the ſoul, the total loſs of his moral image, and his favor forever more, with the miſeries connected therewith, and the eternal pains due to the tranſgreſſion of his holy and good law.

When they had ſinned, they really expected that, within that very day, as now deſcribed, their bodies would ſo die; and that, as they found their ſouls deprived of the moral image of God, they would forever remain ſo, with all the anguiſh and ſorrow, pain and diſtreſs, contained in the malediction, to all eternity; even a duration abſolutely interminable. This appeared in their fearful conduct, when "they heard the voice of the Lord God, walking in the garden in the cool of the day," i. e. in the latter part of that very day on which they rebelled.

No doubt, they thought he was come to execute the ſentence upon them, juſt as he had ſpoken, and as they plainly underſtood. And they knew that this was juſt and righteous. But, to their great and joyful ſurprize, they found it quite otherwife. A dark intimation was given them, in an indirect manner, of the ground God proceeded upon, to avoid the violation of his honor and truth, viz. a fubftitute, a vicar, an atonement, one in their place and ftead, the feed of the woman. The Mediator began to officiate that moment for all the human kind. They were all prefent, all in the firft pair. And he has conftantly officiated for all the human kind ever fince, and will until the curfe is wholly wiped away. Sin reigned unto death, even then immediately upon the fall ; and grace began its operation on the fame day, and fhall reign with an overcoming, prevailing triumph, to the end of the world, and to all eternity. " That as fin hath reigned unto death, even fo might grace reign through righteoufnefs, unto eternal life, by Jefus Chrift our Lord." Rom. v. 21.

At what time our firft parents were renewed, is immaterial to the prefent argument ; but it is certain the Meffiah on that very day, operated, in a bleffed and merciful degree. He fpared their lives. They did not die an immediate and remedilefs death, as they deferved, and expected from God's own mouth. On that day, they were gracioufly pointed to an atonement. The great high Prieft exhibited an oblation before their eyes ; the import of which was, that one of their feed fhould be divinely qualified for a full atonement, and his death fhould ftand for theirs. Then he took the fkins of thofe beafts which were flain, and clothed them. Which denoted that they were accepted, not in their own fig leaves, a garment of their own preparing, their own vile character; but in the character of the future Messiah, the cloathing or garments of his all perfect righteousness. Much grace and mercy was granted them on that very day; and more added, as a gracious Sovereign saw proper. So it is with all their poor, lost children. They have always much mercy and grace from Christ; and he goes on to the consummation of it as a gracious *Sovereign.*

ALL this is only in a gospel way; and so " the gospel was preached to every creature under heaven," even from the fall of man. i. e. Gospel grace was always manifested, or held forth, to all human creatures, in some degree or other. And where Christ begins a good work, as Mediator, he will perfect it, in his own way and time. It will issue in perfection at the great day. " Being confident of this very thing, that he which hath begun a good work in you, will perform it until the day of Jesus Christ." Phil. i. 6.

IT is moreover evidential that this is the doctrine of grace and salvation; because this, and this only, excludes all boasting. *Good distinctions* are the *only* things that men boast of, or at least, what they value as good. If they come in a way of mere grace, without any hand of theirs in them, they always feel more pride in them, than if they came by their own good efforts. How proud are mankind of exquisite beauty; noble birth;

a grand estate descended down from an ancient and dignified family? Every body knows that good things of this nature are all of mere favor or grace, pure gifts of God, in the way of nature and providence.

Say of a man, that he is descended of the most honorable family in the nation; that he has naturally the greatest powers of mind of any man in it; that he carries the greatest majesty, dignity and beauty in his countenance, and in all his gestures, together with the most unaffected, winning behavior; that in vigor and activity, he exceeds all: Add that he was made so, he was born with all this greatness and excellence in his very nature; and is indeed the completest work of God to be found within a thousand miles. You can say nothing that will take hold of the human heart, to make a man feel prouder; though you have not said one word, but what is an expression of free, sovereign grace, as the man himself will acknowledge. Indeed, he is much the prouder, on this very consideration, that so great a Being as God himself, has taken such peculiar notice of him, and singled him out as a special favorite.

Let another man hear it said of him, that he was in every view mean and contemptible by nature; despicable in soul and body throughout; of a scandalous family from generation to generation; but he has taken so much pains to become something, that he is really now, a man that ought to be respected, indeed a very worthy man. He will hardly thank you for the compliment; though you attribute the whole of his virtue and worth to himself.

Very great diſtinction from others, in honor and happineſs, is what men moſt pride themſelves in; and if this be owing to the peculiar notice of ſome great perſonage, it really adds to their gratification. Men are naturally proud of being peculiar favorites of the great. Mr. Pope, the celebrated poet, was a man more free from vanity, than moſt men; but he betrayed much on an occaſion, and at a time when it was leaſt to be expected. In writing his laſt will, when his thoughts were full of approaching death and another world, his pride is apparently moved by a matter of free, ſovereign grace, a peculiar mark of diſtinction from a king. In the bequeſt of a valuable ring, which might have been quite as well deſcribed without telling how he came by it, he ſays, "*the ring which the king of Sardinia gave me.*" All the poets uſed to ſpeak in like manner, and they expreſſed human nature. If they had received only a pipe, or any other ſmall matter of a renowned poet, or any man of great note, as a free gift; they would be ſure to take notice of the manner in which it came to them, valuing themſelves on the mere gracious diſtinction of a renowned man. Such is human nature.

Tell a man that he is bad, how ready is he to keep himſelf in countenance, by enumerating many that do as he does! If he thought himself distinguished from most others in wickedness, he would be far more ashamed. Whether it respects pride or shame, *peculiar distinction* is the grand thing; and if that distinction come in a sovereign way, from a great personage, it is not the less, but the more flattering. To be mean, despicable, and contemptible by birth and nature, or to be esteemed so, mortifies human pride, more than to be so in any other way. Hence men are more mortified to be called fools, than knaves or cunning rogues. It is indeed, distinction from others in a way of excellence, real or supposed, that is in every case, a strong temptation to pride, in whatever way that distinction is made.

The reader may then say, that there will be this temptation to pride among the saints in heaven, to all eternity: For there will be in heaven, great and everlasting distinctions of free grace. But this objection will vanish in a moment, when you consider that all fuel for pride to kindle, will be forever taken away in that world; as no corruption at all will be admitted there; no moral capacity of pride.

You will then say, that from this view of things, eminent advances in grace and favor in this life are strong incentives of pride, in the most exalted saints on earth. They are so. They always were, and always will be, so long as any moral depravity remains, or any principle of pride in their hearts. Paul found it so when God, of his free grace, set him at a great diftance from others, by fpecial difcoveries and divine raptures. 2 Cor. xii. Saints in heaven, will find the fame thing operating in a way of the deepeſt humility, which now takes hold of their corrupt part, as an incentive to pride and felf exaltation. On earth, fpiritual pride hath always been a very dangerous and troublefome enemy to the comfort of eminent faints, indeed to all good people.

If you enquire, how did holy angels find pride originating or moving in them? I anfwer; this is a queſtion that never was folved, nor ever can be, *by man*. It is a fact; but wholly incomprehenfible by us, as innumerable other facts are. This, however, may be faid, faints in heaven are fecured by Chriſt; the fallen angels were not.

In a word, the moſt exalted faints in heaven, will be as much before others in humility, as in any other part of their holy attainments; and will bow as much lower before the throne of God, as they are exalted higher. Thus I am advocating the only rational, gofpel doctrine, that will exclude all boaſting. In heaven, it will be confirmed, when they will view the matter of their juſtification, the righteoufnefs of Chriſt. "to all and upon all, without any difference."

This gofpel doctrine tends greatly to the promotion of practical holinefs and virtue.

The bands of love and gratitude ever were, and ever will be, the proper bands of a man. Fear and terror, never yet had any direct tendency to holiness and a good life. I mean common, legal fear. For it always carries in it, not only terror, but even odium of its object. It never attracts the soul to the object of terror, but quite the reverse. Love, or a sense of goodness, amiableness, kindness, or benevolence, always attracts and assimilates the soul to its object. As God hath constituted immortal souls and their objects, it cannot be otherwise. This is not only the clear doctrine of reason and scripture; but also the doctrine of all called orthodox, since the days of the apostles; remarkably so, since the reformation from popery.

It is true, papists and arminians have often told us that the doctrine tends to licentiousness; and that, if they believed the infinite stedfast, immutable love of God, and faithfulness of Christ, as we do, in respect to our salvation, the certain perseverence of believers and the like, they would indulge themselves in all manner of sinful lusts and pleasures. While their hearts are unrenewed, and while they believe not this glorious doctrine, they may think as they say. But did they believe, and feel the power of it, they would know better, as calvinists have always told them. They would find the cords of such love very different bands from what they imagine, while in ignorance of God and the power of his love.

What great things has slavish fear or terror ever done to make men holy? It will keep them from many open and daring crimes, in the fight of man, it is true: But at the fame time they will be juft as guilty in the fight of God, as if they had no fuch fear. In their very fouls, they will wifh and long to commit them, as much as ever. In this wifh, and longing defire of the foul, lies all the fin, in the fight of God.

PRINCIPLES of fear are managed to good advantage, by the laws and government of men. And without taking this great and good advantage of a principle of flavifh, unfanctified fear, in man, we could not live in human fociety. But the vile, hardened wretch, who is reftrained in his overt actions, only by fear of the whip and the gallows, is as greatly guilty in the fight of God, as if thefe fearful reftraints had never been upon him. The civil magiftrate has much to do with this principle of fear in man. All human laws make great ufe of it; and this is wife, and good for the end propofed. But alas! how little doth this avail as to things invifible and eternal? How little with the habituated drunkard? How little with the inveterate thief and robber? Take away the fear of vifible, temporal punifhment, and does it at all appear that the terrors of eternal damnation have any influence on their conduct? Although they profefs to believe the doctrine, and allude to it in almoft all their converfation, their mouths being perpetually full of hell and damnation. Verily it is a fenfe of the goodnefs of God that leadeth to repentance, a true fenfe of God, *as love*, that meliorates the heart, with a divine power on the life and conduct. "If ye love me keep my commandments." "Walk in love." "The love of Christ constraineth us."

I never yet heard any man pray or preach to any congregation, without building on principles, which, by just, inevitable consequence, would infer the sure salvation of all the human kind, *at last*.

We all agree in these particulars. We pray for the salvation of all. We, in the name of Christ, offer salvation to all on the purchase of his blood. In the name of Christ, we command all to believe. We tell all men that they have a good warrant to believe: That a sufficient foundation is laid for them all to believe; and that if they do believe they shall certainly be saved; and that not at all on the merit of their faith, but the merit of Christ: That their repentance and faith and whatever good may be in them, does not in the least alter the foundation, or object of their faith. We tell them that it is the greatest sin *not to believe*; that it maketh God a liar, as far as they are able. In the name of Christ, we promise them full pardon and life eternal, when they repent, and believe, and obey the gospel; and this, not in the least, *for* their repentance, faith, and obedience. What then, do we make of all these graces *in man*, but only means leading to the enjoyment of an end, not dependent on *these means*, but *they* dependent on *that*: Not an end which these means do establish; but established beforehand, as an immutable foundation, on which alone is built the propriety, use and necessity of *all these means*?

I HAVE often heard much inconsistency, and contradiction in the prayers and preaching of good men; but never heard one performing these duties, who did not adopt many sentiments, which, by just consequence, would infer the salvation of all mankind, made previously sure in the purpose of God, and the foundation he hath laid in Zion. This is consistent. Otherwise, the salvation of man is dependent on *himself*, if any thing can be *on a creature*. He depends on his qualifications and exercises of mind, as the foundation of all his hope. What God hath done is just nothing, or worse than nothing to him, without these distinctions *in himself*, or before he hath them. All God hath done gives him no security. As if one should say, that the will and testament of his father was not his security for the legacy; but his opening and reading of the will, after his father's death, was the only thing that secured him. Would you not tell such an one that he did not speak with propriety; that his whole security was in the will and testament of his father; and that his opening and reading it only gave him knowledge of it and comfort in it.

WE usually pray to God, just as Paul directed, and on the same ground which he has established. We pray for the salvation of all men. This we ought not to do without a foundation in the word of God. If God has decided the point in his word, that many shall be damned eternally, in their own persons, we have no warrant to pray as we do. But the apostle bids us pray for the salvation of all men, even such wicked kings and magistrates as Nero, and the bloody, persecuting magistrates in those days, for all the cruel persecutors of the church, and for every body else, without a single exception; and then gives this as our warrant, "God will have all men to be saved and to come unto the knowledge of the truth." He also enjoins it upon us to give thanks for all men, on the same ground; because "Christ gave himself a ransom for all." At the same time, he plainly intimates, that the time was not then come to pour in all the light that God had designed in after ages; that a progression of light would continue as it had begun, and proceeded thus far; and that the glorious doctrine would be more fully manifest in due time. Read 1. Tim. ii. 1,—6.

The most literal translation that can possibly be given of those words which I have more than once alluded to, is this; *a testimony for times proper.** In the English bible it stands, "*to be testified in due time.*" However, it is scarce worth while, in any place, to correct our last English translation of the bible: For every man that is well skilled in

---

* Τὸ μαρτύριον καιροῖς ἰδίοις.

the original languages, who is also a man of candor, will bear me witness, that there is scarcely a single sentence in the translation, but what will bear, without marring the true sense any wise essentially.

If it is certain, that the word of God, his justice and his glory, do ascertain the eternal, *personal* damnation of many; we ought to pray for that awful event, as explicitly as for any thing else. "*Thy will be done*," ought to run through all our prayers. But how would it strike the minds of any congregation in the world, to hear him that leads in prayer, crying mightily to God, that many, or most of his fellow men, might be the miserable victims of his eternal vengeance *personally*, in hell to all eternity. Many men discern premises well, but do not see the just consequence. We have always seen it a clear gospel duty, founded on gospel warrant, to pray for the salvation of all men, and give thanks for all men, on the foundation laid in Christ. If a great many have not discerned the consequence of such premises, it is no more than what happens in many other cases every day.

I am far enough from being an enthusiast, and believe I was never thought so by any person, but rather the reverse: However, I think it is good and sound reasoning, to argue from our own experience, and from what other honest people affirm to us from their experience. Having had the special

V

care of souls, many years, and been happy in my charge, I have often conversed with persons under special awakenings, and great concern about their souls. I have always kept up the holy law in their view, with all its infinite purity and strictness, and tremendous terrors to the enemies of God; have always told the distressed that they could *in no wise* help themselves, or make any distinction in themselves; charged them to make no dependence on their prayers, tears, reformations, or any thing they feel within themselves, but on the sovereign grace of God, through the atonement of his Son, totally exclusive of every thing else in the universe; always pointing them to Christ as the end of the law, in the stead of sinners.

' I have found numbers that have been by the Spirit of God, brought to this sense of the way of salvation, and have rested in it as a safe way. They have found it attended with evangelical repentance and great comfort. And hence have invited the vilest of sinners to come to Christ, and trust in him, without one moment's delay; telling them there was enough in Christ for their salvation, *vile as they now are;* that the atonement was sufficient to recommend them to God *in their very worst condition of soul and life*; and that they never could obtain any qualification, within or without, that would move the heart of God towards them; but that all things on God's part, are ready.

They have told me, that they never found themselves so unqualified, as when their relief and comfort broke in upon them in a way of *mere faith*; and that they looked far from themselves, even as far as *Mount Calvary*, for all their hope; and that they saw all God had done to relieve their distressed souls, was done, sure and certain, long before they were born. And that they could make no foundation of hope in all that God had wrought on their souls, but praise his glorious name that he has been pleased, in mere, sovereign mercy, to work thus effectually on them, only in order to lead them to the sense and comfort of what was immutable truth before, viz. The all-sufficiency of Christ for the chief of sinners. These persons have generally brought forth fruits meet for repentance, and walked as real christians.

The observation of my fathers and brethren in the gospel ministry, as many of them have told me, is the very same in their concerns with souls, with what I have now mentioned. They have also told me, it is their true experience with respect to their own souls, and all their comfort; and I am certain it is mine. It is well known that all pious protestant ministers have taken this very method in guiding souls to Christ. And all the success they have found, has been by thus cutting off sinners every way, as much as possible, from every dependence, but on Christ alone. God has granted his peculiar blessing on this doctrine, and this way of guiding poor, miserable sinners to a Savior. No minister of the gospel in this land was ever more bleſſed of God in his labors, perhaps, than the renowned biſhop *Stoddard*, of Northampton. Every one that is acquainted with his character and writings muſt be ſenſible that this was his method.

MANY, no doubt, were brought to know Chriſt, in that remarkable period, in the year 1740, and a few ſucceeding years, notwithſtanding the great frailty and diſtraction of human nature appeared much in thoſe days. All, ſo far as I can learn, who became true followers of Chriſt, in thoſe times, built firmly on this very doctrine; that Chriſt alone is the compleat Savior of the chief of ſinners, excluſive of every diſtinction in themſelves, previouſly moving the heart of God towards them, or, in any wife, fitting them for mercy; that all that maketh them to differ from the moſt abandoned of the human race, flows wholly from a previous ſource, alike open to all, and built on a foundation as independent of man, as God was in creating him at firſt. It is well known that the moſt ſucceſsful preachers in thoſe days, dwelt mainly on theſe very doctrines.

THIS doctrine of ſaving, UNIVERSAL grace, *is perfectly conſiſtent with the moſt plain and poſitive declarations of the word of God, that the pains of hell ſhall be endleſs; and that the wicked ſhall go away into everlaſting puniſhment, in all the boundleſs extent of theſe words, and many others that convey the ſame idea of the endless punishment of sinners*, and that in the plainest possible manner of expression.

In their *Surety, Vicar*, or *Substitute*, i. e. in Christ, "*the head of every man*," they go away into *everlasting punishment*, in a true gospel sense. In him they suffer infinite punishment, i. e. he suffers for them, in their room and stead. But how so? The divine nature never suffered, and the human nature was not infinite, nor capable of infinite sufferings; yet by union in person with infinite Deity, the gospel, the divine constitution does account the atonement infinite. The obeying, and the suffering human nature was as much united to all the attributes of Deity, as to any one of them; to Deity in all his infinite perfections; to the eternity of Deity as much as to his omniscience, almightiness, or any other attribute. And the sufferings of Christ are eternal sufferings, just in the same way of reasoning that they are infinite. The same ineffable, hypostatic union of human and divine natures, which connects infinity with manhood in one person, does equally unite eternity with the same. There is the same gospel propriety in calling them eternal sufferings, as infinite sufferings. It is only by personal union with Deity, that either term will bear.

The apostle gives us this idea, as plainly as any other, to lead us to estimate the atonement complete for the sins of the world, and in the gospel account, an eternal punishment. He considers the gift of salvation by Christ, under the idea of a will or testament, that makes the legacy sure; as sure before the legatee knows any thing about it, or has any comfort in it, as afterwards. And, as in all his writings, he exhibits the atonement complete in every other view, so he does in the eternity of it, in the divine account; that none may imagine himself to be exposed to personal punishment in hell to all eternity, for want of an eternal atonement, any more than for want of an infinite one. He tells us that a sense of this, will free the conscience from every bond that might hold the poor sinner under obligation to suffer; and will also become a spring of holy gratitude and living sacrifice to God. " How much more shall the blood of Christ, who, *through the eternal Spirit*, offered himself without spot to God, purge your conscience from dead works to serve the living God?" Heb. ix. No person of judgment will say that the phrase, *through the eternal Spirit*, here signifies, that the eternal Spirit of God supported Christ in his sufferings: For he was then wholly forsaken in this sense, and left, in his expiring moments, without any support at all, as much as ever a victim was, when bound and bleeding on the altar. It was then he cried out, " My God, my God, why hast thou forsaken me!"

We cannot make the atonement sufficient for our redemption in any sense; unless we consider the human nature infinitely dignified, by personal union with Deity, with every attribute of Deity, one as much as another. On this very ground it is, that the merit of the atonement took place, and was efficacious long before Christ came in the flesh. Yea, from eternity, it was efficacious, on our behalf, in the mind and decree of God. And it was, from eternity, regarded in the gracious purpose of the Most High; as he always determined to save sinners in this way and no other. "Then was I by him, as one brought up with him; and I was daily his delight, rejoicing always before him; rejoicing in the habitable parts of the earth, and my delights were with the sons of men." Prov. viii.

The atonement of the Lamb of God, which taketh away the sin of the world, was present in God's view from all eternity; and will be so to all eternity, as much as when he was actually bleeding on the cross, in all his amazing agonies. Thus he is "the Lamb slain from the foundation of the world." Or, if you put the adjective before the substantive, as a late writer does, and as it stands in the original, the idea is the same; "the slain Lamb from the foundation of the world."

Thus, at the great and solemn day, characters shall be separated one from another, as a shepherd divideth the sheep from the goats. God will shew infinite approbation to the *character* of his own Son, the Son of man, as foederal head in union with his redeemed creatures, placing *it* at his right hand; a phrase denoting approbation and honor. And he will manifest infinite wrath, indignation and vengeance against the real character of man, placing it at his left hand; which denotes the utmost detestation and abhorrence. The place of his Son will, on that day, be at his right hand, as it always was, and always will be, and " where I am," says Jesus, " there shall my servants be." The character of sinners, the real character of all men since the fall, was always at God's left hand, and always will be. God never abhorred man as his creature, never hated, and never will hate any thing in man, but his bad character. In Christ, he has no bad character, but one infinitely good. And God will bid all that sustain it, welcome to all the joys and glories of heaven; even all whose sins the Lamb of God came to take away.

When the great Judge shall give final sentence, and thus display his wondrous love to his elect head, and his elect body of human nature, also his tremendous abhorrence of the character of sinners, it will make all human nature tremble. But they will *rejoice* with trembling. Their amazing sense of the holy indignation of God against sin, will not allay their holy joy, which will be in God alone, on that day, and to all eternity. They will see their personal deserts in the *eternal sufferings* of their Head: For in gospel account they are so; though in time endured once for all on the cross. They will, I say, then, and forever-more, see their damnable character and deserts in themselves; and will go away into everlasting punishment, in this sense. This is the true, and only sense of the gospel constitution; which is well called a wonderful mystery, claiming the admiration and astonishment of angels and saints, now and forever.

To behold the redeemed surrounded with the most formidable displays of the wrath of God forever, against their real personal character *while in this world*, and with his awful indignation forever, as a burning flame, against all ungodliness and unrighteousness of men; and to behold the very persons to whom this real character did personally pertain, made perfectly innocent in a substituted character, their robes all washed and made white in the blood of the Lamb, with clean hands and a pure heart, dwelling in this devouring fire, and inhabiting these everlasting burnings, in displays of righteous and holy Deity; and yet perfectly blessed, and even the more blessed, for this their situation; in the midst of all these awful displays, dwelling on high, and having their place of defence the munition of rocks, bread given them and their waters sure: This is indeed a wonder of love worthy of the wisdom of God only wise. Isa. xxxiii.

ALL this glory and terror of divine holiness and justice, we see, and forever shall see, in the sufferings of the Son of God for sinners. And there is no more need of the eternal *personal* damnation of any of the human race further to display and illustrate the glory of God's justice, and his infinite holy anger against sin; than there is

X

need of the dim light of a candle, to help us to behold the beautiful face of the earth in the vernal season, when the sun shines in the meridian, with all his glorious splendor and in his full strength. Even to suppose otherwise, is in full opposition to the sole glory of God and Christ in the atonement. The gospel is, with great propriety, called a "ministration of righteousness." i. e. righteousness displayed, imparted, and applied, even as the ministration of healing medicines, imparted and applied for the recovery of the sick.

It is, moreover, evidential of the truth of this doctrine of free sovereign grace, as now illustrated, that *there is no possible danger in believing, and living according to the genuine dictates of it.*

It will certainly have the same influence on the heart and life, which the common protestant doctrine of grace always had; but only much more powerful in its blessed operations and effects. It is the self same doctrine, in all points but this: It extends the same eternal good will of God to all poor sinners of mankind; which we have been taught, by puritan divines, is confined only to a part; and it may be to a very small part indeed, agreeably to the more natural aspect of their doctrine. It differs no more from the doctrine of *Calvin*, *Owen*, and *Edwards*, and the great body of protestants, than a circle as large as the periphery of the earth, differs from a circle of the diameter of one cubit. Both have all the same properties, and every demonſtration may be built on the one, that may on the other; but only one is much larger than the other.

In this caſe, we hold the great diſtinguiſhing doctrines of divine revelation exactly as they have always been taught, by thoſe called orthodox. Particularly ; the firſt Adam a federal, as well as natural head, for all human nature : Our fall, guilt and miſery in and by him : The kind decrees, and immutable purpoſes of the Moſt High to ſave ſinners : The covenant of redemption with the ſecond federal head, even Chriſt, the ſecond man, the Lord from heaven : The all ſufficiency of his atonement, and his obedience unto death, in the room and ſtead of ſinners : The neceſſity of regeneration by the almighty power, and free grace of God : The neceſſity of repentance, faith, and ſanctification, a holy mind, perſeverance to the end, all through Chriſt, and by the power of his ſpirit and grace. Yet, we think the doctrines of divine love, redeeming love and grace, include a greater number of poor, wretched ſinners, all alike unworthy of mercy ; than good people have, in time paſt imagined. This is the only point of difference.

I believe, God will have all men to be ſaved : That the Lamb of God hath taken away the ſin of the world : Died for the ſins of the whole world : That as ſin hath reigned unto death, much more ſhall grace reign through righteouſneſs to eternal life, by Jesus Christ our Lord. I believe all this, in the common, plain, natural sense of language; and so I do a thousand other plain assertions in the bible as full and direct to the same purpose as these are. Yet, I have every motive, even with additional force, to seek the kingdom of God and his righteousness; to press into the kingdom of God; to make my calling and election sure; that ever was yet urged from the word of God: And so has every man in the world.

We insist on the same qualifications and *in the same way;* as do they who are called orthodox. We know that while we believe not with an holy heart, we shall be damned. We know that except we are born again, we cannot see the kingdom of God, are condemned already; and that the wrath of God abideth on us, unless we are united to Christ by regeneration and saving faith; and that except we repent we shall all assuredly perish. We insist on every medium, every qualification for heaven that ever was insisted on, by any pure gospel preacher. We have every motive to avoid all the ways of wickedness, and use all the means of grace and salvation that ever the renowned *Calvin* had. He believed that all the elect should infallibly be saved, and no more; so do I. He believed, God hath fixed and established the certain number, from all eternity, as immutably as his own being; so do I. And let men cavil as much as they please; there is but just one way to get rid of this doctrine; and that is to deny divine revelation, and the necessary attributes of God. *Calvin* believed that Christ had undertaken to prepare all the elect for heaven, and would most certainly see the work done, in his own time and way; so do I. He insisted on the necessity of the means of grace and salvation, and great propriety of them, and adduced the word of God, and all the reason and nature of things, to demonstrate that as a truth; which he did beyond all rational contradiction; so do I. His idea of heaven and hell was the self same as mine, as to the nature of the happiness and misery of each. I mention Mr. *Calvin*; because his name and character are much known. I might unite with him, the great body of christian teachers since his day.

Now where is the difference between us, in the doctrine I plead for? This, indeed gives a greater display, a more astonishing manifestation of the goodness of the great Father of all, than we have before admitted. The eternal, rich, free, sovereign love of the immense eternal source of love, breaks forth to our view, in more copious, and amazing floods. The triumph of grace is more glorious than heretofore, *in our sense of it*; and gives our souls a most surprizing, adoring, rapturous shock, enough to make us break forth, "O the depth of the riches, both of the wisdom and knowledge of God! how unsearchable are his determinations,* and his ways past finding out!" "For of him,

* κρίματα.

and through him, and to him are all things : to whom be glory forever. Amen."

EVERY judicious reader will see, that the use of means cannot alter the case as to the salvation of the elect, any more on the common doctrine of predestination, than on this I plead for; yet there is the greatest propriety in the use of appointed means. On both principles, the means and the end are inseparably connected, in the eternal gracious purpose of God.

UNTHINKING, unreasonable men have always been wont to tell those who were founded on the pure doctrines of free, sovereign grace, and who trusted all to God and nothing to themselves, and were thence led into pure and holy lives, lives of prayer, self denial, watchfulness, dying to the world, and all the vanities and carnal delights of it; that if they themselves had such a belief of God's character, decrees and dealings with men, they would plunge into all manner of sinful pleasures, and would gratify every lust, in the highest degree. However, they who have indeed received this grace of God, have constantly affirmed that the greater sense they had of the infinite, eternal, immutable love of God to them, the more they loved him and all his holy laws: And the greater assurance they had that Christ died for them, the more they hated and abhorred all their sinfulness of nature and life, which nailed so dear a Savior to the cross: The more they realized their absolute safety in God alone, and the certainty of their perseverance to the end, through the promises grace, and faithfulness of Christ, the more they felt their hearts weaned from the world: The more spiritual and heavenly was the frame and temper of their minds, as they saw more of the vanity of themselves and of all creatures, and that God was all in all.

THE children of God have always spoken the truth in all this. And we can say the same, in answer to the same cavils of a blind world at enmity with God, and ignorant of his nature, which is love. Only we may add, that as we have more extensive views of the love of God, and the glorious harmony of all his attributes, in gathering together in one all things in Christ; so, we trust, it has a more powerful influence on our souls, of the same kind.

IF we really mistake concerning the extent of the merits, and salvation of the Savior of all men; it is at the farthest remove from a mistake, that affects the essentials of religion. It is only a wrong conjecture as to the number whom Christ will save, in one and the same way. There always have been different opinions among good people in this article. Some have been far more charitable than others, on this subject.

SOME, at this day, expect a millennium of three hundred and sixty five thousand years, i. e. a thousand prophetic years; in which long period almost all on earth shall be holy and happy. I was ever in this sentiment; and am full in it now. Yet many good people, at the prefent day and for ages paſt, have faid that they could find nothing in the word of God, but that the day of judgment might be in their day ; having no expectation at all of fuch a latter-day glory. Now, there is an almoſt infinite difference between the belief of thefe two, as to the extent of falvation; yet both are in the fame fure way to heaven, and on the fame effential foundation. There is a much greater difference between thofe that have faith in a millennium, and thofe who have not, as to the number that fhall be faved; than there is between the advocates for the falvation of all men, and the former; at leaſt as to thofe that have already lived on the earth.

Suppose you hear three pious chriſtians difcourſing on the doctrines of grace, and the way of falvation; all in perfect agreement. At the cloſe of the converfation, each gives his opinion with regard to the number, to be faved. One fays, the way appears to him fo exceeding ſtrait, that he believes not more than one hundred thoufand of all the human race, will ever get to heaven. Another fays, he believes there will be more than one hundred thoufand faved, but he is confident not a million. The third, having great faith in a millennium, and naturally fomewhat unhappy in his talent at computation, is perfuaded that there will be more of the human race faved, than there are fingle atoms of matter in this whole globe of earth. You would not imagine that either was in an error, in any thing that concerned his own falvation. From a good acquaintance with human nature, you would only infer, that the firft was naturally a man of a narrow foul and ftingy temper of mind; that the fecond was, in thefe refpects, not fo unhappy; and that the laft was rather inattentive in his computations; but that they might be all in the fame way to heaven. And, indeed, if a great fenfe of the *free*, fovereign grace of God, leads men into vice and immorality, *how comes it to pafs*, as always appears to be fact, *that they who have the higheft fenfe of this, have ever been men of the pureft lives?*

If I underftand the gofpel to be glad tidings of great joy, which fhall be to all people, in the common natural fenfe of language; and another underftands the fame words to mean glad tidings to a few people of all forts, and very fad tidings to the bulk of mankind, as being a fure occafion of enhancing their eternal mifery in an awful degree: Yet, if I have gofpel qualifications to relifh and enjoy heaven, I fhall go there; and fo will he in the fame way. For we both agree in the neceffity of the fame work on our fouls, without which there is no falvation for any. I infift on thefe qualifications, as flowing from a previous allfufficient atonement made for all finners of the human race, and as neceffary to give me fenfe and enjoyment of the benefit of that atonement, to which Chrift has given me a previous title. He infifts on thefe qualifications to make out his title for him, instead of taking it solely from Christ, and as sealed in his blood alone. I believe that, while we were yet enemies, Christ died for the ungodly, and secured them for life eternal, as a Priest; and then goes on, as a Prophet and King, to enlighten and subdue them, and make them know the things freely given them of God. I put the atonement at the bottom, the death of Christ as the chief corner stone, and build all upon that. He supposes the sacrifice of Christ not to be the foundation of all our hope; but when we have got good previous qualifications, then we may make great advantage of it, and bring it in somewhere in the building, though not at the bottom of all, Christ the *only foundation*. Both of us agree in this, that the greater sense and experience of God's free grace we have, the more we shall love and serve God; and that the love of God, or God in his character, which is LOVE, is the only principle that constraineth us to love God, and live an holy life, or that the goodness of God leadeth to repentance.

The general aspect of the *limitarian principles*, is, that a very few, in comparison with the whole of mankind, shall ever be saved; and, indeed, that but a very small part, even of those people that enjoy divine revelation, will escape eternal, personal damnation; and a far less number, in proportion, among all heathen nations. On this principle, the gospel is by no means glad tidings of great joy which shall be unto *all people*, in any common, natural sense of language: But to people and nations, as such, it is very *bad news*, *doleful tidings* to any nation or people, in a collective view, as they are plainly addressed in the text, to which I allude.

TAKE, for example, the inhabitants of the United States, as a people. More than nine tenths of them, the *limitarians* suppose, are, at the present day, going to eternal destruction; and that a very great majority of all that ever lived here, are now in the intolerable flames of an eternal hell, with torments aggravated more than ten thousand-fold beyond what they would have been, had they never heard the gospel. How then are the tidings glad tidings to the people, as such? They are plainly declared as such every where in the voice of the gospel. Yet upon this plan, the people will be far more miserable than if they had never heard the gospel. Suppose one out of an hundred is saved, which is as many as the general aspect of the *limitarian* doctrine will admit; or, if you please, suppose ten among a hundred, which is going quite beyond the charity of the doctrine: You must still allow that all the rest are ten thousand times more miserable, and will be so to all eternity, than if they had never heard the gospel. So that the people, as such, and as they are plainly addressed with good news, GLAD TIDINGS, will be found far more miserable than if they had never heard these tidings. Thus the gospel becomes glad tidings only to a very few individuals ; but dreadful tidings to any people, or all people, as such.

A SOVEREIGN prince has a colony consisting of one million subjects. All much on a level, laboring under the toils and burdens which attend a people, that eat their bread in the sweat of their face, struggling hard for a comfortable provision for themselves and families. The common lot in this evil world. The king sends an herald to assemble them all together, and to address them in the following words :

"BEHOLD I bring you glad tidings of great joy, which shall be to all this people. For it is the immutable decree of your sovereign, that a few of you shall be delivered from all your toils and labors, and shall be exceedingly rich and happy all their days, abounding in every possible pleasure and delight. And that all the rest of you shall be inexpressibly more miserable and distressed all their days, than ever they have been. Their labors, toils and vexation shall be increased more than a thousand fold. Your sovereign will mark the happy few with a distinction, which his own hand and no other can set upon them ; and the multitude, not so marked, shall forever find their woes amazingly augmented."

WOULD not the colony, the people, be filled with horror at the tidings, and think the news exceedingly sorrowful ? Would it not be much happier for that colony, as a people, to live as they did before ;

though many toils and troubles attended them?

Now, should the herald proceed to name the happy few, perhaps one in a thousand; and the multitude of their brethren should see them rejoicing and triumphing in the sovereign distinction, by the free grace of their prince; would they not say that this very joy and triumph was all founded in pride and selfishness, and a total want of benevolence to the community? And should those favorites cry out glad tidings! glad tidings! would not the wailing multitude answer, "*To you glad tidings they may be; but not to the people. The colony is ruined; the people are undone, undone forever!*" And if these *few favorites* of their sovereign had that amiable spirit of benevolence, which adorns human nature, and is one of the glories of the gospel, would they not rather chuse to return to a level with their brethren, and partake with them in common, in all troubles and calamities as before, than to be thus singled out for dignity, glory, and pleasure, when necessarily connected with such augmented woe and misery to the people?

The case now stated, applies to the gospel tidings, on the *limitarian* plan. A few, very few that hear them, are made happy. All the rest are much more dreadfully miserable on account of Christ and the gospel. This is fixed by the immutable purpose of heaven, with all the means, and every step leading to the consummation of it,

I HOLD to the doctrine of predestination as fully as any man in the world ever did, and that in the supra-lapsarian sense, which is the only consistent sense. The absolute sovereignty of JEHOVAH I maintain, in the highest possible conception of it. But, it will abundantly appear, in its proper place, that JEHOVAH is not a God whose attributes and sovereign will can admit of such a predestination as that; such decrees as I have alluded to. God is love, infinite love, sovereign love; and such love admits of no such *limitarian* decrees; and the word of God abhors them, as you shall see in the sequel.

IT is an evidence of the true gospel, that there is no contradiction in it. Every sentiment in it, is in full concord with the whole.

A SERMON is not made up of contradictory parts, if it be wholly a gospel sermon. Now, the doctrine I plead for, is the only plan that ever was exhibited, as consistent with itself. The arminian scheme is full of inconsistencies. See what the late president *Edwards* has made of it; and he has demonstration on his side. Many other great men have opposed it with the same force. The calvinistic scheme, in the *limitarian* sense, is every whit as *full of contradiction* and absurdity; as hath often been objected, with arguments that admit of no confutation. The same may be said of all the rest that ever have been advanced in the world, except this alone. But this has not the shadow of inconsistency with itself. If it be a mere hypothesis, it is a self-consistent one.

On this plan, you may hold up to view the true nature and character of God: That of man in innocency: That of man fallen: The first and second covenant: Give Jehovah his proper place, and man his place: Speak of a work of God on the souls of sinners, as necessary to their salvation: Shew them that without this work they are damned, condemned already, and the wrath of God abideth on them: Tell them what Christ hath engaged, what he hath done and suffered, and for what end; and what he will certainly do: Command all sinners to believe it, on pain of abiding damnation: Tell them the warrant and ground of their faith: That they are not commanded to create truth, or in the least alter it, by all the changes and exercises of their own minds; but that eternal, immutable truth is ready to their hands, and, by mere faith, they must take hold of it and be saved: That this is the way, in Christ, sure as Godhead can make it: That Christ is the way, the truth, and the life, &c. &c.

As this doctrine relates to practice, you may urge every moral duty, with infinite force, from motives truly evangelical; holding up the pains of sin, and the beauties and rewards of holiness, all in most glorious harmony.

The doctrine we have generally heard from our best preachers, since the reformation, hath been of this tenor, viz. " God

" hath elected to eternal life a part of man-
" kind, and Chrift made an atonement for
" that part only." And they have commonly
conveyed the idea of a very fmall part, in
proportion to the whole. " Which part are
" elected to the end, and to all the neceffary
" means and qualifications; which God will
" infallibly beftow upon them in his own
" way and time. All the reft of mankind
" fhall as certainly perifh, and that juftly,
" the fault being all their own. Now we
" invite, and command every one to believe
" in Chrift to falvation, every one alike:
" For in him there is a fulnefs for all." A
thoufand arguments have been advanced to
prove there is no inconfiftency, no kind of
equivocation, or illufion in this way of
preaching; but that it is the pure fimplicity
of the gofpel: While it hath always been
clear demonftration, on the other hand, that
there is great duplicity and illufion in it.
Yet this preaching is exactly right, in every
point but this one; *the extent of predeftination*.
Only extend it to all the human kind. Only
define the decree in the words of the apoftle;
" *God will have all men to be faved.*" " *As fin
hath reigned unto death, fo fhall grace reign
through righteoufnefs, unto eternal life, by Jefus
Chrift our Lord.*" Many other exprefs declarations of divine revelation, of the fame
import, are as fimple and exprefs to the fame
purpofe, as any language will admit. I fay,
thus explain the decrees of God; and all
their preaching would be as free from inconfiftency as any mathematical demonftration.

ONLY begin thus, in the plain, simple sense of the words; "*Christ came that all men through him might be saved.*" Tell people that this is the eternal fixed predestination of the Most High; and that all means and qualifications are connected with it, in the same decree, and made as sure as the end, to take place in his own way and time; yet so as to have the free will and actions of his elect, concerned in them, as moral agents and causes by counsel; which is the only possible way of connecting the intermediate steps with the end. Tell your audience so, I say, and then in all the rest, you may preach law and gospel just as *Calvin* or *Owen* did, or any other calvinistic divine. Then you may indeed proclaim *Glad tidings of great joy to* ALL PEOPLE; and may urge every gospel doctrine, duty and motive, just as we have been wont to hear, without the shadow of contradiction. Then you may call upon all poor, miserable sinners as Paul did. He told them all, that Christ had began his operation in their souls, as Mediator, and would perfect the whole work unto eternal life; dealing with moral agents *as such*, in which the will and activity should have their proper exercise. "Work out your own salvation with fear and trembling. For it is God who worketh in you, both to will and to do of his good pleasure." On this plan the gospel is plain and clear: And the usual preaching of it, is consistent with itself and with common sense.

Z

If any say here, that the use of means is of no consideration, if the end is fixed and certain; they speak in direct opposition to this idea of the decrees of God, and the whole scripture account of them, which ever unites the means and end, in one and the same decree; and against all the common sense and common practice of mankind. Every one that owns the being of God, allows that he *certainly knew* every thing that ever did or shall take place; and that every future event shall certainly be just as God always knew it would be. But this never hinders their using means, in common life. Nothing can be more certain, than that which God always knew would be, is certain. Whatever distinction there is between the foreknowledge and decrees of God; every one sees there can be none in the object, the infallible certainty of the event. Yet there is full room left for all moral agency to operate, with all the liberty that any creature can possibly be made capable of.

If any say, there can be no moral agency at all in creatures; this is a flat contradiction to all the common sense and feeling of man. We all know our perfect freedom of will and action; not by any reasoning or demonstration: For it is too plain to admit of any. It is a prime, immediate perception of soul, which we always have, and constantly feel, and cannot possibly divest ourselves of: Even as I feel heat or cold; or perceive that paper is white, and ink black; or that whatever is, *is*; or that a thing cannot exift and exift at the fame time. So that I have ever imagined that fuch a fenfelefs cavil is worthy of no notice at all.

But to return. The gofpel, on the ground I maintain, is all confiftent with itfelf, with common fenfe and reafon, and with univerfal experience, and with the beft reafoning and practice of all mankind in every other matter. We always unite the proper means with the end, in all other cafes; and there is no other way for moral agents to be treated, as fuch, and to act in proper character. Creatures are creatures, although God is God.

There is a fentiment, or impreffion, on the hearts of all men, concerning the dead, that univerfally favors the argument here advanced.

When the vileft finner in the world is taken out of it, by the moft fudden death, we dare not fay, and it would wound our hearts to hear any one fay, " *that perfon is certainly gone to an eternal hell, to fuffer there in perfon forever.*" Who dare fay of the moft abandoned failor, having his head taken off with a cannon ball, with an horrid oath in his mouth, " *I am certain that man fhall burn forever in hell?*" Yet we might fay fo, with great confidence, on the principle I oppofe. Had you, my reader, a fon of this character, thus taken out of the world, would you be fo deeply affected, in regard to his eternal doom, as if you certainly knew he was in hell? Or had you a fon very dear to you, even as Abſalom was to his father, and of a character to the laſt moment no better, taken out of the world by the hand of juſtice; would not the circumſtances of his death ſtrike your mind deeper, than any certain knowledge you have of his future ſtate? You may ſay the future ſtate of men is inviſible, and we have no buſineſs with it. Be it ſo. Yet, would it be in the power of any man to avoid the moſt dreadful anguiſh of ſoul, in ſuch a caſe, but from a *latent hope* in his heart, ariſing from the power and mercy of God? Would not any man in the world, feel more anguiſh of heart to ſee his ſon hanged as a criminal, than what he ever can feel with reſpect to his future ſtate, ſeparate from the circumſtances of his death? If we have no buſineſs with the inviſible world in ſuch a caſe, yet this does not alter the neceſſary and unavoidable feelings of human nature.

I am perſuaded that any man, who has buried a dear child, in a caſe which is thought the moſt hopeleſs of all, will find, if he is critical to obſerve the feelings of his own heart, ſome *latent* aſſuaging of his grief, in thinking of the unſearchable riches of Chriſt, and the almighty power and infinite mercy of God. Have we not often obſerved much of this nature, in mourning for the dead, even in caſes that would admit of nothing but abſolute deſperation, on the *limitarian* plan? Deſpair, in this caſe, never takes place. There is ſomething in the ſoul of man that will not admit of it. What but the hand of Deity has fixed in the hearts of all mankind this latent hope, in every death?

ALL the pungent pangs of David for the death of Abſalom, may be fully accounted for, on the principles of natural affection, without any conſideration of his future ſtate. Any tender parent would feel as he did, in the like caſe, without looking into futurity.

IT is exceedingly ſtrange, on the *limitarian* plan, that the ſcriptures have never aſſerted that any particular perſon went to an eternal hell.

THE ſtate of no one, perhaps, is more hopeleſs than that of Judas, who betrayed Chriſt the Savior of all men; yet not a word is ſaid of him but what may conſiſt with his ſalvation after death. He is called the ſon of perdition; and it is ſaid that he went to his own place. All this is but juſt what we may ſay of every ſinner, in kind, though of Judas in a very aggravated degree. Every man is a ſon of perdition until new born, damned until regenerated. Judas was a notable ſon of perdition, ſignally ſo, a moſt miſerable, loſt, condemned ſinner, until his death; in perdition until that moment, even until ſoul and body were ſeparated; until then a ſon of perdition in an extraordinary degree. Paul was ſo in a woful meaſure until he died, " *a wretched man,*" with a " *body of death.*" Every man is ſo, in a ſad degree, until the union of ſoul and body, which firſt contaminated the ſoul, is diſſolved; some in a greater, and some in a less degree, according as the Head of every man, i. e. the Mediator, has been pleased to advance, or restrain his prophetic and kingly power and grace upon the soul.

Judas went to his own place, to a very horrible and ignominious death, in awful anguish and utter despair, in his own mind. His soul went, perhaps, to the lowest seat provided for the elect human race, by him who died for the sins of the whole world; to the lowest place among all given to Christ. Judas being one given to Christ, as is expressly declared. Judas was lost in an awful manner; he was lost as an apostle of Christ; lost as to all service in this world; lost with regard to all his comfort on earth; lost as to any hope to support his own soul here; lost with respect to the proper seat of one of the twelve apostles in the world to come, and with respect to that dignified lot, in this world, which Matthias took in his place. He was, in fine, so lost, such a son of perdition, and in such wise went to his own place, as fully to support and justify the most plain and natural import of all the awful things said in the word of God concerning him; without any consideration of positive misery, after death. The same may be said of Ahitophel his type.

With regard to the parable of the rich man, in the gospel, who lift up his eyes in hell, being in torments. It implies no personal misery there; but is one of the many striking displays of *pure justice*, the sanction of the law, in awful terror. Such displays will remain forever, as I have said before, in the full view of all the saints in heaven to all eternity. In the glass of pure justice, they will forever see, not only this Dives, but themselves also lifting up their eyes in torments unutterable. And, in this sense, will dwell with devouring fire, and inhabit everlasting burnings. Though in their surety, they shall personally find a place of defence, a munition of rocks, the bread and sure waters of eternal consolation.

I READILY grant, if this distinction, which I would every where keep in view, between the voice of justice, and that of mercy, the display of law and that of gospel, running through the whole word of God, is without foundation, my whole argument falls to the ground. So does the whole of divine revelation, for ought I can possibly discern, after a most careful inquiry, for many years. And (with awful reverence I would speak it,) I am not able, without this distinction, to vindicate the holy bible from many more flat contradictions, than any other book I have ever read. But this distinction is the peculiar glory and mystery of divine revelation.

WE are expressly told, that even a brother for whom Christ died, may *perish*. 1. Cor. viii. 11. This is a term used for eternal misery, by the *limitarians* themselves, as much as the word *damnation*. The meaning is certainly no more than this: He may fall into snares of infidelity, into many doubts and sorrows in this world; may lose all gospel confolation, and become a miferable creature, all his days on earth.

Moreover, what our Savior hath faid concerning children, greatly confirms the opinion, that he gave his life " a ranfom for all," in the moft natural fenfe of thefe words of the apoftle.

The greater part of departed human fouls have left the body, having never arrived at the age of maturity. Chrift tells us, " of fuch is the kingdom of heaven." Plainly fignifying, that a great proportion for whom he died, are of this defcription. And he does not at all limit his words to the children of his peculiar people, in prefent knowledge of his covenant, and prefent enjoyment of the privileges and comforts of it. This fhews that he is the Mediator between God and man, in general, without any exception or diftinction as to final falvation.

The paffage I have alluded to, may alfo carry in it this idea, viz. That all who enjoy heaven, have a meek, humble, dependent, child-like fpirit given them. This may be one thing fignified thereby; but this militates not in the leaft againft the conftruction I have given, as the main import of the words of Chrift; but is compatible therewith, and the rather confirms it. We hope for the falvation of children of the covenant, dedicated to God by his fpecial feal. The fame merits of Chrift, and the fame power of fanctifying grace, are as adequate to the falvation of all the little ones in the world.

We all fell in our firſt fœderal head, without our knowledge or act in the caſe; and all mankind are reſtored in the ſecond fœderal head in like manner. Otherwiſe grace does not abound *much more;* but indeed *much leſs.* This idea of the kind Parent of all, gives us a father's conſolation when we follow to the grave our dear children, who are often ſwept away by death in ſuch multitudes. Read Jeremiah xxxi. 15, 16, 17. We can yet ſay, " the Lord is good unto all, and his tender mercies are over all." No infant in the world was ever exempt from the mediatorial love of him, who *took little children in his arms and bleſſed them.*

Much is ſaid about being fit to die. There is one fitneſs and but one, and that is by no means perſonal; but in the perfect character of a Covenant Head, a Vicar, or Surety, in the full atonement, and all perfect worthineſs of Jeſus. Whatever difference progreſſive grace may make between mankind in this life, (and great is the bleſſing of all thoſe who are elected to ſpecial attainments of grace in this world) yet every one without diſtinction, is left utterly unfit for heaven, ſo long as the ſoul is in the body, an awful unclean thing. No unclean thing ſhall enter into that world. On the ſeparation, and not before, is any ſoul in its own temper and qualifications fit; but in a relative view, all for whom Chriſt died, are ſo. Their garments are all alike waſhed and made white in the blood of the Lamb.

What was done for David, Daniel and Paul, at the moment of separation, that they might enter paradise with spotless purity, was of the self-same nature, and not twice so much in degree, as might qualify Pharaoh, Ahab, and Judas for the same world: For no man on earth, to his last breath, was ever yet sanctified to the one half, or ever made progress in holiness one half way from a state of total depravity, to a state of complete holiness.

My reader if you are left as you are found at your last breath, you must know that your soul will be too unclean for heaven, or else you know very little of yourself. In Christ, all things are ready for all, and equally ready at all times, without any consideration in the universe, but what is drawn from God alone in a glorious, all sufficient Mediator. God is all in all, and Christ is all in all. Thus the primitive preachers of Christ warned *every man*, and taught *every man*, in all wisdom: That they might present *every man* perfect in Christ Jesus. Col. i. And I am bold to say, that any child of Adam that trusts to any distinction in his own heart or life, in the least to support the heart in a dying hour, or to any thing but Jesus Christ alone and him crucified, *shall be all his life time subject to bondage through fear of death;* and, thus abiding, shall find no relief, until the departed spirit is taught better, in the arms of him who has the keys of hell and of death. The notion of some fitness in a sinner for heaven, whether a penitent or an impenitent sinner, is utterly repugnant to the whole word of God. It is built wholly on a legal fpirit, and on our attachment to the old covenant of works. It wars againſt every evangelical motive of comfort in our fouls, and obedience in our lives. It ſtands in oppoſition to an intire dependance on God in Chriſt, and to every moral virtue. Hence we do not allow God his proper character and place, nor take our own: " We obferve lying vanities and forſake our own mercies."

It is an evidence of the true gofpel: That when it is impreſſed on the heart, it makes men better in their morals than before.

The *limitarians* urge this argument againſt all the cavils raiſed from the doctrines of God's decrees, of free fovereign grace, and of the certain perfeverance of believers. And they have ever well maintained their ground, by dint of reafon, experience and divine revelation. The doctrine I plead for, takes full advantage of every argument they adduce, and enforces them all with vaſt additional ſtrength. They fay, and that truly, that the difplays of God's mercy and love, always draw the heart to love God, and to keep his commandments. How much more ſhall theſe more glorious and extenſive difplays of the love and mercy of God, in the felf fame way, melt the whole foul into the obedience of love, and produce every moral virtue in the life of man?

The queſtion is not, what will be the influence of this doctrine on thoſe who do not believe it, but on those who do? We know that every gospel doctrine is turned to bad account, by impenitent, unbelieving men. They all turn the grace of God into wantonness; while true believers are purified by their faith, and led into all holiness of life. There is not one objection of licentiousness against this doctrine, which does not lie, in full force, and much greater force, against every *limitarian* doctrine of *free, sovereign grace.*

They who have built on the highest principles of sovereign grace, and have most of all set at nought all fitness in men for salvation, but in Christ alone, have ever been the most moral and virtuous in their lives: While, on the other hand, they who could not endure a thought of the absolute decrees and sovereignty of God, and salvation by mere mercy in Christ, exclusive from every qualification in man, to move the heart of God towards him; and have plead for power and merit and free will of their own creating, have too often been a dissolute, abandoned part of mankind. The higher thoughts men have of God, and the lower of themselves; the better their morals always have been, and always will be. Therefore, as this doctrine, which I am supporting, carries these sentiments to a much greater extent than any *limitarian* doctrine: So it will, if cordially believed, produce much better morals.

The *fear of punishment* after death, never

yet had any power to reſtrain an hardened ſinner from ſin; much leſs to make him love virtue.

The moſt abandoned in wickedneſs, in all ages, have believed in the doctrine of hell torments, as much as a hardened ſinner can believe any thing of the inviſible world. They have always been wont to allude to theſe torments, in their common converſation, as a matter indiſputable. They have hell and damnation in their mouths, all the day long. But did all this ever, in the leaſt, prevent their ſtealing, curſing, ſwearing, committing adultery, fighting with one another, or any horrid blaſphemy they were addicted to? Never in the leaſt. Now if any imagine the moſt extenſive doctrines of divine goodneſs will make hardened ſinners worſe than they now are; they have yet to ſtudy human nature, and the common ways of the world.

Give an old, veteran, profane ſailor, a guinea in ſome ſpecial diſtreſs he is in, and he will not uſe a bad word if he knows it will offend you. But threaten him with eternal damnation for his ſin, and tell him his preſent diſtreſs is juſt upon him, and he will curſe you to your face. Men ought indeed, to be deterred from ſin by fear of hell: For hell in an awful degree and the pains of it attend all ſin; and the eternity of hell torments can be avoided in no way, but by forſaking ſin, no more on my plan than any other. But *ought* is one thing, and *fact* is another. Whatever hardened sinners ought to do, and from whatever motives; I say, it is fact in all ages, the world throughout, that they never did mend their ways, from a fear of any thing in the invisible world. It has ever been fact, that when they have had most of hell and damnation in their mouths, they have gone on most daringly in their wickedness.

It is readily granted, that awakened sinners, with whom the spirit of God is on his usual way to bring them to a sense of the salvation of God, will be much restrained from all immorality, under such special awakenings; yet all these will not bring them into the love and practice of holiness and virtue, as will a sense of the love of God's redeeming love. Under all these legal awakenings and restraints from open vice, *they will only change their mode of sinning*, until the grace of God that *bringeth salvation*, appears to their souls: Which alone will effectually teach them to deny all ungodliness and every worldly lust. But then, let it be well noted that the doctrine I plead for, secures every advantage and restraint of awakening grace, as fully as any *limitarian* doctrine ever did, or can. I maintain the same doctrine in the true nature of it; the same necessity of conviction and conversion, that they do. We differ not a single atom, as to the way and manner of application; but only in this, I extend the glorious work of God, and every good influence of it, much further than they do.

From visible, sensible shame and punishment, in this world, the hardened and moſt abandoned are laid under very great reſtraints, without which they would be wholly intolerable; but none, none at all, from all you can tell them of an eternal hell. As for theſe viſible reſtraints, none can plead for them more than I; as will appear in its proper place. It may however be obſerved, that all the conduct of ſinners, under the utmoſt power of their reſtraints, is wholly deſtitute of any holineſs, or real virtue in the ſight of God. Their open ſin in the ſight of the world, is much leſs than before; and there is a good token, that the ſpirit of God is on his uſual way to bring them to ſaving good. There are reaſons enough in oppoſition to ſtupid ſecurity and open wickedneſs: Yet, ſtill the ſoul of one unregenerate ſinner is no more recommended in itſelf to the mercy of God, than that of another. This mercy is " unto all, and upon all them that believe; for there is no difference." Rom. iii. 22. Antecedently there is not a diſpoſition, or thought of the heart, or action in the life, but what is not of faith; and conſequently ſin.

The view of divine love, of Chriſt and ſalvation, as is here repreſented, is the true and only ſource of *goſpel charity*, ſo much recommended in the word of God.

We are taught to love all mankind, and to pray for the ſalvation of all, and to do all we can to promote the ſalvation of every human creature; as the goſpel hath ever been, is, and ever will be preached to every creature under heaven, in a more direct and clear, or in a more indirect and obscure manner, as I have shewn before. But how can you pray for the salvation of all, if you believe it is the fixed will of that God, whose attributes and will are infinitely dear to you, that most of mankind shall go to eternal, personal misery? You love God better than men, and his will more than all the happiness of creatures; how can you feel any disposition to have all men saved? And how can you pray in opposition to the desire of your heart? Or how can you love all mankind when you believe that most are infinitely hateful to God and Christ, and always shall be? How do your will and affections correspond with the will and affections of Christ in such a case?

You are strictly charged to hate nothing in any man, but his sinfulness; *to love the person and happiness of every one.* You may hate the wicked with perfect hatred, only as God does, and as David did, accounting them the enemies of God, i. e. so far as they are so. And thus far, and in this sense, you may hate all present believers, and even your father and mother, wife and children, brethren and sisters, yea and your own self also. This is consistent with a sincere love to your own salvation, and that of all mankind. But, how can you desire that blessedness and extent of salvation, which the highest object of your love opposeth, with an eternal, immutable, holy, and good purpose of mind? I see no way to warrant such desires, exertions and prayers of ours in all this extent, but the warrant Paul hath mentioned, viz. *God will have all men to be saved,* and, first or last, in his own way and time, to come to the knowledge of the truth; and because Christ *gave himself a ransom for all:* A glorious truth to be communicated to the world by degrees, as infinite wisdom sees fit: A testimony to be exhibited in proper times and measures. On this warrant, the way is open and clear, to love all; to pray for all; to seek the salvation of all; to exercise kind and tender affection for all poor sinners in the world; because God hath so loved the world, and Christ hath so loved the world.

THE love of God will make us love all as he does, according to our measure of love, and to be co-workers together with God. A principle of this nature moves tender affection in all other cases. You have a very dear, earthly friend, that is absent afar off, who has left a little child with you. The remembrance of your friend, and how he set his affections on that child, and what tender concern he continually has for the child, will affect your heart with tenderness, pity and love, every time you look on the little helpless creature; even though it be, a perverse child. The love of your most dear friend, will make you always exceeding kind to his child, as an object of his love. Your care will extend to his other property, less

B b

valuable, which you have any concern with, or knowledge of. So, in the present case, when you see any poor, perverse sinners on earth, your love to God and Christ will cause your heart, on the true gospel principle, to say, " My God made them in his love ; and in his great love and pity he preserves them. My dear Savior died for them, in the greatness of his love. God hath a desire to these works of his hands. The heart of my best beloved even bleeds with compassion, love and pity to these poor creatures. My love to my Savior makes me feel towards these unworthy, miserable objects, as he doth. He is exceedingly good to these evil, unthankful creatures ; and the love of God constraineth me to feel towards them, as God and Christ do towards them and me." There is verily no other fountain of gospel charity but this : No other principle that can make us feel towards the vilest of sinners, as God commands us. But this " charity believeth all things, and hopeth all things," certainly not excluding the capital point. This charity is the radical grace in the soul of man, and " the bond of perfectness."

SOME, who have been full in the opinion, that Christ the Savior of the world, will finally triumph over all the power of satan, and all the sins and miseries of mankind, wholly destroying all the works of the devil, seeking and saving that human nature which was lost ; have yet supposed, that pain and misery may attend many of the human race, a long duration after death; even for ages of ages.* This they suppose necessary, to purge, humble, and subdue some sinners; and make them fit for a pure spotless heaven, a pure state of consummate happiness.

The above sentiment is without any reason, or any thing in divine revelation to warrant the supposition. All want purgation at the moment of death, as really as any one. Sanctification is far, very far from being complete, while the sinner breathes, whether a penitent or impenitent sinner. In both there is much unholiness, while life remains. No unclean thing shall enter heaven; and, of certain consequence, not the best saint, not any mere man that ever lived, as he was in the last moment of his life.

Whatever is done before, for us miserable sinners, it is certain, the most of all will be done in the parting moment, to separate us from pollution, and fit us for glory. All then must go into purgation, if any: Though it were granted that a shorter period would suffice for some than for others; which is not true, as will soon appear. Hence the papists are quite consistent with themselves, though not with the gospel, in sending all to purgatory; without a decree of exemption, which, they say, is the pardon of the priest.

A special work of Christ there certainly must be in death; or never one of the mere human kind can get to heaven: For the ve-

* εἰς τὰς αἰῶνας τῶν αἰώνων.

ry moment before we expire, the best do justly cry out, O wretched men that we are; we have a body of death, and who shall deliver us from it! We shall all be poor, wretched sinners in that moment, whenever it comes, and under greater guilt then, than ever before, in ourselves considered: For we shall continually add many sins, and atone for none. The same infinite mercy, power, and faithfulness, which can then separate one soul from all its unfitness for heaven, can another. Christ does but a small part of his glorious work on any soul in this life. He graciously begins earlier with some than others; but he finishes with all alike, even at death. "The last enemy that shall be destroyed is death. I will make this last even as thee."

We are very plainly taught in the word of God, that every soul goes immediately after death, into an eternal, fixed state; which never more admits of any alteration, but in progressive degree; the same in kind, unchangeable to endless duration. The special manner in which Enoch and Elijah went out of the world, does not make them differ from that of all mankind in this respect; viz. That they were both so far from perfect holiness, the moment before their translation, as to be utterly unfit for the pure glories of heaven. Yea, they were much more fit for hell, *in themselves*, as neither they, nor any other man had ever arrived half way to sinless perfection while in the body. Yet, it is sure, they both went direct to heaven. The thief on the cross was miserably unprepared for paradife, as long as he was dying; but when dead, he went there, with the human foul of Jefus. Lazarus went as directly to that world when he died, as the rich man went, *in the voice of the law,* to hell, and as all go there, when they die, *in the fame holy fentiment of the law.* Paul defired to depart, not for fome AGES of purgation and humiliation, but to be with Chrift; although he groaned under his body of death, more than under the dying pangs of his body. And there is every reafon to prove, that all the redeemed finners, for whom Chrift gave himfelf a ranfom, fhall go there as immediately after death, as the poor, hateful thief.

WE are taught the fame truth, from the early periods of divine revelation. All the uncleanneffes mentioned in the mofaic inftitution, and all the purgations there, reprefent, as all allow, our moral or fpiritual pollutions, and our moral or fpiritual cleanfing. A day there denotes oftentimes the day or feafon of life, and the evening, death, or the clofe of life. How many times is it repeated, that the polluted and the unclean, in a ceremonial fenfe, though they wafh their cloaths and bathe themfelves in water, (denoting all the means of grace and fanctification in this life) yet fhall be unclean until the even? But it is faid of all fowing feeds, in like cafes, that they fhall be clean. Levit. xi. And in many other places, needlefs here to quote. Seed fown and fpringing up again, is a well known fimile, denoting our death and refurrection. " It is fown a natural body, it is raised a spiritual body." So in the type alluded to, we die most dreadfully unclean; yet no unsafe consequence shall follow, any more than it was unsafe to sow polluted seed, for fear the pollution would not be taken out in the ground, and that the rising crop would be all unclean.

The human body goes into the grave an awfully polluted thing; but does not arise so. It is sown in dishonor and weakness, it is raised in honor and glory. Our bones will be full of the sin of our youth, which will be buried together with us in the dust; but will not arise with us, except in the holy voice of law: And in that sense all mankind shall awake to shame and everlasting contempt, and abide so forever; but in gospel language and *certain effect*, all shall awake to everlasting life. Sin lies down, but does not arise. " His bones are full of the sin of his youth, which shall lie down with him in the dust." Job xx. Sin and its attendants shall vex and distress the wicked as long as they live; and hurry them on in all its dreadful rage and malignity while they live. It shall even drive them to death, " to the king of terrors;" but no further.

The utmost torment, for a long period, even for *ages of ages*, could have no more effect in humbling sinners of the human, than of the angelic nature. The devils are no better, for their long continued anguish and pain. Afflictions in this world, do not make sinners any better; but are invariably, only an occasion of their growing worse and worfe, if the fpecial, almighty energy of the divine Spirit does not attend them. There is not the leaft intimation of the operation of the Spirit of God, or of any means of grace in hell; in whatever fenfe any underftand that awful ftate, whether as a ftate of real, perfonal fuffering, or as the pure voice or difplay of juftice. The devils have been under thefe perfonal fufferings, for a long time, and are no more humble than ever, no more fit for heaven. And had it been the decree of God, that all mankind fhould be there in perfon with them, ever fo long, they would grow worfe and worfe, through all ages of ages; for ought that their intolerable torments would do for them. Almighty power could create their hearts anew, even in hell, as eafily as on earth. God has power enough to change the natures of all the devils there; but, he has not told us he ever will do it, and we know of no favior provided for them, or that ever will be.

Unto us a Savior is born; unto us God's own Son is given; and he has been pleafed to make known to us his decrees of infinite love and mercy. The love and kindnefs of God to man hath appeared, not by works of righteoufnefs which we have done, or can do; but by his mere mercy he faves man, by the wafhing of regeneration, and the renewing of the Holy Ghoft, which he hath fhed on us, on all mankind abundantly; though on different perfons and people, and in different ages and periods of time, in a very different degree, as the great and holy Sovereign hath seen fit.

Upon the true, gospel doctrine, that God will have all men to be saved, and to come to the knowledge of the truth: That the Lamb of God hath taken away the sin of the whole world: That Christ is invested with regal power, as Mediator, to gather together in one all things in himself: That as far as sin hath reigned unto death, grace shall reign through righteousness to eternal life by Jesus Christ our Lord: And that the last enemy he will destroy is death, crying in exalted triumph, O death! I will be thy plague: O grave! I will be thy destruction: On this plain gospel doctrine, I say, it is wholly without reason or scripture, to suppose that the miseries of man shall reach beyond death.

The contest between the Mediator and his grand adversary, or the two opposite seeds, is very often, and very justly represented under the similitude of a long war, or a long, obstinate battle. It is every where affirmed that the Savior of the human race shall obtain the victory, and a full complete victory too. The adversary shall succeed no further than to bruise the heel; which is not a wound that shall terminate in that death, *everlasting, personal death*, which he aimed at. It shall admit of a cure. But the seed of the woman shall bruise the head of the adversary; give a fatal stroke, where a bruise by almighty strength is certain death; and so far as we know, it will admit of no cure. Such will be the victory of Christ over the serpent.

WHEN two armies go to battle, if the one, only with the loss of an hundred men, slay ten thousand of the adverse party and take almost all the rest prisoners with great spoil; we say there is a great and triumphant victory gained; yea, we are ready to call it a complete triumph, even though the victors lose a few men in battle, and a few more are taken captives by the retreating foe. Just such will be the victory of satan, upon the *limitarian* plan. The rescued of the Lord will be only a very few, amidst the general overthrow of mankind. Satan will obtain a great and awful victory, though not so intire and complete as he could have wished: Not wholly without loss; but almost so. Now is this like the representation of the rencounter, the great contest, in which the Almighty Son of God hath engaged against his adversary, and the grand adversary of his dear offspring of the human kind?

THE point satan aimed at, was to involve us all in death, temporal, spiritual, and eternal. Christ set himself in full opposition to the whole purpose of satan, that no evil, *none at all* on the whole, should accrue to man from all the malice, and all the deadly works of the devil. Christ's aim was as extensive as satan's; as good as the devil's was bad. HE UNDERTOOK WITH AS MUCH BENEVOLENCE, AS SATAN DID WITH MAlice. He aimed at no partial victory, much less at a rescue of a very few, leaving the field and a triumphant victory to his adversary.

The Mediator, the Head of every man abundantly assures us, that his victory shall be complete. " I will ransom them from the power of the grave ; I will redeem them from death : O death ! I will be thy plagues ; O grave ! I will be thy destruction : Repentance shall be hid from mine eyes." Hos. xiii. 14. So in Heb. ii. we find the union of Christ with human nature, *with every man*, as fully asserted as words can express ; together with the end of his undertaking, and of all his sufferings. " That he by the grace of God should taste death *for every man ;*" and " that through death he might destroy him that had the power of death, that is the devil ;" and " that he might deliver them (without any exception mentioned) who, through fear of death, were all their life time subject to bondage :" Which is most of all the case of poor, distressed sinners, who under conviction, feel themselves, of all mankind, the least qualified for heaven, and the most fit for hell : Indeed, all other sinners also, tremble at a realizing thought of death. The great Redeemer speaks without any, the least exception, when he says, " shall the prey be taken from the mighty, or the lawful captive delivered ? But thus saith the Lord, even the captives of the mighty shall be taken away, and the prey of the terrible shall be delivered ; for I will contend with him that contendeth with thee, and I will save thy children." Isai. xlix. 24, 25.

The Holy Ghost speaks of man without any distinction, in words like these: " His soul draweth near unto the grave, and his life to the destroyers; if there be a messenger with him, an interpreter, one among a thousand, to shew unto man his uprightness: Then he is gracious unto him, and saith, deliver him from going down to the pit, I have found a ransom." Job xxxiii. Here it is most plain, that the discovery, interpretation, or display of the Mediator's *own righteousness* is the sole relief of the guilty, without any the least qualification or distinction in the sinful creature.

The holy scriptures every where abound with thoughts correspondent to the passages now cited. There is nothing that looks like a victory of satan over the Son of man, in any part or degree; though it is well known, the whole human kind are the prize contended for. All is quite the reverse. Christ rideth forth conquering and to conquer. " He hath led captivity captive, and received gifts for men, yea for the *rebellious* also, that the Lord our God might dwell among them." Psalm lxviii. " For it pleased the Father, that in him should all fulness dwell; and (having made peace, through the blood of his cross) *by him*, to reconcile all things to himself, *by him*, I say, whether they be things in earth, or things in heaven." " For in him dwelleth all the fulness of the God-head bodily; and ye are complete in him, who is the head of all principality and power." "Blotting out the hand writing of ordinances, which was againſt us, and took it out of the way, nailing it to his croſs; and having ſpoiled principalities and powers, he made a ſhew of them openly, triumphing over them in it." Col. i. and ii. The holy ſcriptures every where announce, not only ſome benefit to mankind by Chriſt, a ſmall, partial reſcue from miſery; ſome valuable ſaving to the human kind; but a redemption, a victory over *ſatan, death,* and *miſery,* FULL, COMPLETE, and ETERNAL.

IT is utterly impertinent for any one to ſay, that this victory may be ſo complete, and yet moſt of the human race, or indeed any of them, may be in perſonal miſery to endleſs duration: And that God may have his own full glory, and the moſt benevolent ſyſtem may be eſtabliſhed, notwithſtanding. We muſt attend to the very thing contended for by ſatan, on the one part, and by the Son of God on the other. On the part of the adverſary, the matter contended for, is the intire, complete, eternal, univerſal miſery of all mankind: The Son of God does flatly, and fully oppoſe ſatan, in this very thing. Otherwiſe there is no war between them. i. e. if the devil is driving at one thing, and the Savior oppoſing another. But the oppoſition is direct and full; as above ſtated.

SUPPOSE ſatan to ſay, "I will have the human kind miſerable with me to all eternity:" And Chriſt to ſay, "So you ſhall, most of them ; but I will have my glory in it." Here is concurrence in the main. The variance and oppofition is very fmall. But we know, that the feed of the woman does oppofe fatan, *in full* ; and will not let him gain that very point he aimed at, either in whole, or in any part: Hence, he makes even the pains of this life, and natural death, not only to turn to his own glory, but to the real advantage and happinefs of man. Satan never fo much as hoped, or in the leaft aimed to obftruct the happinefs or glory of God; for he always knew it was utterly impoffible for him to do it, in the leaft degree. The complete, eternal mifery of all mankind was the fole point he aimed at ; and this is the plain fcripture reprefentation of the matter. The Savior fully and flatly oppofed him in that very point; and this alone can make a proper war, a true and direct contention. The Meffiah did not fay to fatan, " You fhall have your will in the main, and I will have mine too :" But " you fhall not have your will at all, and I will have mine wholly." " I will overcome and conquer you, on your chofen ground, on which you contend to make all the human kind forever miferable. The human kind fhall be as happy, as univerfally fo, and even more completely fo, than if you had never determined on their ruin." This is a proper oppofition ; and in this the Almighty Savior will be victorious.

But alas ! the *limitarian* plan gives fatan a grand victory and triumph, in all he had in view, or ever had any hope to accomplish. It considers Christ as concurring with him, *in the main*, in all that he desired; though, in another way, getting glory to himself, and making the victory and triumph of satan only an occasion of it. Here is very little opposition. The devil has got his will in one thing, and the Savior in another. Satan expected, in his most sanguine hopes, little more than what he will obtain; and Christ never meant to make any *great opposition* to the devil, while seeking whom he may devour; though in another way he would secure his own glory. Consult the sacred oracles throughout, and let common sense say, whether there is any thing in all this, that bears the most distant likeness to the direct and full opposition, between the seed of the woman and the serpent contending *for one and the same thing*, even human happiness.

Satan shall not finally have his will in the least part, or degree; though for a season he may be gratified: For divine wisdom and goodness have ordained, that there shall be a long contention, and the war not soon over. Yet, in the end, satan shall be wholly overcome and disappointed in every view, and in every hope that he has entertained. The prize in contest may be divided for a time; and satan may seem to have the greater share of it. It has indeed been so ever since the fall, to this day; and may be so to the end of this present world. But in the result, satan shall lose *all*; and the Son of

God gain all, even the whole prize in dispute, and even deſtroy him that for a time, a long ſeaſon, has the power of death. His victory ſhall be complete; though for a long time God divides him a portion with the great (adverſary) and he divides the ſpoil with the ſtrong. Since he hath poured out his ſoul unto death, and ſince God hath laid upon him the iniquity of *us all*, and he hath been numbered with tranſgreſſors, and bare the ſin of many, i. e. as many as thoſe, whoſe iniquities were laid upon him, even "us all," all the human kind; he will, in his own way and time, make the application ſure. He will make interceſſion for the tranſgreſſors. Iſai. liii. Not a word of exception or limitation is mentioned in the paſſages now alluded to.

The word *many*, is often uſed in ſcripture to ſignify all the human kind. The reſurrection of all the dead is expreſſed in the ſame manner. Dan. xii. Alſo the apoſtacy of the human race : "By one man's diſobedience *many* were made ſinners." Rom. v. Indeed it is the common language of ſcripture. The reader will multiply quotations as many as he pleaſes. The word *many* ſo uſed, is often explained by the ſynonimous term *all ;* and often the plain ſenſe and connection of the context ſo explains it. So in the paſſage above cited out of the prophet Iſaiah, God laid on Chriſt the iniquity of *us all*, and he bare the ſin of *many*, i. e. the ſame number, the whole number of tranſgreſſors;

and his effectual intercession shall be for just so many, in the final result.

The kingdom of Jesus, in this world, hath ever appeared feeble, like a bruised reed and like smoaking flax ; and the kingdom of satan hath appeared in pomp and power ; but this will not forbid a complete victory on the part of the Mediator in the end. " He shall not fail nor be discouraged, until he have set judgment in the earth: And the Isles shall wait for his law :" He will, in his own time, " open blind eyes and bring out the prisoners from the prison, and them that sit in darkness out of the prison-house. I am the Lord, that is my name, and my glory will I not give to another, neither my praise to graven images." Isa. xlii. 1.—16. Satan hath long led away most of the nations after images, and into various kinds of idolatry ; but Christ will finally reclaim as many as satan hath deluded. " God will gather together in one all things in Christ." Yea, wherever " sin hath abounded, grace shall much more abound." The matter immediately in contest is the weal or woe of the human kind.

" What can awake thee unawak'd by this,
" Expended Deity on human weal !"

It is, moreover, worthy of our special notice that throughout the books of Moses, and indeed through the whole of the old testament, there is very little said of blessings, or of curses, of happiness, or of misery, but what is temporal and pertains to this present life, as every attentive reader of the sacred books will immediately recollect. And when the word *hell* is mentioned any where in the old testament, it very seldom, perhaps never, signifies any other than the grave, or state of the dead in general. The curses on the disobedient are every where mainly such as take place in this world, or terminate in the grave; so are the blessings promised to the obedient. Citations from the scripture would be almost endless, the reader has them in his own memory without number. How shall we account for this, but upon the supposition that no distinction shall remain beyond death, except a distinction in degree of happiness, by the glorious Savior of all men?

Sin is an infinite evil in its own nature; and nothing at all ought, or can be said in excuse for it on our part: Yet, at the same time, it is not amiss for us to know that we do not, *cannot* hurt God by it, or in the least infringe upon his uninterrupted and infinite happiness, or add in the least thereunto by all our holiness and virtue. We do much harm to our fellow men and to ourselves by our wickedness, and much good by our virtues: But the essential glory and happiness of God is untouched by both. "If thou sinnest, what doest thou against him, or if thy transgressions be multiplied, what doest thou unto him? if thou be righteous, what givest thou him, or what receiveth he of thine hand? thy wickedness may hurt a man as thou art, and thy righteousness may profit the son of man." Job xxxv. 6, 7, 8.

With regard to God Most High, his eternal, fixed will and choice was never yet frustrated in any single instance, and never will be. This by no means excuses sin on our part. The mere nature of it is infinite guilt in us, in the first instance. Yet it is certain that every thing, every event in the natural and moral system, does take place just, exactly, as God chose and fixed in his immutable plan, before any creature had existence. Saint Paul grants this, when the thought is suggested even with a view to a bad improvement of it. The apostle gives the proper character of God, as absolute proprietor, absolute sovereign of all things, and sets up his absolute decrees and immutable plan, agreeably to the nature and perfections of such a God. The objector then steps in and says, " why then doth he yet find fault, for who hath resisted his will ?" Upon this doctrine how can sinners be worthy of blame ? Paul does not take back a single word he had said, but most solemnly reprimands the bold objector, who would on this ground justify his sin ; by holding up to his view the holy nature and character of Jehovah, as *absolute proprietor* and *absolute sovereign* of all things ; and he still maintains the principle he had laid down, without the least recantation. Rom. ix.

Much has been said against this true and proper character of God, as fixing his own immutable plan, both in the natural and in the moral syſtem, and ſeeing it executed through all the ſcenes of providence, from beginning to end, without the leaſt poſſible variation. But all is in vain. We never can get rid of it, unleſs we will rid ourſelves of the word of God, and of the plain light of nature, with all our juſt natural notions of the Supreme Being. We may even as well reject God himſelf, his very being, as to deny that all events were by him fixed and certain, in his own eternal, infinite mind, before creation began; or that God had infinite right ſo to eſtabliſh his own plan of operation. Paul maintains this point, and pleads only this, to ſilence effectually every objector, who would on this ground, juſtify the nature of ſin, when it is immediately known and plainly felt in the ſoul, to be, *in its own nature*, directly oppoſite to the nature and attributes of God. As though he had ſaid, " you ſinner, have not fruſtrated the eternal plan of the Moſt High, it is true, and you never can; but it is enough for you to know that your will and heart has been ſet to do it. This very thing is your guilt, and there can be no guilt, no blame worthineſs in the univerſe, in any thing elſe; but in the evil will and diſpoſition, in its nature and operations. You therefore have merited unutterable puniſhment. But I will maintain the character of my God; if I relinquiſh this idea of JEHOVAH, I can find no Supreme Being."

I WOULD add: However wicked and unreaſonable it is to abuſe this juſt idea of God, to indulge in sin; yet we may and ought to make a very comfortable use of it in another way. We ought not once to imagine that we have hurt the MOST HIGH in the least, by all our odious sins, as we hurt our fellow men and our own souls by them. God is infinitely happy in every thing that is done, every event, both in the natural and moral system. The whole is just what infinite wisdom and love decreed, and the whole forms the most lovely and benevolent system, of all possible systems that were in the eternal, infinite view of Deity.

THE nature of sin is, *in the first instance*, an object of sorrow in our hearts; but its *existence, connections, and all its effects and consequences* pertain to the pure and holy, wise and good government of the most high God; all whose ways are holy, just, and good. God need not punish poor sinners, to retrieve any harm they have done him, any damage, any infringement on his happiness. God is, and ever has been, and ever will be, just as happy as his soul hath chosen to be, i. e. infinitely so. With infinite pleasure he sees the operation of his own eternal plan, in every part and every movement of it. And mankind, in God's own time and way, will behold it as God does, and delight in it as God does, according to their capacity. We are in guilt and ignorance and sorrow for a time, and all is just: For the will of God cannot be otherwise. But, as the nature of God is love, he will bring us all, "in due time," to see and approve of his infinite wifdom and love, in all his counfels, and in all his works. " What I do thou knoweft not now, but thou fhalt know hereafter." " In the latter end ye fhall confider it perfectly."

THERE have been, no doubt, many godly perfons that never could endure the doctrine of the divine decrees, in the *limitarian* fenfe. The hearts of good people do not reject the abfolute predeftination and decrees of God, nor ever did, fimply confidered, or juftly confidered. What our hearts revolt at, is the attributing fuch decrees to God, as are contrary to his nature. " GOD IS LOVE." Attribute no decrees to God but thofe of infinite love, in harmony with all the perfections of Deity, and they will fet eafy on our minds. Charge him with no decrees that are contrary to his nature, and they will all appear beautiful. But, when we conceive of a God exhibiting a nature and difpofition oppofite to that of the great JEHOVAH; a God of fome love and of great malevolence ; and then conceive of fuch decrees as fuch a God would make, our hearts fhudder at them. But decrees flowing from the true nature of the living and true God, are all lovely. All our hopes of happinefs are founded on the nature, attributes, and fovereign will of the living and true God. His infinitely good difpofition fecures us. His paternal love and goodnefs makes us fafe ; as all his natural perfections are exerted under the direction of his wifdom and love.

COULD we fuppofe, I even fhudder to

name the suppofition, that JEHOVAH was in all things elfe as he now is ; but only had a difpofition to infinite malevolence, as he now hath to infinite love and benevolence ; poor fuffering creatures could not even then impeach his juftice, fimply confidered : For their whole beings, and all the comfort, and all the pain that could ever affect them, would be God's own abfolute property, to difpofe of, as he pleafed. Their very feelings, of every kind and degree would be his abfolute property ; fince their whole being is fo. But, alas! he would certainly act out his difpofition, and propagate mifery far and wide, and that to all eternity. My reader, is this your God? Have you learned that he hath indeed fuch a difpofition of heart, from his works or from his word? Is this the Son of God that you have heard and thought fo much about, that fo loved the world as to die for the fins of the whole world? Have you fo learned Chrift? To difpute of *meum* and *tuum*, *mine and thine*, with Deity is utterly abfurd; but to hope and truft in the nature, attributes, will and word of fuch an infinitely good fovereign, through the atonement of his own dear Son, is unfpeakably comfortable to miferable, dying finners.

WE are taught, in the word of God, that all our backwardnefs in believing to the falvation of our fouls, lies in the enmity of our hearts ; at leaft, that if this was all removed, we fhould, under gofpel light, readily believe. The underſtanding, and all the powers of our ſouls would act in a ſaving manner towards God and Chriſt, if the temper and diſpoſition of our ſouls were right. This is certainly true. But our hearts are exceedingly oppoſed to God who is love. Therefore, until this enmity is removed, we cannot believe the doctrines of God's ſovereign, ſelf-moved love, pity, mercy, to ſuch horrible ſinners as we are.

WHEN we hear the pure doctrines of free grace, our hearts ſay, "this is too good news to be true." Mankind, in a ſtate of nature, find no ſuch diſpoſition in themſelves, nor in other men like themſelves; and they do, and will imagine that God is, in this regard, "altogether ſuch an one as themſelves:" and ſo cannot believe there is any ſuch ſelf-moved love and mercy in God. They cannot forgive their enemies before they repent, and reform, and become their friends, and make all the reſtitution in their power; and hardly then. They will maintain ſome grudge after all. Therefore, they will not believe " that while they were yet enemies, in due time, Chriſt died for them," and paid their whole debt, while they were in all their enmity againſt God: And juſtified them, as to the law of God, while they were ungodly, working not in any manner acceptable to God, but wholly in enmity againſt him: And that " being juſtified by his death, they ſhall much more be ſaved by his life." i. e. By his almighty all gracious mediation, applying the benefit of purchaſed pardon and salvation, by giving them repentance, faith, holiness, and fulfilling in them all the conditions, in his own way and time. They cannot believe, that "God hath exalted him a Prince and a Savior, to *give repentance* as well as remission of sins:" That " he that spared not his own Son, but freely delivered him up for *us all*, all sinners, will much more with him freely give them all things." They have no such disposition themselves; but quite the reverse: and they cannot believe that God has, when he says, " I, even I, am he that blotteth out your sin for mine own sake." They cannot receive this saying; because, all they know of the temper of their own hearts, and of other men is directly opposite to such free love and self-moved mercy.

A SENSE of divine love, or charity, is never impressed on the hearts of sinful men, but in an almighty work of regeneration, making them feel, in some degree, the same temper and spirit. When they can forgive their most malicious enemies, and love them, and sincerely wish them all good, and pray for them, before they become any better, or ask any pardon at all, as Christ did, and as Stephen did; then they can believe that there is such an heart in God as his word does testify.

A YOUNG man that has been brought up in the family of a nobleman of vast wealth, who has always been a great benefactor to him, and whom he always loved most sincerely, and served most faithfully, giving every teftimony of love, fidelity and obedience, during his minority; well knowing that his benefactor always had the kindeft fenfe of his filial love, duty, and obedience, will, when he comes of age, eafily believe the report, if it be told him, that the nobleman has given him a valuable legacy, in his laft will and teftament. But, a young man that was under the like advantages, who yet always hated his benefactor, rebelled againft him continually, mocked him every day, reviled him in all his converfation, did all he could to kill him more than a thoufand times, and finally purloined all his goods that he could lay hands on, and ran away from him, and continues to hate him worfe than ever; would by no means believe the report, fhould the ftory pafs, that the faid nobleman had given him a fine eftate. His own fenfe of guilt, enmity, and ingratitude, would repel any idea that the news could be true. Juft fo, the glorious teftimonials of God's infinitely free love and mercy, come to finful men. The bleffed gofpel is oppofed by them, on every ground and motive of enmity and unbelief, which can arife from a confcioufnefs of the utmoft difaffection in their hearts to an holy God, and the moft awful rebellion of their whole lives againft him.

This doctrine of infinite, univerfal, fovereign grace, flowing wholly out of the nature and difpofition of God to mankind, is wholly confiftent with his rewarding every man according to his works; and is the only doctrine of falvation that is fo.

The *limitarians* themfelves, have always underftood this doctrine as relating, not only to the different degrees of happinefs among the faved, and the different degrees of mifery among the damned; but alfo *principally* to the great difference in the eternal world, between all who are faved, and all who are damned: Each defcription being compared with the other, or the faved compared with the damned. And this is certainly the true gofpel fenfe of the declaration, fo frequent in the word of God. But then we ought to underftand the word of God aright, as to the true meaning of *falvation* and *damnation*. Which cannot be, in any other fenfe than what I plead for, confiftent with that proportion of reward which is afferted.

No *limitarian* on earth will prefume to fay, that believers in this world are as much better than other finners, as heaven is better than hell: Or that there is, or ever was, fo great a difference in moral character, between any two men on earth, as there is between heaven and hell. There is not a man on earth, nor ever was fince the fall, that can juftly claim a better character than that of a *believing, penitent, abominable finner.* We do not fuppofe that the beft on earth have got half way from the worft character they ever had, before converfion, to that character which faints in heaven fuftain. It is certain that Job, David, and Paul, did not think they had. " I abhor myself, and repent in dust and ashes." " There is no soundness in my flesh, because of thine anger, neither is there any rest in my bones, because of my sin." " My wounds stink and are corrupt because of my foolishness." " I am carnal sold under sin." "O wretched man that I am, who shall deliver me from the body of this death!" " Not as though I had already attained, either were already perfect." Thus spake these men, distinguished by the most eminent attainments in this world; and that without any compliment at all. They spake the truth, as they felt the real weight of it in their own souls. These are true specimens of the best men, and best moral characters that ever were, or will be, on this side death. Now let these three men go into the infinite and everlasting joys of heaven, (and no doubt they are there) and contrast with them the three vilest moral characters, that ever existed since the world began, gone away into the infinite and endless torments of hell, in the *limitarian* sense; and then say, my reader, is there not a greater difference between the reward of these, than there was between their works in this world? All may be in heaven, and yet the difference of reward be as great there as that of character here. In no other possible way can the proportion take place according to scripture.

If believers, in this life, were as holy as they are in heaven, and unbelievers altogether as bad as the devil; yet even then, there would be no proportion of reward to their works, on the *limitarian* plan, unless they had been one eternity *a parte ante* (as the language of the schools is) before they went into another eternity *a parte post*. The time of works, or of exhibiting a moral character in this life, bears no proportion to eternity. Duration, or long continuance in good or bad works, no doubt, hath its due consideration in the reward; but temporal, momentary works bear no proportion to an eternal reward either of happiness or misery. Do not misunderstand me here. I mean not in the least, to countenance the idle notion of those who say, " because sin is but temporary in this world; therefore it is not strictly just that its punishment should be eternal." I have before exploded this idea. I am now speaking only of the *proportion* mentioned in the gospel, between the rewards of mankind in a future state; not of the just demerit of sin. I say, it seems exceeding plain, on the *limitarian* plan, there can be no proportion at all between the rewards of the elect, and reprobate, as measured by their different works in this life. All in themselves deserve an eternal hell, no doubt; but God has been graciously pleased to assure us, that the state of each man in the world to come, shall be in proportion to his works here. This never can be, if some great sinners, who sinned all their lives here, yet believing sinners, are in the next life consummately and eternally happy; and other poor, miserable sinners, that is, unbelieving sinners, are made consummately and eternally miserable. Both deserve it. But we are now availing ourselves of God's own declaration of sovereign goodness in the gospel. I know, and I have already said it again and again; that the law thunders eternal, certain damnation to sinners, and it is the awful voice of justice throughout the sacred oracles from beginning to end; but there is not one word of gospel, glad tidings, or good news to sinners in all this: It is all law, *pure law*, glorious law, denouncing what, *in pure justice*, ought to be. There is not a single word of the gospel in the whole of this, in all these dreadful thunders. The gospel mildly and sweetly announces that all these dreadful things have taken place in Christ, the *head of every man*. And now he hath full power and commission to apply his own redemption, to all those of whom he is the head, and for whom he died; and that in his own time and way.

We all know there will be different rewards in heaven, according to different characters and works in this life. None will be rewarded *for their works;* but *according to them.* It will be so with all mankind that ever lived or shall live. They will, every one of them, bear a proportion to each other, *as to their state in the eternal world,* as they did in their *respective characters and works* here. This never can be, without the universal triumph of Christ over sin, death and hell, and all the condemning power of the holy law, in tasting death for every man. We could easily see all this to be the true spirit of the gospel; if we only knew and felt within our own souls, that the great PARENT of the universe, as much exceeds any human parent, in love to his offspring, as he is a greater being than man ; and that this is the real nature of God.

This blessed, gospel doctrine gives us an admiring view of the wisdom and goodness of God, in the appointment and ordination of his civil ministers in the present world, to make this life tolerable, by the suppression of vice and immorality : Especially as secure, hardened sinners are not at all restrained by the threatnings of eternal damnation, even though they deny not the awful doctrines they hear ; but allude to the truth of them, by most profane and horrid imprecations, in their common conversation. Present, visible punishments strike them with dread, and greatly restrain them. A fine, a prison, a whip, and a gibbet have great influence to suppress their enormities.

God has, in his infinite wisdom and goodness, appointed his civil ministers for good. These powers are ordained of God, for this great and benevolent purpose, to be a terror to evil doers, and the supporters of those that do well. It will give an exalted sense of God to those that know his salvation, to see all those ministers he has ordained for the good of mankind, executing their respective offices well, for the glory of his great name and the good of human society, in punishing all transgressors with the utmost faithfulness and impartiality, according to good and wholesome laws; and in encouraging all the virtuous and regular in the community. We ought to rejoice that they who do all in their power to make their fellow-men happy, should partake largely of that good, which they so much strive to promote and communicate; and that they, who war against the happiness of mankind, should feel in a proper degree, that misery, which, by their wickedness, they would bring upon all. God's glorious decrees of sovereign, rich, self-moved mercy to them at last, do not in the least, excuse them from the due reward of their deeds here; no, nor even those that have already believed to the saving of their souls, when they backslide and do the deeds of the wicked.

There are a great variety of just and terrible punishments from the hand of God's civil ministers, that do, and ought to meet and oppose flagrant transgressors, in all their open wickedness in this world. Those indeed have their visible and sensible effect. The scourge and the gibbet are very terrible to those that are wholly unmoved by every consideration which does not apply to their senses: And how wretched are daring sinners in this world, by the just rebukes of heaven in this way! While they are hardened in vice, all consolation arising from the final mercy of God is wholly shut out of their souls, just as much on the plan I plead for, as on any more limited doctrine whatever. The most glorious truth, without an heart-felt conviction of it, can give no comfort. These poor, miserable creatures are just as we have been wont to say the elect are, antecedent to their conversion; not at all the more comfortable for their election, until they are brought to know the things freely given them of God. How miserable in this life, are thieves, drunkards, traitors, murderers, and such like! Every good law, and every good magistrate, and all good people oppose them with all their might, with one awful punishment after another, until many of them end their lives of fear, trembling and horror on a gibbet, awful spectacles of shame and reproach, and without any comfort in their own souls, from the blessed truth I maintain. For it will fully appear, that no man of the vile character I have been describing, while with such an heart, can derive any comfort from this plan of salvation; any more than any of the elect of God, on any supposition whatever, could have inward divine consolation, while in a state of nature, of unbelief, and utter impenitency. I say, how miserable are such poor creatures in this world! How full of shame and horror, when taken away by the arm of justice! And why should we grudge them the mercy and pity of the Father of their spirits, on whose sovereign grace alone we ourselves are dependent for better conduct, and better circumstances in this life; if he is pleased, in his infinite goodness, through the all-sufficient atonement of him who died, not for our sins only, but also for the sins of the whole world, to give relief, everlasting relief, to these poor, trembling spirits, his own offspring at last, even at the time when the soul, with infinite anguish and the most horrible expectations, is separating from that body, from a union with which, it derived all its awful depravity.

If we have been more favoured in this life, by the sovereign, distinguishing goodness of the common Parent of all, let us be exceeding thankful. We should do well to remember, that, considering all the superior degrees of God's free grace granted to us, against which we have also sinned every day, and every moment, we may be as guilty in the sight of God, as our poor unhappy brethren, that never have been blessed with that prudent foresight, and those restraints wherewith God has been pleased to favor us. We may well acquiesce in all the displays of divine justice which we see in this world, even in those that are condemned to flee to the pit, and our hand should not stay them. But, I think, we can give no reason why the blood of Jesus Christ, which *cleanseth from all sin,* should not save them in another world; which will not lie *full strong* against every hope of our own salvation. If their sins go beforehand to judgment, ours may follow after. An earthly tribunal affords but a miserable decision to determine who are deepest in guilt, in the eye of the Omniscient Judge.

We have exceeding strong motives to religion and all moral virtue, drawn from views of honor and prosperity, pleasure and joy in this life ; and to deter us from the ways of wickedness, from the opposite consideration. *Cæteris paribus*, a man is always happy in this world, in proportion to that degree of true godliness and virtue which forms his real character; and miserable in proportion to the degree of wickedness that governs him. Also great, very great will be the distinction between such different characters to all eternity. Their reward will be as different, as their works have been. And this may be ; yet both of them be in the same world there, as well as here. No man in this world, since the fall, ever had any heart but a bad one, *really and truly so*. " There is none good but one, that is God." No man ever did one good deed, in the strict sense of the divine law. " They are all gone out of the way ; there is none that doeth good, no not one."

When we speak of the good heart of believers, and of their good and holy lives; and when we find these epithets in scripture, they are never to be understood in *strict propriety of speech*, but only in a *comparative sense*, i. e. *less wicked*, in the exercises of their hearts, as to the real matter of these exercises, than unbelievers are, or than they themselves were, in a state of unregeneracy. It is the same with regard to their good and holy lives : i. e. they are *much less wicked*, as to the matter of their conduct, than once they were, or than unbelievers ordinarily are. But it is certain; that, *in propriety* and *strictness* of speech, no positive goodness belongs to any human character on earth; nor can this possibly obtain, unless something be found as pure in all respects as the law of God, which is the only measure of positive moral goodness.

In real propriety of language, all men are great sinners without exception, and some, as to the matter of their character and conduct, much greater sinners than others. I say, *as to the matter;* for I shall consider obligations, motives, aggravations, &c. in the sequel. But in this all men on earth do now, and ever did agree, viz. " *the heart and character of every man, in the sight of God, is an awful, unspeakably bad heart and character.*" And there will be no reward to any in the next world, but a reward of free, sovereign grace, through the atonement and mediation of God's elect Savior, the elect head of every man. All may be in heaven together in God's own time, brought there in his own way, with as great a distinction of reward *there*, as of character here. But if some are personally in hell, and others in heaven, to interminable duration; the difference of reward will be infinitely greater than that of character and works ever was.

All believers are absolutely, positively, and perfectly holy, *in a relative sense*, i. e. in Christ. But this hath no concern with their real character; and their works have no hand in all this. Their own personal character, and their works are just as far from having any consideration in their justifying righteousness, as the character and works of those who never heard of a Savior. They are justified *as ungodly,* by that righteousness made known to the soul, by the medium of faith, which is unto all and upon all them that believe, for there is no difference. There is no difference, none at all, but what exists while the medium of faith and the means of application are suspended: None as to the covenant of redemption: None as to the undertaking of Christ: None with regard to the purchase or faithfulness and promise of him, who came into the world, not to condemn the world; but that the world through him might be saved: None as to merit on the part of man, or any motion towards God in the heart of one man more than another: None, as to the eternal good purpose of God: In this, and every other sense he is no respecter of persons. The language of a God of infinite, sovereign mercy, to his children partakers of flesh and blood, and for the sake of union with whom, his own Son took part of the same, is this, without any distinction; " I, even I am he that blotteth out your sin, for mine own sake."

VERILY there are all the distinctions among mankind, in this, and a future world, which the holy scriptures know any thing of, without our making any distinction, invented by the blindness of the human mind, and the great want of benevolence that is natural to man. Pride, and love of preeminence which is so dear to human nature, will not let us reft eafy, but in a felf-exalting profpect that a very few of us fhall have the pleafure, in the next world, to look down on the great body of mankind infinitely beneath us, and feeling our own happinefs much heightened, and our own glory much augmented, by the contraft of their extreme mifery and fhame. Do you feel this fpirit, my reader? You had need take care, left, on your plan of limiting the Holy One of Ifrael, yourfelf may take the inferior rank among thofe, whom you now view in profpect with a future unutterable contempt.

WHATEVER difference, or *fpecific difference*, if any prefer thefe terms, there may be between the grace given to one and another, in this life, the character, temper and ways of all the human race agree in many things more than they differ! " As in water face anfwereth to face, fo doth the heart of man to man." Bring all the human race together, and their diffimilitude will be very fmall, in comparifon of their general agreement. A prefent believer hath indeed fomething, which a prefent unbeliever hath not; and God knows what a *little fomething* it is. His omnifcient eye fees how awfully we all agree. He never yet faw a reafon, or found a motive *out of himfelf*, to fave any of us all. Had all mankind right thoughts of God, a real true knowledge of that glorious fountain of love, this would make falvation appear *common falvation*, as it did of old. Jude iii. And none would deny it, or even fo much as wifh the doctrine were not true. If that knowledge of God, which all men are commanded to seek after above all things, would establish us in this blessed truth, is not the foundation of it real, solid, and true? Or does our discovery and knowledge of things so glorious, give being to their own objects?

If mankind were wise enough to know in what way to find their greatest interest, joy, pleasure, and delight, even in this present life, they would certainly seek it and find it only in the ways of real piety and virtue, in the ways of true wisdom. "Her ways are ways of pleasantness, and all her paths are peace. She is a tree of life to all that lay hold on her; and happy is every one that retaineth her." All the happiness of heaven consists in true religion, in the highest perfection of it. If it is not happiness as far as we have it, in the present world, it will not be in a future: For the nature of it is the very same, in whatever part of God's vast dominions we are. The nature, tendency, and concomitants of sin are just the reverse. If sin is happifying in this world, it will be in the next; if it gives real joy and pleasure here, it will there. The hell that the devils are in, and that all mankind deserve, and are condemned to, by the law of God, is nothing but perfection of sin, with its inseparable connections and consequences. These remarks being admitted, we are prepared to resume the thought before suggested; comparing one sinner of the humankind with another. I have intimated that there is a vast difference, in many *res-pects*, and yet in *one grand respect* none at all.

WITH regard to this present life, and our connection with human society; and with respect to our own comfort or misery here, there is very great difference between those we call the best, and the worst of men. The former do much good, and inwardly feel much comfort and real, solid pleasure; and are, in the general course of the divine government, of all men most beloved, honored, and promoted. I say, *in the general course of providence;* for special times of persecution and the like, I now leave out of the question. In saying this, I say just what the word of God, in the general tenor of it, abundantly asserts, and what the general experience of all nations of the earth does abundantly confirm.

EVEN, in days of the most bloody persecution, the real happiness and joy of the godly is much greater than that of any other men. Whatever a blind, carnal world may imagine, there is in very deed a great, and most blessed reward of holiness and piety, in the present life. " Thou wilt keep him in perfect peace, whose mind is stayed on thee; because he trusteth in thee." " In keeping thy commandments there is great reward." " And who is he that will harm you, if ye be followers of that which is good?" " If ye obey and serve him, ye shall spend your days in prosperity, and your years in pleasure." No outward circumstances, or adverse dispensations can possibly frustrate this exceeding, real, inward delight and joy in the mind, in the soul, the seat of all rational and spiritual pleasure. " As sorrowful, yet always rejoicing : As having nothing, yet possessing all things." The real, substantial, solid pleasures of believing, godly souls, have a basis very different from all the emotions of the hearts of God's enemies, which deluded souls call pleasure. They are always " like the troubled sea, which cannot rest, whose waters cast up mire and dirt." Whatever false shew of happiness they may make, in the eyes of the world, yet " there. is no peace, saith God, to the wicked." There is truly as great a difference in the real, inward reward of the virtuous and vicious, the godly and ungodly, in this life, as there is in the different temper of their minds, and in the different ways in which they walk.

But now let us compare their desert of punishment, in another world, *solely as it respects the law of God*, the great and only unerring and decisive rule. We all agree in the following ratio of estimating the demerit of sin in the sight of God. We consider the matter of it as one thing, i. e. how far our hearts and lives deviate from the law of God ; and the obligations against which we sin, as another. We compare these two together, and thence judge of the real criminality of a sinner in the sight of God. This is agreeable to reason and the word of God.

Let us set up two men, and try their guilt in the sight of God, or in the eye of

his holy law, by the above rule. Pharaoh
ſhall be one, and Paul the other. The former was a moſt horrible ſinner, in the eyes
of all good people; the latter was one of the
beſt of men, in the ſame view. Pharaoh did
all the harm in his power, and his whole
heart was in it. Paul, after his converſion,
did much good, with a ſincere and pious
heart. Thus far the difference of character
is exceeding great, while we attend only to
the matter of it. Next bring in the obligations. Pharaoh was, perhaps, leaſt of all
mankind favored with tenderneſs of conſcience, or reſtraining grace. He was in all
the groſs darkneſs of paganiſm, and God
did indeed harden his heart, in a moſt ſignal
manner, and that in a way conſiſtent with
his own holineſs and purity. It is here
quite foreign to the argument, to enquire into the manner how. Whether only by permiſſion, or otherwiſe, it is certain God did it.
He was left under the leaſt obligations and
motives to keep him from ſin, we will ſuppoſe, of any man that ever lived; and we
will alſo ſuppoſe, and grant, that the matter
of his ſin, in heart and life, was the greateſt
of any man on earth. Paul, after his converſion, was bleſſed with the greateſt divine
light (we will ſuppoſe) of any man on earth.
His natural powers and education were exceeding good, with moſt eminent degrees of
ſaving grace in his ſoul, abundance of ſanctifying grace, and an equal degree of divine
joy and conſolation. And he ſerved God

in a most eminent manner. Yet he always sinned in some degree, in his heart and in his life; he was never perfect one single moment; far, very far from it, if we may believe his own inspired testimony of himself.

Now, did not Paul's obligations and motives to holiness, as far exceed Pharaoh's, as the matter of his character was better? What made him better, but his motives and obligations, arising from the light, grace, and spirit, freely given him of God? Yet his character was always very inadequate to the purity of God's holy law. All that made him less sinful in heart, and life, was mere obligation from God. All light and grace, and every thing that hath this effect, is so. Multiply the degree of his remaining sinfulness, as to the matter of it, into the degree of obligation and motive to which it was opposed, and what less will be the total amount, in the sight of God, than that of Pharaoh? This abominable prince had obligations, against which he sinned, many and great; as every man in the world has. But compare them with all that a sovereign God did for the apostle, all his light and grace; the difference is exceeding great. God did as much more for Paul, as his heart and life were better than Pharaoh's. All he did for that eminent apostle was mere obligation on him, and the law justly required perfection of him: But he was always very far from it. Obligations on Pharaoh, i. e. light and grace, were as far withheld from him, by a holy sovereign God, as his heart and life was more sinful than that of Paul. Perhaps my reader has not much attended to this thought in time past; but I think it worthy of solemn attention. I am sure it runs through the whole word of God. This will account for those most abominable descriptions, which Job, David and Paul give of themselves, even in their highest attainments in grace, and after all their pious walk with God, and all the great good they had done in the world.

Descriptions of this tenor, which the best of men give of their hearts and lives in holy writ, and which I have always heard the most eminent christians give of themselves, in their solemn and devout prayers, were surprizing to me, in the days of my early youth. I once understood them as humble and meek compliments, which they were disposed to make to the Deity, or expressions entirely hyperbolical. When I so often heard the most godly ministers, and other eminent christians describe their hearts and lives, in the presence of God, bad enough for the vilest and most notorious sinners in the world, I used to wonder how they dared thus to compliment with an heart-searching God, who, I supposed, must know they did not speak the strict truth, and that they knew it themselves. I did not so much wonder to hear a rich man own his poverty; or a delicate lady despise a fine entertainment, an excellent dinner, or supper she had provided, in the presence of her guests. Such compliments I thought might bear having countenance from frequent cuſtom, and an appearance of humility and delicacy. But, I thought it quite amiſs to ſay that to the great, heart-ſearching God, which both the ſpeaker and the object of prayer knew was far from ſtrict and plain truth.

After long attention to the law of God, and the hearts and lives of men, and the obligations we are under to God, very eſpecially for every degree of divine light and ſaving grace; I am at laſt very ſenſible of the propriety of all ſuch confeſſions before God, and that they are wholly without a compliment. The phariſee in the parable was, no doubt, a man of pure and amiable character in the eyes of the world, and deſerved great honor and reſpect from man, for the good he had done in the community, by his ſhining virtues. But, when he was tranſacting the great concerns of his ſoul with his Maker, he might have prayed juſt as the ſcandalous, infamous publican did, and with good acceptance too.

Let beneficent, ſhining characters, the eminent benefactors of mankind receive great honor and reſpect from their fellow-men. Let them ſtand far diſtinguiſhed from the common people, and farther ſtill from all the vicious and immoral: But as they ſtand related to that holy law which conſiders every obligation men are under to perfect holineſs, as well as the matter of their conduct, I ſay, in this view, let every high thought and towring imagination be levelled with the duſt. Let every mountain and hill be brought down, and the Lord alone exalted.

MANKIND have a spirit of monopoly. Nothing is more natural to them. If they have great advantages and honors in the eyes of others in this world, they are apt to infist on those distinctions before God, as an argument for eternal continuance. But, "the last shall be first, and the first shall be last."

THAT which is highly esteemed among men, even all that men call good, in the human character, is so far from bearing the test of God's holy law, that it is, in that relative sense, abomination in the sight of God. Let the best man on earth plead the best of his heart and his life, as a ground of acceptance with God; and he shall find it an utter abomination. The atonement stands by itself alone and unmixed: "The Lion of the tribe of Judah, the root and offspring of David, and he alone hath prevailed." This glorious truth hath ever been deeply impressed on the hearts of the friends of God, in this world, and will be to all eternity. The blind, proud notions of mankind will have no place in heaven, as they have here. There they will know and feel that "the former things are passed away."

THE doctrine which I plead for, has a great tendency to afford believers adoring and submissive exercises of mind, in view of all the sin and calamity they find in the world.

THEY see that God has done nothing inconsistent with his infinite love, and his avowed character in his word, by introducing, in his holy providence, or permitting, if you please, all the moral evil that is in the world. It will all have a glorious issue, conducive to the greater manifestation of his infinite love, and all his amiable attributes, in the wonders of redeeming love. And in a view of all natural and penal evil connected in justice with the evil of sin, the soul adores God and falls in lowly submission under all his holy rebukes. So, when we see so many miserable creatures of our own kind struggling with pain and calamity, through life, we behold them as Jesus does, who died to save them from wrath to come; and our souls are filled with humble submission, and all the astonishment of devout love.

When we read of all the dreadful slaughters of the ancient inhabitants of the land of Canaan, and many millions more of God's own offspring like ourselves, under all the horrors of massacre, by the express command of the Father of their spirits, we shall yet say " God is love." He hath, in all these things given a due testimony of his justice, and his abhorrence of sin. Yet it is not "the rod of an enemy, or the chastisement of a cruel one:" God hath not forgotten that he is their own Father, by creation, and that creation is a dear child of his love. On this plan, we do not stumble at any thing he does; but feel these his words with believing joy, " as I live, saith the Lord, I have no pleasure in the death of him that dieth." When we think of all the awful and terrible judgments that have fallen on the trembling children of men, our own flesh and blood, it is well for us to remember what he hath faid, who died for the fins of the whole world, "and I, if I be lifted up from the earth, will draw ALL men unto me."

LET it not be imagined here, that I would fo much as intimate, that God is under any obligation to fave men finally; becaufe that, in the difpenfations of his government, they have been very miferable in this world: Or that thofe who have been moft fo, have *in juftice*, any claim of reparation on their Maker. I mean no fuch thing. I argue only from the nature and attributes of JEHOVAH, as they appear in his word and works. He is worthy to be God fupreme, by his own infinite worth, by virtue of his own infinitely glorious and lovely perfections. He is *by nature* God, as fome have well expreffed it.

MY hope is founded entirely on his *nature* and *difpofition*, through his own Son made manifeft. In this manifeftation, GOD IS LOVE. His moral difpofition is infinitely amiable and inviting. It is the fupreme joy of all holy, wife, intelligent beings, that there is fuch a God. His nature is the bafis of all happinefs, and the foundation of all hope. It is the fource of all our comfort, that there is fuch a God over all, bleffed forevermore; that he is Creator, Proprietor, and abfolute Difpofer of all things, abfolutely fovereign and uncontrouled; and that he worketh all things according to the counfel of his own will. *For his will flows from a nature infinitely glorious and lovely.*

We have no claim of justice on him who gave us our whole being, whose absolute property we are. Whatever he does with us, he meddles with nothing but his own. Hence, I argue only from the immutable nature of God, infinitely perfect and good, and from his plain word and all his manifestations. I say, these do ascertain the final redemption of a whole guilty world, or, that he will have all men to be saved.

Had there been an eternal, Supreme Being, Creator and absolute Proprietor of all things, as Jehovah is; who in his *moral disposition*, his *moral nature*, had been just the reverse from what he really is. Horrible supposition! but lawful in the view I make it. Had he created innumerable myriads of rational creatures more than ever yet had existence; and made them all consummately sinful and miserable; and had we our place in that woful scale of beings, doomed to endless sin, sorrow, and pain unutterable: Even on this supposition, we could have no claim of justice, on our Maker, as we have upon our fellow creatures who injure us, and bring pain and misery upon us. They take hold of property not their own, but ours, in opposition to their claim; and therefore we may in justice demand reparation of them. Not so is it with regard to the supreme Fountain of all being, who is the Creator and absolute Proprietor of all things, including all the feelings and sufferings of creatures.

Their very pains and all their affections are his property: For their whole being is so.

In such an awful, lamentable case, as above supposed, we could never accuse our Maker of injustice, with any kind of propriety. All we could say would be to howl, in doleful accents, to all eternity; "*the Supreme reigneth, let all creatures mourn; let the multitude of beings lament and bewail!* woe! woe! woe! to miserable creatures, that such is the nature and disposition of him that ruleth over all." I cannot think we do any honor to the blessed JEHOVAH, in ascribing to him a moral nature, in any wise similar to this. One as opposite thereto as we can possibly conceive of, is indeed the very nature of that blessed Being whom we adore. God's will cannot possibly, in the nature of things, be unjust; and by *his own immutable nature*, it is infinitely good, and the spring of all blessedness and joy. Diffusion of being and blessedness flows from the nature of God. This doctrine exhibits JEHOVAH, as the true God, whom angels and saints adore, "Alpha and Omega, the beginning and the ending, the first and the last."

If we carefully attend to the holy scriptures, we do not find any holy men insisting upon terms of limitation with God, as though they thought there could ever be in the disposition, or will of God any possibility of doing wrong to them. They all appear to choose God should be just as he is, or as his own nature does dispose and incline him; and they know he ever will be so disposed towards them. This is their happiness; and in this they put all their confidence. All their hopes arise from this; although they have ever looked on themselves as fit objects of eternal misery, as any creatures that ever God made. His character is often, and with great propriety, called his name. Poor, penitent, believing sinners repair to nothing else, nothing but his character and disposition as manifested in a Savior, in whom only they are righteous. "The name of the Lord is a strong tower: The righteous runneth into it and are safe."

It is truly for the honor of JEHOVAH, that we should all know, that he alone is the absolute source of all being and blessedness: That he is absolute, sovereign, and uncontrouled, in every view, no foreign influence of any kind or degree ever acting on him: That his creatures never can nor shall have any thing else to found their hopes upon, but his own glorious nature and sovereign will: That his manifestations are all glorious and comfortable to every human soul, that understands and believes them: And that it is not the understanding and belief of a sinner that makes them so, but they are so in their own nature.

No sinner of mankind does God any honor, by believing that all his own hopes of pardon and salvation, depend as much on himself, as it is possible any thing can depend on a creature, viz. on some disposition or qualification in himself. This denies God his proper character, in his relation to sinful man. But to believe the blessed God has given qualifications as sure to unworthy sinners, in his own way and time, as he hath provided an all-sufficient Savior for a guilty world, is ascribing to God all his glorious attributes, " working all things (without the least exception) according to the counsel of his own will."

If the *limitarians* could be disposed to think, study and read as much on this point, as the writer hath done for many years past, with an ardent desire to find nothing but the truth to rest in; they would see that it does no honor to the great and glorious God to make eternal salvation, in the least, depend on any creature, as to the certain event of it. Indeed, all the powers of the soul are fitly exercised by a sovereign God, in his own way, in the application and enjoyment of all that flows out of the mere goodness of his own nature, in a way honorable to himself, by the substitution and mediation of the second man, the Lord from heaven.

I can find no plan of religion but this, that can ever warrant the great charity, and union among men, which is so much recommended in the sacred oracles. If we consider ourselves as distinguished from most of our fellow men, in the eternal purposes and views of God: That we are destined to his infinite, everlasting love, and most others to his hatred, wrath and vengeance forevermore; we shall hardly find it in our hearts to exercise that pity, and tenderness, love and good will to them, that the gospel requires. If we think our God will be their eternal enemy, and delight himself in their eternal destruction; we shall hardly feel ourselves friendly to our God, in loving and pitying all mankind, and striving all in our power for their salvation. You cannot more displease your fellow men, than by manifesting great love and tenderness to their enemies.

Again; In conversation, or in hearing the word preached, or in reading the multitude of good authors that have written on our most important concerns, we cannot upon any other plan, maintain gospel candor. We shall find the light and communications of God to men so various; and their channel of preaching or writing, in many respects, so devious from one another; that we shall be ready to scruple whether there is any truth in the doctrine of a special revelation from heaven. We shall fall away, at least, as far as Deism. But, on the plan, for which I am pleading, the whole difficulty is obviated: As every writer uninspired, every preacher may be wrong in many things, and some in many more than others; yet all be essentially right. By them God communicates light and truth to the world, in various measures and degrees. Perhaps, it has not as yet been fit, in the sight of God, in the former, or present gradations of divine communication, to enlighten any author, or preacher fo, but that all have been involved in more darknefs than they have feen of the true light. Hence arifes great bitternefs of fpirit towards many, or univerfal fcepticifm. But on the gracious principles I am fupporting, we can reft contented, that the infinitely wife Being fhould caufe the light to dawn and increafe juft as faft as his own wifdom and goodnefs dictate. And we can love one another as the gofpel requires; though under various degrees of inftruction, and under various modes of thinking.

Thus, if I read an author, or hear a fermon which I look upon one half according to truth, and the other half not fo; that part which is good, ought to fet as well on my mind as if the whole was fo, and I ought to love the writer, or the preacher, and blefs God that they are enlightened fo far as they are. This I take to be a gofpel fpirit, and if fo, it is according to the truth of the gofpel. It is for want of fuch a fpirit, that many will reject all that is good in an author or preacher, becaufe of the many miftakes, or fuppofed miftakes found in both. But, in good truth, if we will be inftructed and edified by none, but thofe who are right in all things, we deprive ourfelves of the whole benefit of inftruction, or edification from any man uninfpired.

The doctrine I am pleading for, is much in favor of gofpel love and charity, harmony and peace. This is one mark of the truth of it. The true tendency of this principle is so far from disposing those who believe it, to contend and quarrel with the teachers and ministers of the christian churches, wherewith they are now furnished, that it will induce them to love them more than ever, and to treat them with all possible kindness. At the same time, we shall wish and pray, that it may please God to lead them further into those glorious truths, which they understand but in part. Thus it will have that quiet, and peaceful influence among ministers and people, which so much adorns the gospel.

The true import of the initiating seal among God's covenant people, both in the former and present œconomy, confirms the doctrine which I am advocating.

The whole Jewish church, and the great body of christians, who practise the initiating seal in infancy, have ever understood it to be a seal of the covenant of grace, to which even the infant seed of covenant parents, have a right, and are thereby sealed in the covenant of grace and salvation; even though they have always allowed, that such children are personally no better than the infants of heathen. An infant among the Jews, at eight days old, was supposed to be no better, *personally*, than any children of other nations; yet they were sealed by circumcision in the covenant of grace and salvation; even as they are now by baptism.

The church of God and the ordinances of it, from the days of Abraham to this day, were designed and instituted as a light or lamp which God holds up in the world, to beam forth by degrees, and fully manifest, in due time, his purposes of mercy and salvation to a guilty world, through that Mediator which he appointed to take away the sin of the whole world. Hence God hath commanded that all the infants of covenant parents should be sealed, though personally in the same unregenerate state with the world in general, as a testimony that all were purchased by the common Redeemer of sinners, and should be brought to actual enjoyment of salvation, in the time and manner most fit in the eyes of infinite wisdom and goodness. Hence any child of a pagan has right to the seal, if its lot is providentially among God's covenant people, and under proper circumstances to be trained up in the nurture and admonition of the Lord.

Accordingly, the commission given to the apostles, was, to go forth and teach all nations, and to command them to believe that divine truth which bringeth salvation, and to baptize all nations to whom they preached, both parents and children, (if they would submit to it) as a seal of the common salvation. This was not a token that they had done, or ever could do any thing toward their own salvation; but that Almighty God, Father, Son and Holy Ghost, had engaged to accomplish the salvation of a guilty world, and had made all sure, and would seal it by baptism.

We can, upon no other principle, make use of the seals and special ordinances with any consistency. How shall we seal, in the covenant of grace and salvation, persons destined and decreed to eternal personal damnation? How shall we admit those to the holy supper, a seal of our eating and drinking with Christ, at his table, in his heavenly kingdom, who may be, for ought we know, not only in an unrenewed state at present, but also under an irreversible decree of eternal reprobation? Would the Most High, in any wise, allow his seals to be so used? God never would have set such blind creatures as we are, about the work of admitting into the church, and exercising discipline, or to handle the seals of grace and salvation, had his own plan been a *limitarian* plan, or had he sent his Son into the world on any other errand than that the world through him might be saved.

DISCIPLINE must indeed be kept up in the church; and the body elected to such special and glorious privileges, out of a world, as yet buried in darkness, must be kept visibly pure, as bearing a proper, visible resemblance to its pure and holy head. Those members that do not bear this visible resemblance, must be delivered to Satan, yet only "*for the destruction of the flesh.*" A dreadful thing it is, to be in a state of excommunication from the privileges and consolations of the people of God in the world; but there is nothing in it that affects the certainty of eternal salvation at the great day: For the express end of every final censure on earth, is, "*that the spirit may be saved in the day of our Lord Jesus.*" 1. Cor.

v. 5. Whatsoever is thus bound on earth, shall be bound in heaven, both as to its propriety and good tendency in this world, and its glorious issue in the world to come, even the salvation of the soul in the day of the Lord. Hence an excommunicated person is still a brother, and not to be " treated as an enemy; but admonished as a brother."

Many souls for whom Christ died, have justly experienced the awful sentence of excommunication from his church on earth: Even Moses and Paul were willing to suffer the same, if it might redound to the glory of God and the salvation of souls. i. e. As most have understood them. Yet this doth by no means frustrate the irreversible and extensive plan of redeeming love, to gather together in one all things in Christ, and to make all men, in due time, see the glory of this mystery, which for many ages and generations lay hid in great obscurity.

God's church on earth, his visible covenant people were always designed, in his infinite wisdom and goodness, as a lamp, a light to the world, a city set on an hill, to manifest and hold forth to a lost world what God hath done for them, and what he would do. The church is a present, visible representation of divine love and mercy to sinners, to a lost world. The church holds forth to the world the glorious God with all his divine attributes and blessed purposes, and the Savior of all men, in all his glorious offices, and the Holy Spirit, in all his infinite and almighty energy. "By the church is made known the manifold wisdom of God." Eph. iii. 10. The church was not set up in the world, to shew us how much better some men are than others, or what a respecter of persons God is, in his purposes and operations; but rather to witness that God hath concluded all under sin, that he might have mercy upon all. Not to hold forth the worth and riches of any community of poor sinners; but rather, the unsearchable riches of Christ.

ANOTHER argument against the *limitarian* scheme, is this : *No man,* on their principles, *can do his duty; even if his whole heart and disposition were perfectly right.*

IT is our duty to acquiesce in God's will in every event. But an holy heart cannot do this in such an event as his own eternal damnation, or that of any of his fellow men. The principal misery of that eternal damnation they plead for, lies in an eternal, fixed and growing opposition of heart to an holy God, and the horrible rebellion proceeding from such an heart. It is certain an holy and right heart, which is full of love to God, cannot feel willing to be thus at enmity with God, and hate and rebel against him to all eternity. It is equally certain, that an holy man, that loves his neighbor as himself, and values his neighbor's happiness as his own, and is exceedingly averse to any dishonor done to God, any opposition against him, as much if it be in his neighbor as in himself, cannot be willing that his neighbor should thus hate and sin against God to all eternity. If we do not so love our neighbors in all things as ourselves, we fall short of that perfect benevolence required of us.

BESIDES, the nature of this opposition to God is infinitely evil and odious, whether in ourselves, or in any of the human kind. Hence if our hearts are right, we shall feel a great opposition to it, and can never be pleased with it, or reconciled to it. We must be exceedingly wicked, to be reconciled to such great and eternal wickedness.

IT is true, the redeemed will in the true gospel sense see the smoke of their torment ascend up forever and ever, and shout Alleluia in the view of it; but this will be in the manner I have before taken notice of, only in the glass of *pure justice*, in the glass of the divine law. Thus they will eternally see all the human race, and themselves as well as others, forever dwelling with devouring fire and everlasting burnings; while, in *very fact* and in *person*, they shall from their munition of rocks shout Alleluia, finding the bread of life sustaining their happy souls, and the waters of everlasting consolation made sure.

IT never can be found in a holy heart to take any more satisfaction in the rebellion of others against God than in his own; both are infinitely hateful to a soul obedient to God. The *limitarian* plan, if fully considered, and realized seriously in the soul, (which is very little done) can never meet with the

approbation of the friends of God. They
will feel their hearts inclined like the infinitely benevolent heart of God, who will have
all men to be faved, and to come to the
knowledge of the truth. They will pray for
the falvation of all, and plead this warrant
fo to do, viz. It is the will of God and
our Savior, who gave himfelf a ranfom for
all, to be teftified in due time.

FURTHER, the charitable hope and defire
of good people, fuch as the gofpel requires,
is certainly agreeable to the word of God.
Now fuppofe all the race of mankind that
ever have lived in the world, or ever fhall
be in it, were to pafs before any godly man,
individually in fucceffion. Afk that good
man, as he views them paffing before his
eyes one after another, with regard to each
in particular, " Do you hope and defire that
in the infinite mercy of God through Chrift,
that man may be faved ?" He would fay *yes,
with all my heart*. So he would fay of the
firft that paffed before him, and fo of the
fecond, and the fame of every one. To anfwer otherwife, would indicate a fpirit not
regulated by the word of God, i. e. not according to truth. But thus to exprefs our
defire and hope of each individual of the
human race, would certainly include the
whole. Yet a man deftitute of fuch defires,
hopes and prayers, we fhould not look upon as poffeffing a gofpel fpirit, or fuch a
friend to fouls as the gofpel requires. What
fhould we think of a man that would fay, I

defire moft of thefe may be in the greateft mifery to all eternity?

THE prayers of good men for their moft malicious enemies, for the vileft creatures in the world; fuch as the prayers of David, and that of Stephen when he was dying, under a fhower of malice from his enemies and the enemies of God; thefe prayers, I fay, were not without faith, and a good foundation of faith; and of confequence, were heard and anfwered of God. Yet, if any are to be eternally damned in their own perfons, we fhould imagine that fuch malicious perfecutors, and murderers would certainly be found among them. We fhould think that the murderers of Chrift, at leaft fome of the many thoufands combined in that moft malicious of all fins, would be objects of God's eternal wrath; but it is as certain they were all forgiven, as it is that the prayers of Chrift were always anfwered, and all his petitions granted at all times. *" And I knew that thou hearefl me always:* John xi. 42.

IF it were poffible for people to diveft themfelves of the long, deep, and rooted prejudices arifing from the *limitarian* fcheme, every man would moft clearly fee that we have no foundation or warrant, in reafon or fcripture, to pray as good people ever have done, or as Chrift did for the vileft of men, for their pardon and eternal falvation, but a warrant of this nature, viz. It is the will of God and our Savior, it is his will, without any equivocation or collufion, that all men shall be saved, and, in his own way and time, come to the knowledge of the truth ; and that confiftent with his truth, holinefs and greateft honor, by a proper atonement ; as Chrift gave himfelf a ranfom for all to be teftified in due times, or fit feafons. 1. Tim. ii.

If we were to fingle out any one of the multitude combined in the murder of Jefus, as being the worft of all, perhaps we fhould pitch upon Judas to be the man. And he indeed met with an awful and aggravated damnation, in the higheft fenfe of the term, in the true fcripture meaning of it, as it relates to any mere man perfonally. What this his damnation or perdition was, I have before fhewn. But it is juft as certain that he was forgiven of God, in his own time, and all the reft of the horrible, blind, malicious multitude, as that Jefus cried to his Father with his dying breath, *" Father forgive them ; for they know not what they do."*

Christ never made but one conditional prayer, and that he made for this fpecial reafon, to leave an everlafting teftimony to the world, that fin, whether actual or imputed, could never be difcharged without a full fatisfaction to the divine law. That prayer related to his own fufferings, and was introduced with an hypothefis, and clofed with full fubmiffion to the will of God. See Mat. xxvi. and other parallel records in the evangelifts. All the reft of his prayers were peremptory, without any condition. On the ground of his atonement, all having the force of a juſt and abſolute demand. "*Father I will,*" is the tenor of all the prayers that ever Chriſt made for guilty men.

It is proper for us further to conſider, that God will accompliſh the higheſt glory of his own attributes; and that it is certain, they are all more glorified in the ſalvation, than in the perſonal damnation of any ſinner, or every ſinner on earth.

In the ſalvation of ſuch vile, guilty creatures as we are, every divine attribute doth ſhine moſt glorioufly, and all in perfect harmony. No attributes are more glorious than the infinite pity and mercy of God to ſinners, with his power and good will to ſave them freely. This moſt bleſſed part of the divine character is not ſeen, it makes no diſcovery of itſelf with regard to many millions, on the *limitarian* ſcheme. Neither can the holineſs and juſtice of God, ever ſhine ſo glorioufly bright in the perſonal damnation of any ſinner, or of all the poor ſinners in the world, as in the great atonement, exacting full ſatisfaction of a perſonage infinitely greater and dearer to God than any mere man, or all the mere human race. If you leave room, in the glorious plan of our redemption, for all to be perſonally damned; you take away all the glory of it: And you derogate from this glory, in juſt proportion, as you hold, that any number ſhall be perſonally damned, be that number more or leſs.

That doctrine which represents all sin, all moral evil, in the most odious and abominable aspect, has thence, one evidence of being a true doctrine.

There is no other understanding of the word, nature, and character of God, that makes opposition to him and rebellion against him, appear so full of mischief, and ingratitude, as this I am pleading for. To oppose such a God, as I consider Jehovah to be, on this plan of creating, governing and redeeming the world; how abominable! All the glorious attributes of God would be effectually obstructed, in their displays and operations; and the whole creation, that wonderful child of divine love, would suffer the most barbarous murder, if sinners might have their perverse wills gratified, in all their necessary consequences. The infinite, eternal fountain of love, being and blessedness, would be wholly dried up; and rebellion against such a character, would leave nothing but consummate woe and misery in the universe. To rebel against infinite power and knowledge, if united with a disposition opposite to that of infinite love, (could such a being exist) would not be like rebelling against our infinitely kind and merciful, heavenly Father. To rebel against the cruelest tyrant that ever was cloathed with despotic power, might be a perilous thing; but not like rebelling against the kindest, most compassionate and loving ruler that a happy people was ever blessed with.

Will not every man on earth agree with me in this one point, at leaſt, that no other doctrine ever advanced, can make ſin againſt God, hatred of God and oppoſition to him, look and feel ſo horribly as the doctrine I maintain? For ſurely the nature and native tendency of ſin is wholly to overthrow a God, ſo infinitely glorious and amiable as JEHOVAH, in this view appears, and to ſtifle in the birth all his emanations of being and felicity. This is the nature of all ſin, and not the leſs odious and abominable, becauſe God counteracts the whole by his almighty power and love; but the odiouſneſs of ſin is rather enhanced and aggravated for this very reaſon. The real nature and diſpoſition of our God is, to emanate being and bleſſedneſs far and wide, and that forevermore. The nature of ſin is to obſtruct all this, and therefore no words can expreſs the odiouſneſs of it. For ſin is to be infinitely hated only for its nature. Merely as an event, it belongs to the pure and holy plan, and good government of Deity: Who, even in infinite love and goodneſs, ſaw fit not to hinder the exiſtence of it, however infinitely hateful; and will certainly turn it all to good account, (even contrary to its nature) to the greateſt happineſs of his creatures. Thus the whole ſyſtem of being ſhall, in the reſult of all, be the perfection of love and happineſs.

But, were the moral diſpoſition of a Supreme Being ſuch as to propagate ſome happiness and abundance of misery, and that eternal, though, in regard to his absolute property in all things (which I have often mentioned) we might not accuse him of injustice; yet most of his creatures could do no other than lament their fate in bitter howlings and deepest agonies of soul, because being and misery had been forced upon them. Our glory and blessedness lies in this, that JEHOVAH is what he is. "I AM THAT I AM." To be disaffected to such a God, oh, how criminal!

MOREOVER, that salvation is ensured to sinners, by the death of Christ, without the least dependence on any qualifications in them; but, on the contrary, that all the qualifications necessary to their enjoyment of the benefit are insured by his death, is manifest expressly from Heb. ix. as well as from the whole tenor of the gospel. A testator insures the legacy, at his death, without any regard at all to the present disposition, or even the knowledge of any one of the legatees. He has made the testament, and, when he dies, it becomes unalterable, and the heirs take the benefit, whenever it comes to their knowledge. This is the idea of the apostle to the Hebrews, on this point. To the same purpose he writes Titus iii. 4, 5, 6. "After that the love and kindness of God towards man appeared, not by works of righteousness, which we have done; but according to his mercy he saved us, by the washing of regeneration and the renewing of the Holy

Ghost; which he shed on us abundantly through Jesus Christ our Savior." So it every where appears from the holy scriptures, that the atonement, in all cases, insures qualifications, or the application of the whole benefit; and *not that our qualifications insure an atonement*, in our behalf; that the undertaking and purchase of Christ is at the bottom of all, leads in the whole of the salvation of sinners, makes all sure; and that the whole application and all qualifications are but consequences, through the kingly and prophetic offices of Christ, co-extensive with his priestly impetration.

No man on earth can ever obtain assurance of his safe estate, or any good hope towards God, on any other foundation than the real and universal grace of God. For, while believing, penitent sinners are laboring to build any hope at all, on good distinctions, and good qualifications in themselves, they can find nothing but what points them out for eternal destruction. And they will sink deeper and deeper in despair, in this way, as they look deeper and deeper into their hearts and lives for any ground of hope. God, and he alone is "the hope of Israel and Savior thereof, in the day of trouble." "Other foundation can no man lay than that which is laid, which is Jesus Christ." In such a God and such a Savior, the vilest sinner on earth may find comfort and salvation. "Look unto me and be ye saved all the ends of the earth; for I am God and not man, the Holy One in the midst of thee."

We may add, that this understanding of divine revelation, not only leaves the holy bible free from all contradictions and inconsistencies; but also takes away the main ground of all *deistical* scruples and doubts.

Many are inclined to deism, under the light of divine revelation, because they see such an infinite variety of opinions among revelationists, innumerable different sects among those, who in common, hold the sacred bible for their rule of faith. They are all alike concerned in the great things contained therein, and alike sincere and honest in what they profess to believe; yet, there is such variety of opinion, and such opposition of sentiment, in many points, many are thence inclined to doubt whether the doctrine of such a special revelation is not wholly groundless; and so fall away into infidelity.

On my plea, all this inducement to deism is removed. We consider the all-wise and sovereign God, as enlightening mankind in various measures and degrees, in his own time, way and manner. All are right in some degree, more or less, and none but what have much darkness mixed with the best light they have. All agree in one, as far as light is given to each respectively. They differ not, on the account of their knowledge of the bible, so far as they understand it; but only for want of more knowledge of it, and a better understanding of its true meaning. Thus all sects in the world, all opinionists, however diverse in many things, do indeed confpire and unite in confirming the truth of the facred bible.

When I hear all that *papifts* fay of religion, though I perceive great ignorance and darknefs in them; yet I have thence great confirmation that there is indeed a fpecial revelation from God, and that the fame is contained in the old and new teftaments. When I find *mahometans* defending the old teftament, though they deny the new, I am by them confirmed in the truth of both. Yea, when I hear any *pagans* in the world, talk about their own religion, (for none are without religion) I eafily fee fomething they have derived from the bible, in fome indirect way or other: Even as we have light from the fun by way of the moon, and many other media of reflection; all witneffing alike that there is a fun. So every fect of pagans on earth confirm me in my faith. I find they are all taught of God, as the bible teaches, fo far as they are taught at all. Their many errors are all owing to negative confiderations. i. e. Where light extends no further, darknefs will remain on their minds. So far as God has been pleafed to lead them to the knowledge of truth, they are right; and in all befide they muft be wrong. So when I take a view of the great variety of opinions among *proteftants*, whom I look upon more enlightened than any other people in the world; they all confirm me in the belief that the bible is from God; though they greatly vary in many things, and oppose one another in points almost endless to name.

If I am right in my understanding of God's design and method, his merciful and wise plan of operation to save a guilty world by his dear Son; then my faith is justly confirmed by all these things, which, on any other principles, will tend greatly to confound the mind. On any other Scheme of salvation, a very few there be, but what are destined to eternal, unutterable torments. Who alas! are those few that shall escape? *All are damned by each other;* and I think with equal authority. But, blessed be God, the great Judge is THE SAVIOR OF ALL MEN, and hath taken away the sin of the whole world.

I AM edified, and comforted by every serious, honest man, that I hear talk upon his religion, whatever degrees of light God hath been pleased to give him, be they more or less. I am most edified where there is most light; but truly the light is sweet, even in the least degrees of it. I find something from God given to every sect, and party; and that gives me delight. So it is with me, and so it must be with all that receive divine revelation in this light. Which, I think, is one mark that it is the true light, in which we ought to understand it; as it bears the stamp of its divine Author, who " is the true light, which LIGHTETH EVERY MAN that cometh into the world." And oh! what charity, love, and mutual friendship must flow from such a view of God and his ways! This is that charity which is the bond of perfectnefs.

There is no other doctrine of grace, that will fo encourage the ufe of all the means of grace and falvation, and fo enforce upon our minds the fitnefs and propriety of all the inftitutions of the gofpel.

I consider the whole divine plan connected indiffolubly: All made fure; not in any diftinction of means and end; but all in one indiffoluble chain. So that it is as true and proper to fay, that none can be faved without regeneration, repentance, faith, and holinefs, as to fay that the extreme link in any chain cannot be drawn forward, by an hand at the oppofite end of the chain, unlefs every link in the fame chain is moved. It is always true, and always will be, that he that believeth not fhall be damned, and is indeed damned perfonally, fo long as he remain in that ftate. " He is condemned already;" " the wrath of God abideth on him," and will fo abide, until he is brought out of that ftate of infidelity and impenitence.

The greater our hope is in the ufe of means to obtain any important end, the greater will be our exertions in every cafe, without exception. Full affurance of fuccefs will excite the greateft exertions of all, provided we know that fure fuccefs is only in this way. So, when Paul told the failors, from the mouth of an angel, that not one of their lives fhould be loft by the fhipwreck,

Acts xxvii. they exerted themselves much the more vigorously to obey his directions afterwards, in using the means, as he told them it was the only way in which they could be saved. Every careful observer of human nature, and of the force of motives, well knows it is so in every case. If the end is very important in our view, and there is but just one way to attain it; yet, if success in that way is altogether dubious, and most likely our labors and efforts will be all in vain, we might probably exert ourselves in some degree, though with a faint heart. But, let us know assuredly we shall attain our important end, if we will exert ourselves with all our might, and that this is the only way; this will animate all the powers we have, and we shall engage to purpose. The case is just the same in this matter of infinite weight, as in other cases of a temporal concern; excepting only that our exertions are excited with much greater force.

MOREOVER, the infinite reasonableness of religion and the service of God; the unspeakable pleasure of it, and the superior reward in heaven, *in proportion* to our signal obedience and piety in this state of probation; the great and good influence of religion and virtue, as relative to the spiritual, and even temporal good of our fellow-men, and many other considerations, too many now to specify, all recommend the careful use of the means of grace and salvation, and a life of piety and virtue in this world. In this of piety and virtue in this world. In this way of faving finners, God manifefts his infinite wifdom and goodnefs in laying out for rational creatures and moral agents, work adapted to their rational, moral natures, and full of comfort, pleafure,. and joy. Salvation, however, was not appointed for the means of it; but the means, for eternal falvation, which was eternally made fure, in the covenant of redemption, to that race of beings whofe fin the Lamb of God came to take away.

It has ever been the fenfe of the moft enlightened part of chriftians, that the doctrine of election, and of the certain perfeverance of believers, were doctrines tending to engage them the more in the ufe of means. The doctrine of election, as I have defined it, hath a greater influence of the fame kind, as it difplays a more extenfive love of God to men, and gives us more enlarged views of free grace, and makes poor finners more dependent on God in every view.

If this doctrine does indeed take hold of our fouls, oh! what a facrifice of love fhall we offer to God, even our whole fouls and bodies! How fhall we love God and all his creatures for his fake! How fhall we love our dear Savior, and all for whom he died, for his fake, whether to us friends or enemies, known or unknown, Jews or gentiles, barbarians, Scythians, bond or free! Jefus hath died for them all; he loves them all; and he will bring them all into his kingdom. He will reconcile the world to himfelf, not imputing iniquity. The ends of the earth shall look unto him and be saved.

It is another token of true gospel faith, and truly evangelical principles, that, in the exercise of them, good people find themselves happy in their own lot, and are not uneasy or envious towards others.

Whoever has that sense of the word of God, which I maintain, will enjoy this happiness. They are quite willing that all mankind should enjoy every favor and blessing God is pleased to bestow. They delight in the gracious communications of God, every where. If the friends of God have many blessings, they delight therein; and if they that at present know not God, abound in outward good things, they delight in God's mercy thus far towards them. They would by no means exchange their own enjoyments, whatever their circumstances may be in worldly things, for all the enjoyments of those in a state of darkness, and ignorance of the great salvation. They well know that their real happiness is as much greater than that of the unrenewed, as are the manifestations of divine light and love to their souls. They feel themselves happy in the knowledge of God and Jesus Christ. This is life and heaven to their souls. Their acquaintance with God is perfect peace. Their sense of the sure, final mercy of God to all men, whom indeed they ardently love, does much add to their consolation. One that loves and pities all sinners, as the gospel requires, and as all that have a gospel spirit do, *cannot* feel so happy in a persuasion that most of them will be eternally damned, as they do, who believe that " God will have all men to be saved."

They who have that sense of God and salvation which I plead for, are exceeding happy at all times, in such a God and such a salvation. Indeed their souls desire no more. " Whom have I in heaven but thee? and there is none upon earth that I desire besides thee." Such well know that godliness carries its own comfort along with it, even in the present world, having promise of the life that now is, as well as that which is to come. I am very confident in affirming, that they who know God and his salvation, in the light I have represented, will be filled with exceeding joy, and will envy no person on earth; but will rejoice in all the good that any enjoy. If this be the effect of these doctrines wrought in the heart, they are doubtless according to godliness.

I am very sensible no man will, or ever can fully and cordially believe in such a character of God, and such a salvation, without the special energy of divine power and grace, which is fitly called regeneration. Others may have a doctrinal belief of these things, in some sense; but to feel the reality of these glorious truths in the soul, requires a supernatural work on hearts so disaffected to God as ours are in a natural state. We judge of God's feelings towards us, by our towards him, as all natural men do. Therefore, none but new creatures, can believe such glorious, astonishing truths as these, with all their hearts, without hesitation, and with joy and peace in believing. No man can be fully satisfied with this doctrine, until God has created in his soul a friendship towards himself. When he knows by experience that he loves God, he will believe that God can love sinners freely. They that truly know God, have a very different sense of the love of God, from that of a blind world, whose eyes are fast closed in infidelity.

THESE thoughts, moreover, lead us to see the great duty, and propriety of supporting, and maintaining gospel ordinances and institutions in the world, and giving all due encouragement to the best instructors in the way of salvation, that we can obtain, whether God hath been pleased to enlighten them more or less. The blessing of such instruction and ordinances is great in every view, temporal and spiritual. This is God's wise and merciful way to make us know the things freely given us of God, and to give us great present comfort in these things, and glorious hopes of eternal, consummate happiness in the life to come. No other plan of religion can ever so much animate a people, to attend the worship and ordinances of God, to hallow his sabbaths, and reverence his sanctuary, and to love their spiritual guides most cordially, and account them worthy of double honor, for their works sake, especially those who labor in word and doctrine. In a word, these principles, if they really take hold of the heart, will have every happy effect that the gospel requires of us.

AGAIN; It is an evidence of true, gospel doctrine, if, when cordially believed, it will make us willing and joyful that God should be at the head of the universe, *almighty, absolute Sovereign in all things, God over all, blessed forevermore;* also if it make creatures willing to keep *their own* proper place, at the feet of JEHOVAH, and rejoice to be absolutely dependent on such a God, and at his absolute, sovereign disposal forever and ever.

THIS idea of God, and this understanding of his word, will have such a blessed effect on every believing soul. We shall see clearly, that JEHOVAH is *by nature* God, and worthy to be God over all; and we shall exceedingly rejoice that we, and all creatures are in his hands, as the clay in the hands of the potter. We can trust him with as much joy, as safety. And we see, that all the world may well rejoice in his absolute, sovereign rule. Then we shall break out in raptures of holy joy, " The Lord reigneth, let the earth rejoice, let the multitude of the isles be glad thereof." Then we shall cry out with unfeigned lips, " Praise the Lord all his works, in all places of his dominion: Bless the Lord, O my soul." When God hath given souls this understanding to know the truth, they will exceedingly rejoice that God is what he is, and that they are his creatures, in the proper relation of creatures; that is, in a state of intire, absolute, and everlasting dependence on such a being as JEHOVAH.

THE *limitarian* scheme never can have this operation on our souls. God himself has fixed his own laws, in our souls, that absolutely forbid it. *The law of nature is as really and truly the law of God, as the written word.* Those natural and inevitable feelings, which are common to all rational creatures, whether holy or sinful, whether angels or men, or of whatever rank or description, are indeed the laws of God. The whole law of nature is the law of JEHOVAH, the Author of nature; and a pure law too. By this law of God, he has made it forever absolutely impossible that any creature should cordially, without any aversion of soul, freely consent to be forever and ever in the most inexpressible pain and torment. God's law of nature cries out against it, with all the authority of the divine Being himself. Much less can any holy soul be willing to be an eternal sinner, an everlasting enemy to God, which is the grand, essential thing in that hell the *limitarians* plead for.

GOD does not set his own laws in opposition to one another. He does not, by one law, call upon us to avoid pain and misery as much as we can, and by another bid us be pleased with it. Much less does he, by one law, command us to be holy and love him fupremely, and ferve him in all holy and perfect obedience, and, by another law, command us to be quite willing to hate and rebel againſt him to all eternity. For us to obey two laws directly oppofite, is as impoffible as to ferve two oppofite maſters. But on the plan which I fupport, we may, if our hearts are right, keep all the laws of God in glorious harmony, and find that, in keeping them there is great reward.

THE *limitarians* do indeed tell us, that all, under their eternal decree of reprobation, ought finally to be willing to be damned. Many of them fay, that every man muſt be brought to this willingnefs, before he can be faved!! God grant them further light, that they may better underſtand his nature, character, and wife, harmonious laws.

ON the prefent plan, I can will all that God wills, and do all that God bids me, if my heart is right, and that with great alacrity and joy. I am willing to keep *my own place*, as a creature of God, and I rejoice that my God will forever keep HIS, that JEHOVAH will fit on the throne of abfolute, univerfal government to all eternity. I rejoice that he doeth his pleafure in the armies of heaven and among the inhabitants of the world, that none can ſtay his hand, neither may any fay unto him what doeſt thou ? I want no fecurity but what I have in the nature and character of God, as difplayed in his works and word, through his own Son, the brightnefs of his glory, and the exprefs image of his perfon.

I think thofe principles cannot be wrong that have this native effect on the foul; nor thofe right, which require of us oppofite things and abfolute impoffibilities.

I have before obferved, that perfonal damnation in hell, is not once afferted in the bible, of any particular perfon; nor a word of that nature faid, but what, agreeable to the whole genius and tenor of divine revelation, points to a fubftitute. I add, in this place, that no fuch thing is faid even of Judas himfelf; though, as the englifh words ftand, in our tranflation, there is more that feems to favor fuch a tenet, than in any other paffage of facred writ.

In our englifh bible we have the words thus, " It had been good for that man if he had not been born." Mat. xxvi. 24. and, in Mark xiv. 21. " Good were it for that man if he had never been born." Now if this tranflation were ever fo exact and literal, it would by no means overthrow the general tenor of reafoning from the nature and word of God, which we have been led into. It might, without any unreafonable ftraining of words, be underftood, only as one of the many awful denunciations we have of the voice of juftice, all filenced and fatisfied in the great furety. I appeal, however, to every learned reader, that the tranflation of thefe words is not juft, nor grammatical. The following words are exaɛtly literal and grammatical. "*Good were it for him, if he had not been born that man,*" or such a man.* Much better indeed, had it been for Judas if he had not been born such a prodigy of wickedness. So much the divine spirit says. But by no means, says that Judas, or any other man, shall be a loser by existence, on the whole. This I notice by the way *as just*, though not essential to the grand argument.

It is also evident that we have a right understanding of the character of God and his word, if we are thence affected with holy fear and trembling, mixed with holy joy and engagedness of heart to serve God.

This sense of God and salvation, now maintained, hath certainly such an effect on the soul. To think of such a God, whose absolute property we are: To consider what sinners we indeed are, and how justly deserving of his awful wrath and vengeance to all eternity: And that we can do nothing to help ourselves, and no creature can help us: That all our hope originates from the nature and sovereign purpose, and decree of God, utterly contrary to all our deserts: To think what we must be to all 'eternity, if justice should only take place upon us, (and let God do what he will with us, we can never

---

* καλον ην αυτω, ει ουκ εγεννηθη ο ανθρωπος εκεινος.

open our mouths with any charge of injustice on the absolute Proprietor of all things) this will fill our whole souls with fear and trembling. Also, to find the nature and disposition of the great and terrible God so displayed in his word, as to see that *this*, and *this* alone, is our full and everlasting security: That our everlasting safety lies in the nature of the great God, and no where else: This I say, will fill us with exceeding joy, and engage us earnestly in all the means of salvation, which such a great and glorious God hath appointed. Knowing that this awful and endearing JEHOVAH saves, *only in his own way;* how thankful shall we be that he has told us the way, and marked out the path! Most certainly, this will make us work out our own salvation with fear and trembling. We shall indeed serve the Lord with fear, and rejoice with trembling.

No view we can have of the way of salvation, but this, will affect us with that undissembled, unfeigned humility, which the gospel requires. But this will make us esteem others better than ourselves, and that without any compliment at all; not only some others, but, in the natural sense of the phrase, others in the general view.

EVERY man that feels the truth and force of this doctrine, will really feel and know that he is worse than other men, yea, than any other man that ever had existence; because he knows so much more of himself than of any other man ; alfo, becaufe the belief of this doctrine is attended with real, gofpel charity towards all men, even that charity which hopeth all things. Such a fenfe of God and falvation, and fuch a view of himfelf, will make any man cry out, in the utmoft fincerity, and without fo much as the fhadow of a compliment, furely I am more brutifh than any man : I have not the underftanding of a man : I neither learned wifdom, nor have the knowledge of the holy : I abhor myfelf and repent in duft and afhes.

Such indeed is the very nature of all mankind, that, while they build their confidence of God's eternal favor, on good marks, and good diftinctions in themfelves ; and thence conclude they fhall be faved and moft others damned, it will feed their pride, and puff their fouls up with haughtinefs. They may fay what they pleafe, of "*mere grace,*" "*mere favor,*" "*free grace,*" "*free favor :*" Not the lefs proud will they be for all this ; but quite the reverfe.

Nothing in the univerfe hath a more powerful operation on human fouls, to make them proud, than that great, exalted, renowned perfonages have fingled them out as fpecial favorites. A full confidence that the infinitely exalted Jehovah hath done it, will make every man, while in this world, feel juft as the pharifee did, when moved by the fame inward fentiment. Merely a fenfe of the greateft favors will make no man proud ; but bring in the idea of comparifon and diftinction, and it will make every man so, while under the moral infirmities of nature which attend us in the present world. But on my plea, every valley is filled, and every mountain and hill is brought low, and the crooked is made strait, and the rough places plain, and the Lord alone is exalted. This will bring down every high thought and imagination, that exalteth itself against the knowledge of Christ, and bring all into subjection to the obedience of faith.

It is very natural for many to make inferences, and draw consequences from what is said concerning the salvation of mankind, and apply the same to other ranks and orders of beings, which we know little, or nothing about.

Thus, they apply these doctrines to the case of the miserable, fallen angels. I think we proceed upon very uncertain ground, in all such reasonings and applications. God has been pleased to acquaint us a little, and but a very little, with any other intelligent creatures, whether holy or unholy, but those of our own rank and order, our fellow men. Yet, as it does, in certain respects, concern our duty and practice in this world, to know something of holy angels, and also of evil angels, we are made so far acquainted with their respective dispositions and circumstances as relates to our practice, and no farther.

We are taught, that many of the angels have been very sinful and very miserable a great while, and that they are very affiduous, crafty, and malicious to oppofe the happinefs of the human race, and promote all the fin and mifery they can. We are told that the holy angels are of a direct contrary difpofition and character. And we are taught, in the word of God, how to conduct ourfelves relative to both. This is as much as God hath feen fit to reveal to us on this fubject. I have often thought, that the immodefty of mankind is as much difcovered in many pofitive affertions about the angels, as in any one thing.

This, however, I fuppofe we may fay concerning the miferable, condemned angels, that they are as great finners, as we by nature are, in proportion to the quantity of being they poffefs; and greater finners than we are by nature, only in confideration that they are of an higher rank than we, and have a greater meafure of exiftence; but lefs finners than we in one very capital view. For they have not finned againft a KINSMAN REDEEMER, and the proclamations of fuch a gofpel as we have defpifed.

We may alfo fay, that even to this day (for ought we know) they have as much caufe of eternal defpair as the human kind once had, during the fpace between the moment of our original rebellion, and the firft intimation of a Savior: That they juftly deferve endlefs damnation, by the very nature of their criminality, as well as we: And that they will certainly be eternally damned, in the voice of juftice, and we know of no declaration of grace that relates to them, any more than the human kind once did, with regard to miferable, *damned*, or *condemned* finners, of our own order.

We may further fay, that God can certainly do them no wrong, any more than he can us. If their mifery is endlefs, or if ours had been fo; the will of God is necefsarily juft, and the only ftandard of all juftice and righteoufnefs, for this grand, all important reafon, which I would not fo often repeat, were it not of the utmoft confequence that it fhould fink deep into our fouls and never be unthought of, viz. his abfolute, underived, univerfal, and everlafting property in all things.

If we fay more than the above, I apprehend, we do no honor thereby to our profefsion of gofpel humility: Or rather, that we tranfgrefs in exercifing ourfelves in great matters, or things too high for us, that we know not; and darken counfel by words without knowledge. Who can fay that the fame God who found a way for our recovery, can find none for theirs, throughout an interminable eternity? Or who can fay, that even our own all-fufficient Savior will not, in fome way, unknown to us at prefent, be found hereafter the Head of all principalities and powers, in a more gracious fenfe than we have imagined, even in an infinitely merciful fenfe to the father, the devil, as well as to his children? Who can fay that a Savior, of fuch unfearchable riches of grace, fuch boundlefs wifdom and power, will not, in his own way and time, make every knee bow to him, in one and the same sense, and every tongue confess, from one and the same spirit, that he is Lord of all to the glory of God the Father? Who can say that God will not, in some future period of endless duration, *gather together in* ONE, ALL *things in Christ, both in heaven and on earth and under the earth,* in the most plain and simple understanding of the terms? Who can say, that he will never wholly conquer death, though it be the last enemy, and shall survive every other conquest of his; even death, in the most common, scripture sense of the word, including spiritual death, which includes all sinfulness, as well as natural death?

WHO can say, that the greatest sufferers, and those who are thrown into the greatest distress and horror, save ONE, shall be on the whole losers by their having been called into being, by the almighty power of God, who is love? Since it is certain that the greatest of all sufferers, and he who, in a legal view, was justly charged with the greatest guilt, is the greatest gainer of all creatures by his existence. I here speak just as our most enlightened, and most orthodox divines have always spoken. They all agree in the perfect holiness and purity of the man Christ Jesus, in a personal sense; yet, in a vicarious sense, and as by the covenant of redemption he stood related to the divine law, they all agree, he was justly charged with the greatest guilt of any

creature that ever God made, even the sins
of the whole world. As he stood related to
pain and punishment he never had an equal.
And this is the great, essential, capital doctrine of divine revelation, whereby the bible
is most of all distinguished from all other
books. I say since this greatest of all sufferers, on account of sin, is the greatest
gainer of all the creatures of God by his
existence, on the whole, who can say God
cannot deal in a similar way with all who
suffer on account of sin? For whether you
are an original debtor, or a surety, there
is no difference as to your just obligation to
pay the debt.

ARE we not rather immodest and arro-
gant, when we positively affirm, that we
certainly know, God has called into existence innumerable myriads of intelligent
creatures to be extremely miserable, to endless duration, under his own fixed eternal
decree? God indeed saw it best, on the
whole, that much evil should take place,
both moral and natural; otherwise he certainly would have hindered it. But who can
say that God himself, with all his wisdom,
power and love, is not able to answer all
the wise, good, and glorious purposes he
designed, by the existence of all evil, moral
and natural; yet so as to leave not one of
his offspring a loser by existence?

As to the man Jesus Christ, he had ten
thousand times more guilt to answer for,
than any other man in the world, and no
doubt more than any miserable, fallen angel.

And he was juſt as much obligated to ſuffer pain, miſery, and puniſhment, as if it had been perſonal; yet that man Chriſt Jeſus is, on the whole, the moſt dignified and happy creature that ever God made. "Being found in faſhion as a man, he humbled himſelf and became obedient to death, even the death of the croſs; wherefore God alſo hath highly exalted him, and given him a name which is above every name: That at the name of Jeſus, every knee ſhould bow, of things in heaven and things in the earth, and things under the earth; and that every tongue ſhould confeſs, that Jeſus Chriſt is Lord, to the glory of God the Father." Phili. ii. 8, &c. " For the joy ſet before him, he endured the croſs, deſpiſing the ſhame, and is ſet down at the right hand of the throne of God."

Do we know enough about the extent of divine wiſdom, power and love, to affirm that moſt, or even any of God's own offſpring ſhall be infinite loſers by exiſtence irreſiſtibly forced upon them, by the infinitely kind Fountain of all being and bleſſedneſs? When we get ſo far beyond our line in reaſoning, we tread on very uncertain ground. Let us then let the fallen angels alone. But if any of us muſt needs enquire more about the eternal fate of the angels that fell; it is well for us to remember that they are our ſuperiors, in the ſcale of creation, and ſtand related to us as the offspring of the great, common Fountain of

being; and are no worse than we in their
temper and disposition, only as no mediator
hath operated on their minds, as upon ours,
in a way of restraint, or by any kind, or
gracious operation, as upon the human
kind ever since the fall.

CHILDREN are to hate their father the devil,
only as they are to hate their natural parents
and all their fellow men, and even themselves.
*Not with personal hatred; not with feelings of
malevolence; not as creatures of God;* but all in
them morally evil in its own nature, all that
is opposite to the moral nature or character
of the common Fountain of being. Thus
we are to hate father and mother, wife and
children, brethren and sisters, yea, and our
own life also; and thus, and in no other
way, we ought to hate every thing in which
moral evil appears. But if we feel any malevolence towards the devil, as a creature of
God, or wish him evil; we feel towards him
as he does towards us, and shew his moral
likeness in this our malevolence, as might
be expected from devils only. If we wish
the fallen angels may all remain eternally damned, and that the common Parent
of all may never display and glorify his
great name in their deliverance, from enmity, sin and pain, even if he is able to do it;
if we heartily wish they may be the objects
of almighty vengeance to endless duration,
then, *we feel towards them, as they do towards
us.*

IF our natural parents are very wicked,
and, by necessary consequences, very mise-

rable, we do well to wish, that God, of his infinite power and grace, would make them better and happier. We know he can do it, if he pleases. And since we know not, but that infinite wisdom, power, and mercy can, if God please, take hold of our infernal parents; we shew a spirit too much like theirs, in wishing they may continue to endless duration, in all their sins and in all their torments. It is certain the great JEHOVAH may, in pure justice, leave them so forever; the very nature of their sinfulness does merit this, by every rule of pure righteousness, without any consideration in the universe separate from the very nature of sin. And God might have left us in like manner, and in the like pure justice. But, for my part, I am quite willing God should make me holy and happy, for the glory of his own name, and all my fellow sinners without exception, if he please. I am willing the Lord should be thus "*good unto* ALL," and his tender mercies thus be over all his works, which are capable of holiness and happiness.

If we knew ourselves better than we do, we should not look upon ourselves, by nature, so unlike to the fallen angels as we are apt to imagine. I think it, however, our wisdom to enquire no more about any order of beings, than we have some *data*, some means of knowledge to assist our enquiries; and no more about the devils than may concern our practice, that we may not bear their image, and may guard against their malice and evil influence.

AND now, to take up another thought, I apprehend that the way of salvation I am defending, has this further mark of truth. *It exhibits God to our view, as conducting the affairs of our salvation analogous to all his other conduct.*

THE all-wise and good God does influence, move, and govern all his creatures, in a way suitable to the natures and faculties he hath given them. This is to be seen every where, and in every thing. With regard to all our temporal enjoyments, though they are the objects of his eternal decree, made eternally sure in his all-glorious, immutable plan; yet he gives us all these things, in a way suitable to our natures, as rational creatures and free moral agents, by the exercise of our minds and bodies, that we may have, at all times, proper exercise; for this is wholly necessary to our felicity. This is all the reason why God does not give us all our food immediately fit for eating, and all our raiment ready to put on: If he did so, we should be without that exertion and employment suited to our natures as active creatures, and necessary to our comfort. Therefore, though our exertions are required, it is not to make these enjoyments more sure to us, than he could have otherwise made them, or than even his eternal decree made them. It is just so with regard to our salvation. The means are all laid out for us, and enjoined upon us, and connected with the end, just as much as in all temporal things, only because this gives proper exercife to the immortal soul, attended with unspeakable pleasure and delight; and is suited to our rational natures, and the relation we stand in to God. Our working out our own salvation, is only a reasonable duty, not preceding the certainty of it, in God's view; but following as a fit and happy *consequence*, in his eternal plan, and in the order of his communication of blessedness made sure before the foundation of the world.

So there is every reason, and all manner of fitness, that we should inculcate upon all mankind, the use of the means of grace and salvation, that can possibly be in any case in the universe. It is our reasonable, fit, and happy service, and not only with regard to all the powers of our souls, but of the whole man, even our bodies also. Hence did Paul say, " I beseech you therefore, brethren, by the mercies of God, that ye present your bodies a living sacrifice, holy, acceptable to God, which is your reasonable service." Rom. xii.

It is proper to say, in every case in the universe, and in every case alike true, that the actions and exertions of creatures never alter the previous and eternal certainty of any thing; neither did God design them for any such end, or with any such view. God has ordered and commanded all the duties that are to be done by all his creatures, to carry into effect, and to accomplish his own fixed, good and merciful decrees, in the only fit way, that is, in a way suited to the natures he has given them, and in certain connection with the end. All thefe are in the immutable univerfal fyftem, as much as the end. Hence we fee the great propriety of God's encouragements and promifes to the virtuous and obedient; and of his threatnings to the vicious and rebellious. They are all fuited to the nature of man. And hence we fee how fit it is, that obedience and virtue fhould be attended with delight and joy, as it always is; and that all fin fhould be attended, or rebuked with pain and forrow, which never fails to be the cafe.

They, whom God has fet up in this world to rule and govern mankind, fhould, under him, enact good and wholefome laws, in favor of all virtue, and good conduct; and in terrible oppofition to all wickednefs, all that oppofeth the nature of God, and the good and happinefs of the creatures of God. This is exceeding fit and proper among men, wifely adapted to their natures. The Moft High, no doubt, could fupprefs vice and iniquity in fome other way; but none appears to us fo well adapted to the natures of men. Hence there is every reafon for rulers and ruled, to unite in the moft vigorous efforts for the beft poffible civil government.

This view of the way of God, and this underftanding of his revealed will, is fupported, in that it opens to our fight another grand doctrine of revelation. Which is, *the amazing unreafonablenefs of fin, and fin-*

ners; and how they will pervert all truth and reason, to the vilest purposes.

MANY will say, if all these things are so, if all things, all events, are eternally made certain; men and devils are not to blame for their sins: Just as though the blame of sin did not lie in the nature of it. Many will say, if salvation is finally secured, as here represented, then it is very eligible for men to indulge all their lusts in this world, and live in all manner of vice, as they please: Just as though vice and wickedness were attended with happiness: Not considering, that perfection of wickedness, with its inseparable connections, does in very deed, make the whole hell that the *limitarians* plead for; or that rectitude and virtue in its perfection, does, in very deed, make the heavenly happiness we hope for. They are so blind and unreasonable, as not to see that if sinfulness, or hell, which are for substance the same thing, are not hateful and horrible in this world, they cannot be hereafter; and that if virtue, holiness, or heaven, which are essentially the same thing, are not desirable in this world, they cannot be in the world to come.

THIS plan, moreover, helps us to the best possible solution of the question, which so often arises among men. *Why did God ever bring moral evil into his eternal plan, or suffer it to exist?* For, upon this plan, we see that God doth so display and exercise his own perfections, in opposing the nature of sin and *its effects*, as we cannot see he otherwise might have done. And we also find many exercises of mind; many employments and efforts laid out for his rational creatures, in opposing sin and its awful attendants and consequences, in obedience to God; and much exercise of humility, and thankfulness, and all graces which we can see no room for, had God's eternal plan been otherwise.

This doctrine is further supported, by the doctrine of God's unlimited wisdom and power.

All will allow, that if all the good ends could have been answered and accomplished, without the eternal misery of a multitude of mankind, then it had been better, and then God would have chosen it; because all grant, that such misery is, in its nature, a great evil, and very undesirable, yea very horrible. To suppose that God could not have answered all these glorious ends, without this eternal misery of so many creatures, is to suppose that he was limited by the very nature of things; or that it could not, in the nature of things have been otherwise. But, pray, what is the nature of things? And whence does the nature of things originate? Certainly from God and his attributes only. For in that period of duration when there was nothing existent but God, where was the nature of things, or the necessity of nature, but in God only?

To suppose there was any limitation upon the eternal Being, when no other being did exist, is to suppose that his own infinite, unlimited attributes did limit, and set bounds to his conduct, or to the emanations of his infinite love and benevolence. It is to say, that God would have done better if he could; but that he could not: He acted out himself with as much kindness as he could, and wished to have been more kind, had it been possible, in the nature of things; that is, in the nature of his own perfections, which give nature to all things else: That his infinite wisdom, power and love, could do no better than to exhibit a system glorious in the main; but at the expence of the unutterable, endless misery of countless myriads of his own offspring. This lays a limitation on the Most High, arising from his own attributes; because thence flows the whole nature of things, as their nature cannot flow from non-entity.

But, a just idea of the great God is this, he can indeed do all that the infinite goodness of his heart is disposed to do; and he never gave a nature to things to obstruct the emanations of his love. *" What his soul desireth even that he doeth."*

The *limitarians* suppose God hath formed a system as full of happiness as was possible, and a glorious system on the whole. That he would have kept out of this system the eternal misery of any creature, if he had been able; but was not able, through the necessity of his own attributes, so to do; therefore formed the best system he could.

O o

A syftem much better than none, and even good on the whole, in a high degree. How does this correfpond with juft conceptions of JEHOVAH, God Almighty, all-wife, and infinite love?

IT is in vain to fay here, that this argument would equally exclude out of the fyftem, all the moral and penal evil that ever did exift, or ever will. Becaufe, on the *gofpel plan*, according to my fenfe of it, all the evil of every kind that hath exifted, or fhall exift, is real good in the whole connection; not only to the *fyftem in general*, but to *every individual* in it, capable of rational happinefs. No one fhall be lefs happy, on the whole, than if no evil had ever taken place. Moral and natural evil never did, or fhall exift, at the expence (if I may fo fpeak) of any one of the creatures of love, or of God who is love. Eternity is long enough, to make every creature as happy on the whole, as if there had never been any experience of evil of any kind; at leaft, we can by no means prove the contrary. That fentiment of the poet has ever been admired—

" The bleft to day, is as compleatly fo,
  As who began a thoufand years ago."

CREATURES may fuffer evil a great while, yet have as long duration before them to be happy in, as if they had never tafted of evil. To fay that any duration of evil, or any degree of it, certainly, makes fome deduction, and a proportionable deduction from our quantity of happinefs, though it may afterwards commence and be endless thenceforth, is to say more than any creature can know; unless we can find a creature who comprehends eternity and all things belonging to it. It is also saying, what stands in full opposition to the common sense, and faith of the protestant world, in several other cases. Take only the following well known instance instead of many.

We all believe that the saint that last goes to heaven, shall have as great a reward of free grace, as the saint that first went thither; provided their moral characters are equal in this life. Of this we doubt not, and the scripture is full to the purpose. We also agree in the opinion of the eternal, progressive happiness of the saints in heaven, and that they who went there several thousand years ago, are far advanced in glory and blessedness beyond those who go there at this day; and further still before those, who may go to heaven thousands of years hence. All this we believe, also, that all equal characters shall have an equal reward of glory in heaven, whether they live and die sooner or later. " I will give unto this last even as unto thee:" " The first shall be last and the last shall be first:" i. e. all equal on the whole, if their moral characters and services have been so in this world. These are points not controverted among protestants. Yet it is easy to see, that the same objection, if any, lies against this doctrine, as against what I have asserted, viz. that experience of evil, for a given time, may be consistent with the same quantity of happiness in endless duration, as if the evil had never been suffered.*

I would, indeed, never be positive, when I reason about infinity and eternity, which are incomprehensible to all beings, but God himself. And I only mention this instance,

---

* Suppose a rational creature to exist any given period of time, more or less, in great misery, and then, at the end of that certain period, to exist just as much longer in as great pleasure and happiness, so as exactly to counterbalance all his former pain and make him even on the whole, neither a gainer or loser by his existence thus far. Then suppose it to be the good will of his Maker, to continue him in being to endless duration, in a state of progressive happiness. Suppose also, that it is the pleasure of the Most High to create another, of equal capacity, at the moment when the former has arrived at the end of the second period aforementioned, viz. at that moment when he is just as well off, and no better than if he had never been created. Let these two beings exist thenceforward to endless duration, in equal degrees of progressive happiness, and it is easy to see that both, on the whole, shall be just alike happy, i. e. the former will be, at the moment of his counterbalance, in the self same predicament, in this respect, as if he had been created that very moment. So that it is evident enough, that if our uncontroverted opinion, that all equal characters in this world shall have equal happiness in the eternal world, whether they are born sooner or later, be true; then it is true, that a rational creature may suffer great pains, for any given period of time, and yet be so far from being a loser by existence, that he may be just as great a gainer thereby, on the whole, as any other creature of equal capacity who never tasted of any evil at all, and who hath his beginning of existence in a later period of duration. I beg none would imagine from this remark, that I think the great Jehovah bound in justice to repay any of his creatures for their pains, by an equal balance of happiness. I have no idea of any such demand of the clay on the great Potter, or of any creature on his Maker. The will of Jehovah is necessarily just, and the only criterion, rule and standard of all righteousness. Let men or angels be in whatever predicament they may, it is the will of God that hath placed them there, and they may not impeach their Maker of injustice, or by any means make on him a claim of reward. I only take refuge in the infinite sovereignty of the divine will, flowing out of the INFINITE GOODNESS OF THE DIVINE NATURE. To know what this is, I turn to all his works, and to his revealed will.

as I might many more, to fhew, that the objection I am refuting, is built on no certain foundation; and that in the fair application of it, it muft overthrow many articles of faith in which we are all well agreed, and bring into confufion the *limitarian* fcheme as well as any other adopted by chriftians.

But it is plain, at firft view, that, if innumerable of the offspring of God, rational creatures which he hath called into being, or even any number of them, are in extreme fufferings to endlefs duration, in that cafe, they muft be infinite lofers by that exiftence, which the God of love forced upon them. Yet even on this fuppofition we might not impeach the *juftice* and righteoufnefs of the abfolute, fovereign Proprietor of all things. But, I would afk my reader, is this your idea of the true character of the GOD OF LOVE, God who is love, even in the abftract; or of Chrift, who fo loved the world, that he gave himfelf a ranfom for all?

It may here be added. On the *limitarian* plan, they who are faved will be faved by their own works, being juftified by their own works, in Paul's fenfe of juftification by works, or in any other poffible fenfe in which we can conceive of any fuch juftification. Yea, *they are faved by their own merit, fo far as we can have any notion of merit in a creature.*

All the idea we can poffibly have of merit in creatures, or claim on the Deity by any good works, is the following: That there is something good in the creature, which God considers as a condition of his salvation; and which in the order of nature, precedes his security of eternal life. The question is not, whether we are wholly dependent on the free grace of God for all this good in us, and all these conditions and terms of justification and salvation? We all agree, that every creature is absolutely and entirely dependent on God, for all good of every kind, both inherent and external. If we consider any good in us, whether faith, repentance, holiness, or any thing else, as a term or condition, previous to which, *as a condition in God's view*, he hath not made eternal life sure to us; we arrogate to ourselves all the claim of merit that can possibly enter into the proud heart of a sinner, and all that Paul so much opposeth; we claim to ourselves every thing that man can possibly boast of, unless we claim entire independency of God, which no man ever pretended to.

To say we have, indeed, certain good qualifications, and certain good distinctions, *through grace*, which give us claim to salvation; is to say all that the proud pharisees ever did say, and all that the proudest man on earth ever did, or can say; even though we are ever so ready to own, that God freely gave us all these good qualifications and distinctions. But the feelings of a soul are exceedingly different, who considers salvation made sure to him, by God in Christ, under the idea of a moſt ungodly wretch, and without any diſtinction of good in him more than in any man on earth, or any fallen angel in hell ; that God juſtified him in Chriſt as *ungodly*, wholly ſo, and then ſent him all the diſtinctions, all the qualifications of repentance, faith, &c. merely in a way of application of that ſalvation which, with God, was made ſure to him before the world began.

It is certain we can form no other idea of ſalvation by works, or merit in a creature, than this, viz. That God, by his own free grace, hath made ſome good and valuable diſtinctions in that creature, hath freely beſtowed ſome good qualifications, making that creature better than ſome others ; and then that God on that conſideration, beſtows eternal life ; and that the good he hath already beſtowed is a condition that binds him ſo to do.

Every one who thinks he has got hold of a diſtinguiſhing, or ſpecial promiſe made under a condition, will readily acknowledge that it was wholly owing to the grace of God, that ever he come up to the condition. Faith, repentance, holineſs, and all thoſe things that are called terms and conditions of ſalvation, are wholly of the free grace of God, as we all grant. Yet, all theſe are good works in the creature ; yea, the chief, the capital of good works. Now, to ſay that we may plead our title to ſalvation, as grounded on any of theſe, or all theſe, is only to offer the plaineſt and greateſt plea of merit in us, or of our own works, that any man ever did offer or rely upon. To own we had our qualifications, which we plead as conditions of the promises, from God, only in a way of mere grace, does not militate in the least against all the pride and confidence of our own merit; but does rather enhance it, as I have shewn before. The more distinguishing notice we imagine God has taken of us, to make us better than other men, the more we shall feel like the pharisee in the temple. Indeed there is no salvation, on the *limitarian* plan; but the same that was so pleasing to that devout pharisee.

But, on the GOSPEL PLAN, the idea, and the feelings of the heart are quite different. Christ alone is our security for eternal life, wholly distinct from all conditions or qualifications *in us.* Our hope is laid up in heaven. Jesus Christ is our life. He hath taken away the sin of the world, even before we knew any thing about it: And now, by his holy spirit, sends to us the means of salvation, and makes them operate effectually on our souls, to make us meet to be partakers of the inheritance of the saints in light. He first insures salvation, and then makes the application of the benefit, in his own way; which is the only reasonable and proper way, the only way adapted to the rational natures he has given us. God looks on no terms, no conditions in poor sinners, however believing and penitent they are; nor on their inward holiness, otherwise than as fit gradations he himself is taking, to apply to them that eternal salvation which, *with him,* was equally sure to them in their very worst estate. " If while we were enemies we were reconciled to God by the death of his Son: Much more, being reconciled, we shall be saved by his life." Rom. v. 10. He that gave himself a ransom for all, will take his own way and time to make the application; but the day shall come when without a single exception, " the ransomed of the Lord shall return and come with songs to Zion, and everlasting joy shall be upon their heads; they shall obtain joy and gladness, and sorrow and mourning shall flee away."

It is a certain truth, that good qualifications and valuable distinctions, conferred by a sovereign God on his rational creatures, will always operate in a way of pride and haughtiness, if they consider these as terms and conditions obliging God to confer great things on them in future; how much soever they may acknowledge free grace in all these excellent endowments. It is equally certain, that all these graces will operate in a way of meekness and humility, if considered only as God's fit and proper means, or gradations to confer benefits, founded on Christ as the only condition, and his atonement as the only foundation to make them sure. Thus, although there will be great distinctions of grace and glory in heaven to all eternity, among the redeemed race, they who have

P p

moſt glory there, will excel others as much in the grace of heavenly meekneſs, as in any thing elſe. They will caſt down the brighteſt crowns; and in doing this, will bow, with the moſt lowly reverence, before the throne of the great and glorious Sovereign of all.

It may not be amiſs here to reſume a thought before ſuggeſted, with ſome addition. I have ſaid that, on the *limitarian* plan of ſalvation, the old covenant with Adam, and the new covenant in the goſpel are entirely one and the ſame, in every thing eſſential or material; the difference is only in words, not in reality.

Are we, under the goſpel, wholly dependent on God for every good qualification? So was Adam before the fall. Was real goodneſs, holineſs, or virtue required of him as a previous condition of eternal life? The ſame things, in kind, are required of us on the *limitarian plan* in the ſame view, only not in ſo high a degree: For an *holy heart* is at the bottom of all the conditional accompliſhments they plead for, as making out our claim, in the ſight of God, to his eternal favor. Did God ſay to Adam you ſhall produce or ſhew your qualifications in heart and life, or elſe there is no foundation of hope from the conſtitution you are under? Juſt ſo the *limitarian* preacher ſays to us under the goſpel. So in all other reſpects, the old and new conſtitutions are, *in their nature, ſubſtantially* the ſame.

But, there is one difference to be taken

notice of, which makes the new covenant much more difficult to obtain eternal life by, than the old. It is this; the terms and conditions God required of Adam were such, as, at the time they were made, Adam had both natural and moral power to comply with: Whereas we now have only the natural power, but no moral power within our souls. Though moral impotency is very far from excusing us from guilt; yet, nevertheless, this shews us that they who now hear the gospel, are, on *limitarian* principles, in a far more perilous condition than man was, when placed under the first covenant; or that Jesus Christ preached in all his infinite fulness, is not so good a foundation to rely upon, as the covenant of works was. And is this the account God hath given us of the foundation he hath laid in Zion? You may answer and say, Christ hath undertaken and engaged for sinners, to work all things in and for them. This is indeed a GLORIOUS TRUTH. Yet upon the *limitarian scheme*, are not the great multitude of mankind left out of this engagement, and under an eternal decree of reprobation too? And not every one of them commanded to believe and repent and become a new creature, and that upon pain of damnation most dreadfully aggravated? And is this good news to all people? Is this gospel, or good news to every creature under heaven? Is not this ground of hope to a lost world, much more perilous, than to man under the first covenant, which yet saved him, not from total ruin?

I must freely confess, that, after a very long and very critical consideration of this matter, I cannot see but that, if any obtain eternal life on the *limitarian plan*, they do it essentially in the same way, in which Adam was to make it sure by the first covenant, i.e. by their own qualifications. These are no more of free grace than his must have been. Nor can I see, but that the foundation of hope laid in Christ for man, since the fall, is far more perilous than his ground of hope by the first covenant: But, blessed be God, Jesus Christ is preached in the TRUE GOSPEL, as a sure foundation and fountain of life to *every* guilty sinner, and to all alike; and every sinner is alike commanded to believe on him. "This is a faithful saying and worthy of all acceptation (the acceptation of all sinners without a single exception) that Jesus Christ came into the world to save sinners; of whom I am chief." 1. Tim. i. 15. And, I never yet could pray or preach according to the gospel, to satisfy my own conscience, without saying those things which, by *unavoidable consequence*, do plainly infer, that God will have all men to be saved in the end; and that Christ is the Savior of all men, in the *full, direct and most natural meaning of the words;* though he is especially so to those who now believe, as I have before noticed. Nor, did I ever yet hear an evangelical sermon from any man, or a devout prayer, without premises from which the same consequence is inevitable.

I am very sensible that it has been common for great and good preachers to mix much of the old and new covenant together; though they never yet could make them unite in one. So far as the new covenant has been attended to with clearnefs, as *pure gofpel*, they have always faid thofe things which cannot poffibly be true; unlefs, Chrift hath given his life a ranfom for all; and died for the fins of the whole world; and will have all men to be faved; and will draw all men unto him, in the *plain, fimple fenfe* of language, without any comment at all. Every fentence and exhibition of pure gofpel, from the firft to the laft page in the book of God, does fully announce or imply the fame; though the defert of man, on the covenant of works, is all along kept in our view, with all the dreadful thunders of a broken law, and the tremendous wrath of Deity againft fin every where difplayed as a flaming fire. The gofpel and the law over againft each other, even as in their ancient types, mount *Gerizim* and mount *Ebal*.

It is my very humble, though very firm conclufion, after all poffible attention to the nature of things, and to the word of God, that whatfoever miferable finner of the human kind is difpofed to collect the leaft ray of hope from any diftinctions, or qualifications in his heart, or in his life, however he may come by them, to embolden him to depend on eternal life, as promifed in *confequence* of thefe things; but not *infufed* in the Mediator previous to all, or any of thefe qualifications, and that moft abfolutely in the covenant of redemption; that man, I say, does still virtually desire to be under the law. And he shall hear the law too, until the spirit of God shall be pleased to furnish him with a more honorable sense of the true God, and Jesus Christ whom he hath sent; and more exalted views of the glory of JEHOVAH, in the manifestations of infinite, eternal, self-moved love, and in his displays of sovereign mercy to a lost world.

I WOULD now resume and illustrate a thought which I have before introduced. It is a common thing among men, that a man is condemned in one character, and justified in another, even the same man. A judge may be likewise general of an army. He may appear exceeding well in one of these characters, and very bad in the other. He may be justly damned or condemned as a general, having ruined his country in his military character; and yet be much approved or justified as a civilian. He may be justly amerced to the amount of ten times the value of his estate, and cast into prison for life; yet be wholly justified in the latter character. A sponsor may step in and redeem him, and he may after that enjoy the blessings of his good character; although his bad one will remain forever condemned, and not the less so because he is redeemed from the penalty of it.

No fair, candid reader will cavil at this simile, because it does not *quadrate* in all respects: Since it does intirely in the point designed to be illustrated by it, which is, that we may be forever condemned in one character; yet juſtified in another, and alſo may be delivered from all the pains and penalties juſtly due to our condemned character and conduct. To ſay that both characters in this ſimilitude are perſonal; whereas, in the way of our ſalvation, *one* is only imputative, is nothing at all to the purpoſe. For the imputed character is, in the account of our great Judge, and by the covenant of redemption, juſt the ſame as to our redemption from the pains of hell, and our title to heaven, as if it were perſonal.

THE common ſenſe and practice of mankind, in many caſes in common life, approves of the condemnation and juſtification of the ſame perſons, in different relations and connections; and of the indemnity of men moſt juſtly condemned, in a real character, which they have perſonally ſuſtained. And though men cannot be happy and miſerable at the ſame time; yet they may be happy, in their perſons and real enjoyments, while forever conſcious they have merited nothing but ſorrow and woe.

IT is further an evidence of true goſpel faith and hope; that they work by love, and purify the heart and life. Faith operates in a way of love to God and man; " and every man that hath this hope in him purifieth himſelf even as HE is pure."

I HAVE already obſerved, that the faith and hope for which I am pleading, always have ſuch an effect, and, in the very nature

of things, always will, while men and moral
agents remain what God has made them.
Also my own experience does indeed witness
to this truth. I suppose that my own soul
is formed on the general, the universal plan
of human nature: And I am certain that
such a view of God and the way of salvation
as I am pleading for; such a view of man,
and of all creatures, and of their entire, absolute, and everlasting dependence on God;
such a sense of the guilt and misery of man
by nature, and the exalted glory of Christ,
and of infinite, free, and sovereign grace,
has, of all things, the most powerful effect
on my own heart to lead to repentance,
odium of all sin, the mortification of every
inordinate desire, and every worldly lust,
joyful resignation to the will of God in all
things, in all afflictions, however painful to
nature, and to make me feel towards God
and all his creatures, in imitation of the
feelings of the blessed Redeemer. I am
certain that if I have, in any degree, the
same mind which was also in Christ Jesus,
I have it in this way. When I have the
deepest sense of these things, the world and
creatures appear to me as nothing, yea, less
than nothing and vanity, and God all in all.
Therefore, if other human souls are like
mine, I have not the least fear that understanding the way of salvation as I do, will
do any harm to any child of Adam; but
quite the reverse.

I cannot contract my views of the great
salvation, the *common salvation*, within nar-

rower limits, without limiting the Holy One of Israel, even as to the capital glory of all his ways. Yet after all, I am happy in this, that if my dear kindred of the human kind, or many of them cannot, at present, extend their faith beyond the *narrow* bounds of the *limitarian plan;* yet they are still in the sure way to eternal salvation, if they fall not short of their own understanding of the way of life; that is to say, if they have that repentance, *faith*, and holiness which they hold necessary; which is exactly the same as that which I maintain necessary, and in a way of free grace only. I well know that every man is *at present*, in the way that leadeth to destruction, who hath not these graces. If many suppose, that the great Mediator hath never engaged, in his own way and time, to give these graces, except to a few of the human kind; let them see to it that they be found among those few. If they do this, they shall never fail.

Their faith falls short in no essential point: Their unhappiness lies only in this, that they do not draw all the blessed consequences and comforts they might draw, from premises truly evangelical and saving. The premises are not unsafe, as far as they go. If inwrought into the soul, they shall lead to safety. We ought, however, to satisfy ourselves in the inquiry, WHAT IS TRUTH? Yet it is not our believing, or not believing, that there are many or few who shall arrive at glory, which will save or ruin any of us. Believing the great, essential doctrines of grace, and living agreeably to the power of them; believing on the Lord Jesus Christ to the saving of our souls, and following him in the regeneration, whether that work be done for us sooner or later, these, as God's means, will end in glory. No man shall see the Lord in glory, without *holiness*, and that in a far more perfect degree than ever any man had in this world since the fall, or ever will have while breath remains, or the soul is in union with this mortal body. Most blessed however, are those elect of God, chosen in Christ to early conversion, piety, and holiness, and to a life of faith, godliness, and divine pleasure all their days.

LET those who believe, that, in the most *plain* and *literal sense*, Christ is God's salvation to the ends of the earth: That as sin hath reigned unto death, *much more*, shall grace reign through righteousness to eternal life, by Jesus Christ our Lord: And that as, by one man, judgment came upon all men unto condemnation; so, by the righteousness of one, the free gift came upon all men unto justification of life: I say, let all such see to it, without delay, that they become new creatures. Such should be immediately reconciled to that God, in the actual temper of their souls, who is *truly reconciled* to them, in the covenant of redemption, and the atonement of his dear Son; and they should walk worthy of him, who hath called them to his kingdom and glory. For, in very deed, there is the same necessity of all this, in order that we may be happy in the world to come, on the doctrine here advanced, as on any limited plan of salvation, that ever entered into the minds of any of the lost human race.

The great business of the preachers of righteousness is little concerned, in telling, *how many shall be saved;* but rather, how guilty, miserable souls shall be saved. They are to hold up to the view of all men, the true character of JEHOVAH, and of fallen man: And the relation in which man stands to his Maker and his Judge, his Redeemer, and the Sanctifier of the polluted human soul: What Christ hath done to lay the sole foundation of all his hopes: What must be done on his soul to bring him to the fruition of that blessedness which alone can happify his immortal soul: What man must be and do, as indispensably necessary, in its due place, to give him true comfort in this world, and introduce him to the inheritance and enjoyment of a kingdom prepared for the elect body of Christ, and, with God, made absolutely sure to that whole body, before the world began: And to point out and inforce all relative duties, and every moral virtue, agreeably to the reason and nature of things, and the word of God.

They are also to shew the horrible nature of all sin, vice, and immorality; that it is even death, hell, and damnation, so long as the soul continues impenitent in the ways of it. They are to dissuade from it, by every gospel motive, and by every motive from God's pure, holy, and infinitely amiable law. They are to give hope and relief to the sinking, despairing soul, *in Christ alone*, and comfort to the children of God in *him only*: To lead in the holy and joyful solemnities of divine worship, in the high praises of God and the Lamb: To preach the *unsearchable riches of Christ*: And to manifest their solemn sense of all these things, by a pure and holy life and example. Yet when pressed with arguments against that glorious, divine revelation God hath made to a lost world, which never can be fully and fairly answered on any more limited plan, I think it a duty, and highly expedient to take refuge in that *very gospel* which, for ages and generations, has lain in great part, hidden from men, in all the extent and glory of it. In which all the infinite honors of Deity are secured, and also the final recovery of a lost world. Thus, they are to open the word of God as fully as possible in that true sense, against which there can lie no solid charge of inconsistency. Thus it will forever appear in the utmost divine beauty, and in glorious harmony, from beginning to end.

Could I possibly conceive of any way,

in which the great and holy God might be more glorified in the eternal *perfonal* damnation of many, or moſt of mankind, than in extending final redemption to them all; I certainly ought to acquiefce in fuch a fearful event, yea, even to wiſh for it. But as it really appears to me, from the nature of God, from his word, and from all his works, and above all, from the character, atonement and commiſſion of his dear Son, and from the covenant of redemption and of grace, that the moſt high and holy God cannot leave one human foul forever, under the power of fpiritual and eternal death, confiſtent with his own higheſt declarative honor, and glory; I ought not, I cannot believe he ever will.

My reafon is weak, very weak indeed; yet it is my duty to keep clofe to the dictates of it, under the all-facred authority of divine revelation. I cannot pofſibly fee, but that, in the eternal, perfonal damnation of one human foul, the Moſt High would caſt a great reflection on the full and complete atonement of the Son of his love, and alfo on the Father himſelf, as the Son is the brightnefs of his Father's glory, and the expreſs image of his perfon. The diſhonorable reflection appears to me would confiſt in this; it would fully imply and indicate, either, that the atonement of Chriſt was not infinite, nor his power and faithfulnefs; or that the love, pity, mercy, and grace of

God, was not infinite; or that the satisfaction of Christ could not be adequate to the divine law.

To imagine there is any need of the *eternal personal torment* of any sinner of the human race, in order further to illustrate the holiness and justice of God, the infinite evil of sin; or further to impress the minds of the intelligent system with a sense of the infinite odiousness of sin, and the infinite purity of God, and his infinite hatred of all sin, is plainly to suppose that the great work of the Son of God can admit of some amendment; that in very deed it is not a finished work. For any man to think this necessary or expedient, or any such thing, is an amazing reflection on him who said " IT IS FINISHED," when he bowed his head and gave up the ghost. It is infinitely more absurd than it would be for a nobleman, whose galleries are adorned with the inimitable performances of a *Raphael* or a *Titian*, afterwards to employ the most contemptible of all painters, to come and retouch them, in order to their greater embellishment! *God is a rock, his work is perfect*. The work of redemption is most emphatically so. Of all that pertains to this work, must it be said, " Whatsoever God doth, it shall be forever: Nothing can be put to it, nor any thing taken from it; and God doth it that man should fear before him."

In good truth, I can learn nothing from

the nature, character, word, or works of God; nothing from the emanations he has been pleased to make of himself, that leads me to a single idea that the most holy God, since what hath been done and suffered by the Son of his love, can derive any glory to himself, or communicate any instruction, any good to the intelligent system, from the eternal, personal damnation of any poor, miserable, guilty sinner of the human kind; or that such a thing can be without manifest opposition to the blessed nature of God, who is infinite love, and to the glorious and merciful covenant of redemption, and all the most glorious and tremendous work of the Son of God, which he finished on the cross. I cannot see, but that the nature of God is now open, (if I may so speak) the nature of eternal, infinite, unlimited, boundless love, is now free to take its spontaneous course, without the least obstacle, from any opposing claims of justice, standing in the way of the final salvation of a whole guilty world. If it be so, do we in any wise, displease God in ascribing such "salvation to our God who sitteth upon the throne, and to the Lamb? Saying, Amen: Blessing, and glory, and wisdom, and thanksgiving, and honor, and power, and might, be unto our God forever and ever. Amen." Rev. vii.

I am constrained to think, that it is this very plan of redeeming wisdom, power, and love, that the four and twenty elders, the representatives of all the redeemed on high, hold in rapturous contemplation; **and also all the blessed in heaven, when they fall down before him that sitteth on the throne, and worship him that liveth forever and ever, and cast their crowns before the throne, saying, thou art worthy, O Lord, to receive glory, and honor, and power: for thou hast created all things, and for thy pleasure they are and were created."** *Thy pleasure*, most emphatically, as all things were made for, and result in the glories of redeeming love. Rev. iv. Nor can I, on any *limitarian plan*, or on any in the universe, but that I am pleading for, account for that glorious display. Rev. v. " And I beheld, and I heard the voice of many angels round about the throne, and the living creatures,* and the elders ; and the number of them was ten thousand times ten thousand, and thousands of thousands ; saying, with a loud voice, worthy is the Lamb that was slain, to receive power, and riches, and wisdom, and strength, and honor, and glory, and blessing. And every creature which is in heaven, and on the earth, and under the earth, and such as are in the sea, and all that are in them, heard I, saying, blessing, and honor, and glory, and power, be unto him that sitteth upon the throne, and unto the Lamb forever and ever. And the four living creatures said, Amen. And the four and

* Zöon.

twenty elders fell down, and worſhipped him that liveth forever and ever."

IF we attend only to the voice of the holy law of God, as it ſounds every where through the bible, we muſt forever deſpair, not only of the ſalvation of this loſt *world*, but of any *one* of the fallen race; unleſs we conſider this law, in all its maledictions, and in all its holy demands, *wholly* ſatisfied in the ſecond man, the Lord from heaven. This indeed, is pure goſpel truth. When we ſo conſider it, the door of ſalvation is wide open for all, and open alike for every child of Adam. The whole debt is paid, and why ſhould not all the priſoners be diſcharged? Chriſt paid it not for himſelf, but for them, and that according to divine ſtipulation, and the entire good pleaſure of the Father. "Meſſiah ſhall be cut off, but not for himſelf."

HE has as much power and love, as he has of merit; and his *kingly* and *prophetical* abilities are equal to his *prieſtly*. All power is given to him, in heaven and in earth. Shall the infinite love, that brought him to the croſs to die for the ſins of the whole world, ſtop at the croſs? Will he not make the application, finally, as extenſive as the merits of the purchaſe? If not, it cannot be for want of power, it muſt be only for want of will and merciful diſpoſition of ſoul. Is it any honor

R r

to Chrift, that we reftrain the bowels of his love in our own minds? Or is it agreeable to his word? Ye are not ftraitened in him; but ye are ftraitened in your own bowels. Certainly we fhould more honor and pleafe God, and the Son of his love, if we had not fuch narrow, limited thoughts of DIVINE LOVE.

You, my reader, know, in your own foul, that you fincerely and cordially love your neighbor, and daily give him every poffible proof of it; yet he fo hates you, that he cannot, he will not believe that you love him, and is ever complaining of you as the moft bitter, cruel enemy he has in the world. Does he not abufe and difhonor you? But what proof did you ever give to any man on earth, that you loved him and wifhed well to him, in any meafure comparable to the teftimonies of love, mercy, pity, and real good will which the Redeemer does daily produce, to prove his real, wonderful love, mercy, and pity toward every child of Adam? He beftows more real kindnefs on the vileft finner in the world, in one day, than ever you beftowed on any perfon on earth, in your whole life.

After all this, for us to fay, that it is his will and difpofition to damn moft of mankind in perfon, to all eternity, appears to me not honorable to the true character of Chrift, or agreeable to his word. To fay, he is willing to fave every finner, that he taketh no pleafure in the death of him that dieth, but that he would turn and live; and yet that God Almighty will not fee that effected in his own way and time, in which he fo much delights, and *that*, after every obftacle is removed by his Son, which ever ftood in the way of man's falvation, I think, is very far from doing honor to the character of the living and true God. Our heavenly Father would have us argue his love, and that of his Son towards unworthy finners, from all the manifeftations of love, kindnefs and mercy he hath made to them, in all the paths of his providence, and, above all, in the wonders of redeeming love. It is our great blame that we do not know that the goodnefs of God leadeth to repentance, and that repentance takes hold of a fenfe of pardon and eternal life.

For my own part, I feel afraid to fpeak, or even think of my heavenly Father, in the *limitarian* view of him; left I fhould awfully abufe that character which claims my higheft reverence and love. If my own children will think and fay, that, *for my own pleafure*, I will make them as miferable as I can, after all the fruits of kindnefs in my power, which I have conferred upon them with an unremitting hand; I fhould think them very wicked, a fhame to their father, and bitternefs to her that bare them. Why fhould we imagine, that our heavenly Father is pleafed to have us entertain fimilar thoughts of him? " If ye then being evil, know how to give good gifts unto your children, how much more shall your Father who is in heaven, give good things to them that afk him?" Matt. vii. 11.

The work of Chrift is a *finifhed work*. The covenant of redemption is fulfilled on his part, *in every iota of it*.

The blood of Jefus Chrift cleanfeth from *all* fin, from *impenitence, hardnefs of heart, and blindnefs of mind*, as well as practical fins. Indeed, if it did not, it could cleanfe from no fin at all: For *thefe* are the fountain of all other fins and the greateft of all. All fins are alike forgiven to men, and done away in the atonement; and regeneration, repentance and faith, are communicated on the fame ground, and their office is to make us " *know the things freely given us of God*." God fent his beloved Son into the world, that the world, through him might be faved; and he " tafted death for *every man*." The prophet forefaw this, and he fpeaks of the bleffed confequence, without a word or thought of limitation. He confiders a loft world all alike prifoners of juftice, and caft into one and the fame doleful pit together; yet proclaims aloud, " By the blood of thy covenant, I have fent forth thy prifoners out of the pit wherein is no water." Zech. ix. 11. Nor had Ifaiah any thought of limitation, when he fpeaks of the anointing of the Son of God, " to proclaim liberty to the captives, and the opening of the prifon to them that are bound; to comfort ALL that mourn."

Ifai. lxi. " That thou mayeft fay to the prifoners, go forth; and to them that are in darknefs, fhew yourfelves." Ifai. xlix. 9. And it is worthy of our notice, that when the Savior was commenting on thefe paffages, he immediately took occafion to open the extent of his falvation to the audience. Luke iv. This was as much to their furprife and offence, as the moft extenfive doctrine of the falvation of finners now is to the moft tenacious retainer of the doctrine of a *partial falvation*.

As I have already hinted, whatever doctrinal perfuafion may be in the mind of any unregenerate man, that the way of falvation, and the extent of it, according to the nature and word of God, is fuch as I maintain, this doctrine will never quiet an alarming, polluted confcience, and fet the foul at reft from awful fears and terrors; until it is acquainted with God and *reconciled* to him.

While total enmity to God remains in the foul, there will be diftreffing fears in feafons of reflection. Nor is it poffible in the nature of things, that creatures that hate God as we do, in our natural ftate, fhould have that exalted fenfe of his love, which is manifefted in the gofpel, and is indeed the glory of it. Blind, unrenewed finners will meafure the love of God, and the motives on which they fuppofe God acts, much by their own.

We muft indeed know the living and true God, and Jefus Chrift whom he hath fent, in order to have a feeling apprehenfion of our eternal life, as manifest in the gospel; whether we have a more confined, or a more extensive understanding of it. *Never can we have comfort in the reconciliation of a friend, to us; until our hearts meet with him in that reconciliation.* If our enmity remains, it will exclude us from comfort in his friendship. How important then is an immediate reconciliation to God, by a new creation in Christ Jesus, and by repentance and faith in his blood!

THE infinite importance of immediate reconciliation to God, is even more forcibly urged on the doctrine I have advanced, than on any more limited principles. The great apostle Paul hath in a few words, virtually said all I have been pleading for; and from premises arising from the most extensive view of the atonement of Christ, he does most forcibly inculcate the immediate reconciliation of sinners to God. " For the love of Christ constraineth us, because we thus judge, that if *one* died for *all*, then were all dead; and that he died for *all*, that they which live, should not henceforth live unto themselves, but unto him who died for them, and rose again. And all things are of God, who hath reconciled us to himself by Jesus Christ, and hath given to us the ministry of reconciliation; to wit, that God was in Christ reconciling *the world* unto himself, not imputing their trespasses unto them; and hath committed unto us the word of reconciliation. Now then we are ambassadors for Christ, as though God did beseech you by us: We pray you in Christ's stead, be ye reconciled to God. For he hath made him to be sin for us, who knew no sin; that we might be made the righteousness of God in him." 2. Cor. v.

ALTHOUGH this apostle did also preach the law abundantly, and found the voice of pure justice in all its tremendous terrors; yet he never preached or wrote one word inconsistent with what I have just quoted. Whenever in his preaching or writing, he held up the gospel to view, it was of the same tenor. The same may be said of all the other apostles, and of all the prophets. They learned it from Jesus Christ himself, in whom the only foundation was laid, and who announced the same glorious tidings.

AND, truly, as I have before hinted, I never read or heard any discourses of eminent and pious protestant divines, but what were built on premises and arguments which fully infer that glorious, final extent of salvation, which I maintain, however inconsistent they may have been, in some parts of their writings or sermons. Indeed, all I have now written, is nothing more or less than the common, genuine, protestant doctrine of grace, set free from all the contradictions and inconsistencies that have so long been intermixed with it, and the genuine and glorious confequences of it more openly and explicitly difplayed. And thus I read thofe writings ftill, and ever fhall, with great edification and pleafure. And the inconfiftencies I find intermixed with fuch pure and glorious truths, give me no more offence, than the bones I find in delicious fifh or fowl at my table.

To clofe the whole, as a confiftent IMPROVEMENT of this doctrine of falvation.

HOW fhould we love, fear, adore, and obey fuch a God, whofe nature and character is fuch as here exhibited to our view! How ought we to fubmit to him in all things, and rejoice in him evermore! What a foundation is here laid for the relief of the moft guilty, even the chief of finners! What high and honorable thoughts of God fhould we ever entertain, and what fhould we think of Chrift his Son! What comfort and even joy does this doctrine afford us in all fcenes of divine providence, in the whole government of fuch a God!

HENCE how are we taught to love one another, to love, pity and pray for all our fellow finners! How will the firm belief of this doctrine lead us to prize the word and ordinances of God, and to delight in his worfhip, and to call on all creatures to praife the Lord, whofe mercy endureth forever, and to hate all fin, all that is oppofite to the nature and commands of such a God! How will these principles, if really in the heart, produce a feeling sense that all sin, vice and immorality, is no other than death, hell, and damnation; and that holiness and virtue is heaven and divine glory! How will they lead us to live religion, for the love and pleasure of it; and to mourn for, and shun all disobedience to God, all moral evil as hateful beyond all expression, in its own nature, and as that which cost our best Friend, our blessed Redeemer so dear! How will these truths, if really believed and wrought into the soul, promote love, union, and harmony among all the ministers of Christ, and every branch of his church redeemed by his own blood, of *whatever denomination they are!*

These principles cannot make those who do not believe them, either worse or better: For they can have no effect upon them. And as for all those who do really *in their hearts* believe in this salvation, I am certain the effect will be very great and good. Their hearts will be enlarged, and they will run in the way of God's commandments. Our misery consists very much in the want of high and honorable thoughts of God and of Christ. And we fall short in nothing more than in our ideas of the divine love. There is not a miserable sinner on earth, and never was, who would not trust in God, if he had a knowledge of his true character. " They that know thy name will put their truſt in thee." Pſal. ix. 10. But all that know not God, are in a ſtate of condemnation. There never can be any danger of our having too exalted and enlarged thoughts of any of the attributes of God, no not of his love : For GOD IS LOVE. And to keep ourſelves in the love of God, in all the infinite extent of it, can never bring us into condemnation.

You, my dear reader, as well as the writer, muſt ſoon die, and appear at the awful bar of an omniſcient and holy Judge. We muſt ſoon make trial of the foundation of the hope upon which we build. Our diſtinctions from other loſt ſinners, will probably be no greater then, than at this very moment ; and where ſhall we look for ſupport then ? To things within ourſelves, or to Jeſus Chriſt ? To our good qualifications, or to God alone ? *Will you, my friend, venture into the eternal world with any hope, or any mixture of hope, but what is built on* JEHOVAH *alone, as manifeſt in his beloved Son ?*

WHATEVER men may plead, in days of health, in favor of marks and diſtinctions *in themſelves,* to feed their vanity, or ſupport their hope ; I never yet diſcourſed with any dying man in the exerciſe of his rational powers, who did not entirely ſet at nought every ſuch ground of hope. I have invariably found every one who felt within his ſoul in that awful, trying hour, any hope at all, has fixed it wholly on the glorious nature and attributes of God, as difplayed in the great Redeemer. And whatever our *refuge* may be now, you and I, my dear friend, muft make *this* our laft refuge. Death is too terrible, and the tribunal of the great Judge too awful, to admit of any confidence but in Chrift alone.

We fhall not feel ourfelves fo much better than others, when death and the judgment ftare us in the face, as we are apt to do, in days of worldly profperity and pleafure. Whatever we imagine now, we fhall then be fully convinced that a fole, unmixed dependence on God in Chrift can alone fupport our trembling fouls; and that every other refuge is but a refuge of lies. We fhall then find our need of Chrift for wifdom, righteoufnefs, fanctification, and compleat redemption in every view, and in every part of it, for Alpha and Omega, the beginning and the ending, the firft and the laft. God, in his Son, will be all in all. And in that trying hour, we fhall all find, that it is our fole refuge and only confolation, that, OF HIM, AND THROUGH HIM, AND TO HIM ARE ALL THINGS, TO WHOM BE GLORY FOREVER.

A M E N.